Dreams to Dust

Dreams to Dust

*A Diary of the
California Gold Rush,
1849–1850*

By Charles Ross Parke, M.D.

Edited by James E. Davis

University of Nebraska Press

Lincoln and London

The paper in this book meets the minimum
requirements of American National Standard for
Information Sciences—Permanence of Paper for Printed
Library Materials, ANSI Z39.48–1984.

Library of Congress Cataloging-in-Publication Data

Parke, Charles Ross, 1823–1908.
Dreams to dust: a diary of the California gold rush,
1849–1850 / by Charles Ross Parke;
edited by James E. Davis.
p. cm.
Bibliography: p.
Includes index.
ISBN 0-8032-3674-3 (alk. paper)
1. Parke, Charles Ross, 1823–1908—Diaries. 2. Overland
journeys to the Pacific. 3. West (U.S.)—Description and
travel—1848–1860. 4. California—Description and
travel—1848–1869. 5. California—Gold discoveries.
6. Pioneers—West (U.S.)—Diaries. 7. Pioneers—
California—Diaries. I. Davis, James Edward, 1940–.
II. Title.
F593.P28 1989
978'.02'0924—dc19   88-27763   CIP

*To my mother
and to the memory
of my father*

Contents

List of Illustrations

Acknowledgments

In undertaking this work I have enjoyed the assistance and encouragement of many people. The Huntington Library not only kindly granted me permission to edit for publication the gold rush diary of Dr. Charles Ross Parke (call no. HM 16996), but the members of its fine staff also rendered much valuable assistance. Especially helpful were Peter Blodgett, Winifred E. Popp, Mary L. Robertson, Jon Stephansson, Susan A. Watson, and David H. Woodward. Personnel at the Library of Congress also provided help. Maxine Brennan of the Historical Society of Pennsylvania helped locate material on Parke's medical training. The Philadelphia Free Library yielded information on Parke's early life, and Wesley Sollenberger of the Chester County Historical Society was especially helpful in ferreting out such information. Much of my knowledge of overland narratives I owe to the outstanding holdings of the Beinecke Library and the helpful people there. I also owe much to the staffs of the Bentley Library, the Burton Collection in the Detroit Public Library, the Newberry Library, the Chicago Public Library, and the main library at Illinois State University. Gregory Koos at the McLean County Historical Society unearthed a great deal of information dealing with Parke's years in Bloomington and elsewhere in Illinois. At the county courthouse in Whiteside County, Illinois, Marvin Van Zuiden and his staff rounded up records on Parke and his overland companions. The Sterling Public Library in Whiteside County also assisted me. As has been true for many years, the fine people at the Illinois State Historical Library and the Illinois State Archives assisted me and encouraged me in every possible way. At the library Roger Bridges, Laurel Bowen, Sandy Stark, Cheryl Schnirring, and George Heerman provided immense help, as did Wayne Temple at the archives. Personnel at the Missouri Historical Society and the State Historical Society of Wisconsin filled in a number of bothersome gaps, Myrna Williamson at the latter institution helping to find and obtain drawings by James Wilkins. The Bancroft Library, University of California, Berkeley, granted me permission to publish excerpts from David Carnes's diary, "Journal of a trip across the plains in the year 1849." I owe a great debt to the staff of the Bancroft Library. Bonnie Hardwick, Irene M. Morgan and Annegret Ogden were especially helpful and considerate. The California Historical Society provided useful details on some overlanders and life in California. Additional information on the gold rush was found in the Denver Public Library and the Colorado State Historical Library. At the Nebraska State Historical Society, Anne P. Diffendal was very helpful in locating some emigrant material. My visits to all of these institutions were made productive and highly pleasant through the efforts of these fine people and others.

I give hearty thanks for the communications from Nelle V. George of the Schuyler County Historical Society, Missouri, and John R. Ward of the Louisville Free Library. They helped clear up some puzzles. The Cleveland Public Library and the County of Los Angeles Public Library also extended thoughtful responses to my inquiries.

Local libraries have contributed to the effort. Schewe Library at Illinois College has, once again, performed yeoman's service in securing sources, and I am in debt to Richard Pratt, Thomas Merchant, Martin Gallas, Sharon Zuiderveld, Jacqueline Bicket, Patricia Schildman and Laura Sweatman. Ronald Daniels and Penelope Mitchell at Pfeiffer Library at nearby MacMurray College also rendered assistance. At another local library, the Jacksonville Public Library, I was ably assisted by Harry Heusted.

Several grants financed several research trips and other facets of research. A summer stipend from the National Endowment for the Humanities enabled me to conduct research in libraries on both coasts and at points in between. Faculty travel funds and faculty development grants from Illinois College were instrumental in my research and are much appreciated. Support from the Ernest G. Hildner Fund at Illinois College also enabled me to further my work.

As has been true for many years, my colleagues at Illinois College provided advice and encouragement. The president of the college, Donald Mundinger, and the dean of the college, John Nies, took a lively interest in my work and supported it with sizable grants and other forms of help. Wallace Jamison, former dean of the college, also provided a great deal of help. Constant encouragement came from the chairman of my department, Donald Tracey, and from such colleagues as Richard Fry and Karen Dean.

I teach two courses at the Illinois State Historical Library for students at Illinois College. Over the past few years, a number of students in these courses have conducted research for this project at the Illinois State Historical Library: Bruce Koehler, Beth Downer, Lee Scropos, Mary Merris, Elliott Turpin, Kirk Caponi, Mike Early, Ray Gillmore, and Dennis

O'Leary. They brought to this undertaking intelligence, diligence, and imagination. Their enthusiastic work is remembered warmly.

As always, my wife, Joanna, was consistently patient, supportive, and understanding. Our daughters, Kathi and Mary, also lent loving support to this project.

Introduction

The year 1848 was a momentous one. On March 10, the United States Senate narrowly ratified a treaty ending the Mexican War, a treaty in which Mexico ceded to the United States nearly all of the present-day Southwest, including California. The ending of hostilities prompted from certain quarters in Europe and the United States sputtering explanations of how young America accomplished the herculean task of winning the war. America's self-confidence and faith in its republican values and institutions surged to new highs. The war did much to strengthen the nation's sense of mission to peoples still laboring under despotism, and it vindicated republicanism as a form of government and the concept of volunteer armies as the means of defending the Republic. Less than three weeks before the Senate acted, revolutions began to shake the ancient monarchies of Europe, doubtlessly inspired, some ardent republicans believed, by the stunning victories of hastily organized citizen-soldier volunteers over professionally led and experienced Mexican forces that were vastly superior numerically to the invading Americans.[1] Many Americans and others assumed that the class-ridden, corrupt monarchies of Europe would soon topple in the face of surging forces of reform and enlightenment. In the U.S. general election in November, military success catapulted General Zachary Taylor to victory, and he took office the following March. The end of the year, however, ushered in ominous news: deadly cholera was again coursing along the nation's waterways and elsewhere, bringing death and fear.

Vying with cholera for newspaper space in the winter of 1848–49 was another event of 1848: the discovery of gold in California by James Marshall, a foreman in the construction of a sawmill on John A. Sutter's property on the American River. Despite efforts to keep the discovery secret and despite persistent skepticism, by May 1848 a stampede had begun, attracting miners from Chile and Peru, woodsmen from Oregon, prospectors from Australia, and merchants from the Hawaiian Islands. These were the forty-eighters.

So great was the frenzy to get to the gold fields that more than half the adult male population of the Oregon country flooded into California, perhaps three-fourths of San Francisco's population deserted the city, and scores of ships lay abandoned along the coast, their crews having disappeared inland. At a time when many laborers on the East Coast eked out a living on less than a dollar a day, enough miners earned thousands of dollars in just a few weeks to excite the imagination of those contemplating a journey to California and sustain them along the way. By September 1848, the discovery at Sutter's Mill and subsequent strikes were the talk of the day in New Orleans, Washington, New York, a thousand other places in the nation, and even in western Europe. Exaggeration and wishful thinking combined to make each strike larger than the last, and everywhere groups and individuals made plans to go west in the spring of 1849.[2] These were the forty-niners.

On December 5, 1848, President James K. Polk, a lame duck who perhaps wanted to justify his role in helping to spark the Mexican War, delivered his annual message to Congress, describing in glowing terms the gold of California. With this executive blessing and with confirmed official reports from California, the nation erupted with enthusiasm. Portions of Europe resonated this enthusiasm, some of those who fled the upheavals of the failed revolutions of 1848 making plans to go to California.

The dramatic events of 1848 were interrelated in a number of ways and unfolded against a national backdrop of sweeping change, occurring as they did after decades of westward expansion, sporadic conflicts with Indians, dizzying commercial growth, profound breakthroughs in transportation and communication, rapid urbanization, a shift in immigration toward Ireland and the German states, bubbling anti-Catholicism, continued agitation for the annexation of Canada, growing interest in the Caribbean world, a vague but pronounced romantic spirit, a myriad of reforms that sought to address a wide range of social ills, exuberant nationalism, and lingering (if somewhat latent) tension between a bustling North and an increasingly embattled South. These diverse conditions and developments helped to shape, channel, and focus the course of the gold rush.

Emigrants could get to California in at least six basic ways: the long voyage around stormy Cape Horn; a sea-land journey via Panama or Nicaragua; by sea to Veracruz, overland across the waist of Mexico, and then by sea from such ports as Acapulco; the Santa Fe Trail to the Gila River route, which took emigrants through the blazing Sonora; a route that led overlanders from the southwestern states to El Paso and into what is now southern New Mexico before joining the Gila River route; and the great central route via the Platte and North Platte rivers and the Sweetwater to South Pass, after which there were several options. (The route along the

1. The Overland Route. Frontispiece from Alonzo Delano, *Life on the Plains and Among the Diggings* (1854).

Platte to South Pass is aptly called the Great Platte River Road, and it is a near certainty that in 1849 it took more emigrants to California than all the other routes combined.) The sea routes around Cape Horn and to Central America appealed to people from New England and elsewhere along the East Coast. Southerners often went through the Southwest or Central America, although a number of companies and individuals from the South ventured west via Missouri and the Great Platte River Road. Travelers from nearly all parts of the nation—especially from the Upper Mississippi Valley and the Middle Atlantic States—used the Platte route, many of them funneling into Missouri via the Ohio River and other waterways.

In early 1849, gold fever struck the village of Como in Whiteside County, Illinois. Dr. Charles Ross Parke and eight other men organized the Como

2. Charles Ross Parke, M.D. From *Illustrated Bloomington and Normal Illinois* (Bloomington, 1896).

Pioneer Company on April 1 and left for California on April 7. In several ways, their group was similar to hundreds of others formed throughout the nation that winter and spring. Practically no one attempted the long journey on his own, although some individuals and small groups waited until they had reached a staging area, or jumping-off place, in western Missouri or elsewhere before combining with others.

Although the household had been the basic migration unit as the frontier moved west, this was not the case now. Unlike those of 1850 and later, nearly all—perhaps 95 to 98 percent—of 1849's emigrants going to California via the overland route were adult males, and this was reflected in the Como company. In the years that followed, the majority of those making the journey were male adults, but the percentage was much lower—perhaps 67 percent or so.

Other social and economic characteristics of the Como organization matched those in the larger overland population. The economic status of the average member cannot be determined with precision, but the company did have men of means and standing, and there is no evidence that any member was destitute. As was true of nearly all other such groups, religious considerations appeared not to have been a factor in the selection of Como members. And the education level was quite high, which was probably true of the general overland population. The percentage of emigrant physicians was surprisingly large, and the presence of one in the nine-member Como party probably raised the average. In terms of overall economic and social well-being, Como probably was fairly similar to many 1849 overland companies.

Charles Parke noted in his diary that the basic objective was the "search of gold and sight-seeing." Implicit in this was the idea of adventure. The motives that propelled tens of thousands of overlanders westward varied, but they seem to have included the hope of self-improvement, excitement, and renewal and a desire to take part in a vast undertaking. News of the gold strikes in California seemed to be providential; it was heady, and scores of thousands, especially young men, saw in it adventure and profit. But some journeyed west to improve the condition of their families, one individual writing, "I ought to make all the endavors [sic], I can, to place that dear wife & family of mine if I can above want."[3] Another, a physician, wanted to break away from society's artificial constraints "and try for a while the life of liberty and unrestrained indulgence; the future will show the result."[4]

Those who streamed across the continent seemed buoyed by a spirit of optimism and expectation. At least a few wrote that the long walk—the vast majority walked most of the way—improved their health, and at least a few went west with this intention. Writing to his mother from California in December 1849, Bolivar Krepps observed, "I have enjoyed the very best of health ever since I left the States and so have the other boys."[5] (The important fact is that he felt good about the trek and its effects on him, not

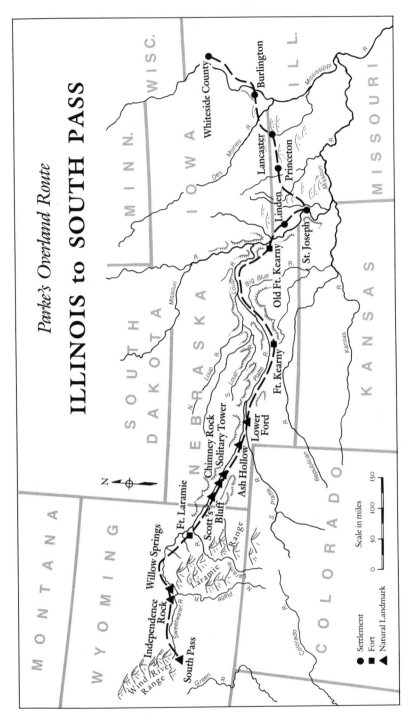

Parke's Overland Route from Illinois to California

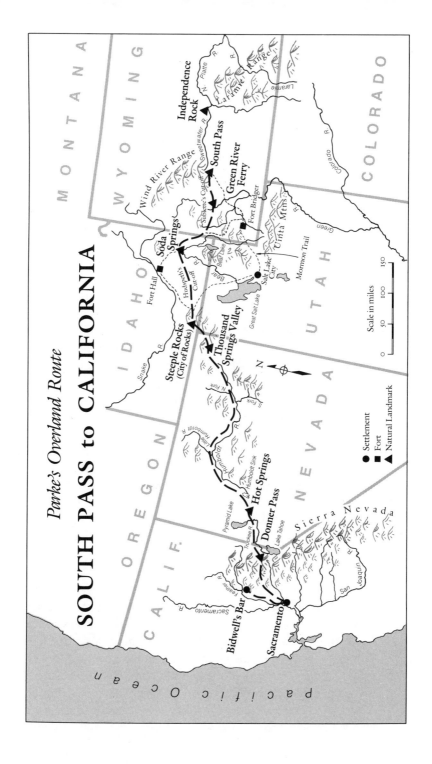

Parke's Overland Route

SOUTH PASS to CALIFORNIA

that he died less than a month later.) It is possible that many of the forty-niners never really understood the motive or set of motives that caused them to leave their homes and venture into the unknown, but most seemed to be aware that they were participating in a momentous event. Perhaps many never really understood why they made the journey, other than feeling some vague urge to do something different with many other people and possibly become wealthy in the process.

In their quest for adventure, many emigrants were eager to encounter obstacles, overcome them, and bask in the knowledge that they had triumphed. They were willing to endure inconvenience and hardship and even risk death. They wanted to "see the elephant" (an expression that was enormously popular among forty-niners).[6]

Two facts are fundamental in understanding the gold rush of 1849: it was the product of voluntary acts of thousands of individuals, and essentially it was privately operated. Except for a minuscule number of slaves who were taken along, no one was forced to go. Nor did those who went call upon the federal government to organize expeditions, subsidize them, guarantee profits, or bail out those that foundered economically. The government, of course, ultimately did operate a thin chain of military posts in the West, such as Fort Kearny and eventually Fort Laramie, and ammunition and weapons were sold at cost to some emigrants. However, aside from these acts of assistance and treaties that opened the West to settlement, there was precious little government encouragement or support. Moreover, the groups that pushed into the plains and mountains were virtually without public regulation, which allowed for spontaneity, creativity, flexibility, and informality as well as occasional irresponsibility, deceit, and even disaster. Writing to his wife from Salt Lake City on September 18, 1849, Dr. Caleb Ormsby observed:

> This emigration may be regarded as one of the greatest anomalies in the history of man. In enterprise and daring, it surpasses the crusades, Alexander's expedition to India, or Napoleon's to Russia. These originated with Potentates and religious enthusiasts—were supported by the combined wealth of nations, and urged forward by the power of Kings, Emperors, Pontiffs, and a Religious mania. This is the spontaneous exhibition of the enterprise and daring of the American character. Tens of thousands voluntarily rush forward, unaided by any national treasure and unprotected by any political power; each one acts as his own sovereign, directs his own time and

mode for travel, and feasts or starves at pleasure. He asks no aid but such as he has a right to call his own—no protection but health, strength, and a trusty rifle. With these, he is ready to encounter the beasts of the forest, and the savages of the mountain wilds. Acting on obedience to no political power—urged on by no religious zeal, he is actuated solely by his love of adventure, and his love of gold.[7]

Again and again the overlanders were thrown back on themselves for solutions to problems and again and again they produced them, becoming different people in doing so.

Although some of the overlanders were seeking new beginnings, most were not desperate, nor were they eager to abandon completely the social and political arrangements they had known; quite to the contrary, it appears that the vast majority sought to replicate these in countless ways. Views on such matters as division of labor, observance of the Sabbath, due process for people accused of crime, protection of private property, and other matters were perpetuated on the overland trail.[8]

One way in which social relationships were altered, despite efforts to preserve the status quo, surfaced in the roles played by men and women. The latter were scarce, both on the trail and in California, and this did much to change, at least temporarily, male-female relationships. Parke took keen interest in female activities and roles throughout his travels in the West and in Central America. In his diary, he notes Indian women, female emigrants, a young woman smoking cigarettes and dealing cards, women who were snappish to their husbands, and attractive Hispanic women who caught the eye of young overlanders. In addition, he notes on May 17 that he had to "do my own washing for the first time in my life." The washing of one's own clothes was a mystery into which many men were initiated that summer, Alonzo Delano undergoing the rite somewhere on the Platte River: "A number of us took our dirty shirts, and going to a pond nearby, commenced our laundry manipulations, for the first time in our lives." He added, significantly, that "we thought of our wives and sweet-hearts at home, and wondered that we were ever dissatisfied with their impatience on a washing day."[9]

Because some men loathed this type of work or were inept at it, they were exceedingly glad when women showed up, hoping the newcomers could be cajoled into becoming laundresses. James F. Wilkins was still in western Missouri when it dawned on him that it would be desirable to have a woman around. When an Englishman and his wife joined the company,

Wilkins was delighted, writing, "Altho' it will cause us to be more crowded and ill-convenient in some respects, still she will be able to do the cooking and washing up, which is a great relief [to Wilkins]."[10] Apparently, some women accepted traditional roles and thought nothing of it. On April 24 some strangers, including a woman, camped with the Como party; one of the Como men suggested that she bake biscuits for everyone, "and she consented, delighted to think she could add to our comfort." Women were not always available, however, and countless men had to do "women's work" for the first time in their lives; and some finally had to do some "men's work."

Besides trying to master firearms, which most seemed very eager to do, some men were called upon to have their first serious discussion with draft animals. Wrote one: "This day I was thirty-five years, eleven months, and two days old. I had never yoked an ox; but I was now about to commence driving my own teams." He took his job seriously, and after much practice he mastered the art of yoking and driving oxen.[11] Responses varied widely, but most men realized that changing conditions, including imbalance in the sex ratio, demanded new roles, at least temporarily.

A manifestation of conservatism was the tendency for overland companies to adopt constitutions and bylaws for the trip. Some constitutions were relatively brief and flexible, others elaborate and intricate, attempting to deal with every possible contingency. Most were remarkably reasonable and reflected the considered thought of reasonable men. The documents reflected contemporary social conditions by allowing virtually all white male adults to vote on constitutions and bylaws, elect officers, vote on such matters as admitting new members or determining routes, and, finally, to decide whether to dissolve the company. Not considered were wealth, religion, length of U.S. residency, or tenure in the company. Even youngsters voted on occasion. Women almost never did, although some expressed their views before a vote. There is no evidence that black men were permitted to participate in any significant way.

Many wagon trains stopped periodically for a day or more to rest and thrash out important matters. Nearly all had factions or individuals who became unhappy and left peacefully, and a few trains expelled miscreants.[12] Similarly, the constitutions and bylaws of most contained provisions for granting individuals and small groups full and immediate membership, the newcomers being required to abide by existing conditions, as was the case in the Como company. Generally, though, the trail communities were open, inclusive, fluid, tolerant, and participatory, and for the most part they operated within the broad framework of written law.[13]

There was an optimum size for overland companies. They needed to be large enough to permit division of labor and allow for unforeseen problems, yet if they were too large, they were difficult to manage and overtaxed fuel, water, and feed supplies. Almost certainly the Como Pioneer Company was too small when it left home, which probably accounts for the fact that it quickly expanded and reorganized.[14]

Occasionally, outfits were set up as both emigrant and mining companies, the expectation being that members would mine together in California.[15] Some of these were organized months before the journey and boasted elaborate constitutions and regulations, but the ones that made it to California without disintegrating usually did not remain intact for long.

Parke and his associates were convinced that once they left their jumping-off point they would be set upon by swarms of ferocious Pawnee Indians and that if they managed to make it through Pawnee territory, other Indians would make life miserable for them the rest of the way. In their youth, the Como men and other emigrants had imbibed tales of Indian onslaughts, and before they ventured onto the plains they armed themselves to the hilt and honed their martial skills.[16] All overland companies posted sentries at night, and some companies went so far as to organize along tight military lines and fancied themselves to be military units. Reality was far different from what they had envisioned: in all of 1849, perhaps only thirty-three emigrants were killed by Indians.[17] Even the dreaded Pawnees proved to be no threat. As a matter of fact, many overlanders did not see an Indian on their way west in 1849.

Parke's party and others took far too much with them. Most travelers crammed their wagons full of heavy furniture, bulky utensils, large quantities of food, weapons and ammunition, items of sentimental value only, and even bogus gold-mining equipment foisted on them by unscrupulous merchants. Newspaper advertisements in early 1849 urged gold seekers and other emigrants to take many things for which there was little or no need.[18] As oxen and mules became fatigued, nonessential possessions were discarded in mounds, some being pitched after only a few miles. The chore continued well into what is now Nevada.

Oxen were chosen as draft animals by Parke and his associates, as they were by countless other outfits.[19] The Como company had at least some familiarity with some earlier accounts of the West.[20] These accounts gave overlanders basic advice and introduced them to place-names and conditions they would encounter. The accounts were also misleading at times, giving false mileage figures or indicating the presence of wood for fuel where none existed. After reading them, some emigrants expected to travel for days before seeing another human being or feared they would become lost. Reality was radically different. Again and again, overlanders expressed amazement at the number of wagon trains they were able to see at a glance, and at night the landscape frequently sparkled with hundreds of camp fires. So thick was the overland traffic, in fact, that there was relatively little chance that a company or even an individual would get lost.

That spring, cholera stalked the land, bringing with it irrational fear, bizarre cures, swift death, and sometimes a feeling of shame for the victims and their families.[21] Cholera, smallpox, accidents, and other grief thinned emigrant ranks at jumping-off places, and the men from Como were not immune to it. Diarrhea afflicted nearly every train, causing Parke and others to wonder whether it meant cholera.[22]

The daily routine of the Como Pioneer Company was similar to that in countless other wagon trains. The emigrants rose early for the most part, traveled through the morning, nooned for at least an hour and sometimes for several hours, and selected a campsite by late afternoon or early evening.[23] They measured their mileage with odometers, often called roadometers.[24] Parke walked all but about three hundred miles, which was the case for most emigrants that summer, places in the wagons being reserved for the sick, the very young, pregnant women, and others in need. Being part of a vast procession passing through a largely unwooded region from the Missouri River to the other side of South Pass, Parke and his mates used buffalo chips for cook fires.[25] In the evening, at least two sentries were posted, each man taking his turn. In many companies, however, physicians were excused from this duty and others, so the fact that Parke took his turn on guard duty suggests that the Como company was so small that everyone had to pitch in.

Fearsome thunderstorms swept away tents, played havoc with the animals, and lit up the skies with their brilliant fury. Such storms did much to increase the forty-niners' toil and suffering and discourage them.[26] Adding to their misery were such unexpected surprises as voracious mosquitoes and the towering Sierra Nevada Range. In countless small ways and some large ways as well, the overlanders were constantly surprised and constantly had to adjust. This led to grumbling and sniping, but Parke's group apparently was not afflicted as much as other companies, where sometimes the end result was violence.[27]

The Como people made frequent and sometimes prolonged contact with other wagon trains. They quickly learned that the Indian threat was relatively slight, and many seized the opportunity to be alone for the better part of the day, sometimes riding off to visit another train or hunting fresh meat for the evening meal. Perhaps the contact with other trains caused overlanders to feel somewhat less attached to their own and may have weakened unity, but in any case the vast majority of wagon trains broke up before reaching the gold fields or shortly thereafter. Even those that remained intact had relatively little success in the gold fields, and aside from Captain Sampson, who met with a fair amount of success, few people in the Como company did much more than make a living. Most who engaged in mining were richer only for the experience. The fact that relatively few found gold and the fact that their adventure had worn thin produced discouragement. Compounding this was the fact that inflated prices gobbled up most of the profits of even moderately successful miners.[28]

The Como company had had its shakedown by the time it arrived opposite Old Fort Kearny (present-day Nebraska City) on the Missouri River. Its members had made camp, decided issues, suffered tribulation, displayed petty jealousies, and had pretty well settled into established routines. Compared with other companies, it arrived in California relatively unscathed.[29] At least a few trains did not travel on Sundays, but Parke and his companions did.[30] The major difference between their group and others, however, was this: its route to western Missouri was used by very few other companies, if any, and at no time did it travel on waterways.

Most of the overland companies failed to produce an extant diary or journal. Very few produced two or more surviving diaries, and most of these groups were large, in some cases the diarists barely knowing each other. Of the original nine men in the Como organization, two, Charles Ross Parke and David B. Carnes, kept diaries that have survived; another diary that touches upon the travels of the Como men was kept by Carnes's cousin, William B. Lorton. The Parke and Carnes accounts complement and supplement each other nicely. Even so, we know relatively little about the Como company. For example, we do not know where in Como the organizational meeting took place or who called it. Some members of the company—Levi Strope, William Cushing, and Frederick Stimam—remain obscure. A Levi W. Strope is recorded as buying land in Como Township on July 10, 1847, but there is no other county record of him or the other two men. It is entirely possible, moreover, that Levi W. Strope is not the same man who went west with the Como party. None of the three appears in state records of the time, and it seems that none returned to Illinois. Since Parke referred to Cushing as "Our Dutchman" and since all three men traveled together and apparently remained together as messmates, it is reasonable to assume that they were recent arrivals from the German states.[31]

Many overland companies received attention from newspapers as they organized and made their way across the continent. This was especially true of groups established in or near towns that had newspapers, those that passed through St. Louis or other towns where newspapers gave extensive coverage to overland trains, those that loitered for a few days in one of the western Missouri staging areas before shoving off, and those that had some distinctive feature, perhaps a well-known individual or a unique goal. The Como party had none of these, and news of its formation, departure, and progress to California was never printed in newspapers. There were no papers in or near Whiteside County, and those beyond the immediate vicinity—in Chicago, Rockford, or Galena, for example—were too far away to notice. Papers in such places as Burlington, Iowa, and Oquawka, Illinois, devoted much space to overland enterprises, but even they failed to notice the Como company.

The Como Pioneer Company was not like the Pioneer Line, an ill-fated commercial passenger venture which was the subject of newspaper advertisements, articles, endorsements, and other attention for months prior to its departure; which was the object of great interest to many emigrants as it stumbled westward; and which was still newsworthy as late as December 1849, long after its survivors staggered into California.[32] There was nothing novel or outstanding about the Como company; it simply was not newsworthy. It is possible, too, that decisions made by Captain Simeon Sampson and Dr. Parke and possibly others steered the Como men away from most contact with correspondents and other writers.

The life and activities of Dr. Charles Ross Parke were far from ordinary, but his early life did exhibit characteristics that were quite typical of the era.[33] Born on June 25, 1823, in Parkesburg, Chester County, Pennsylvania, he was the son of George Washington Parke and Mary (Ross) Parke. Charles Ross Parke's great-grandfather was William Parke, a man of Scotch-Irish extraction who left his home in the north of Ireland and settled in America. During the American Revolution, he served as a member of the Committee of Safety in Pennsylvania and as a member of the state legislature. George Washington Parke, Charles Ross Parke's father, was a native of Parkesburg and, after inheriting mill property, thrived as a farmer, miller, and tanner. He served as justice of the peace from 1828 to 1837 and register of wills from 1842 to 1845. His first wife, Mary Fleming, died in 1817 when she was thirty-one.[34] In 1820 he married Mary Ross.[35] She died in 1863 at the age of eighty-two, and he died in 1860 at seventy-nine. Both were Presbyterians, a faith in which Charles Parke was reared but did not formally join.

Charles Parke received his primary education in nearby schools, working on the farm and in the mill during his spare time. When his father was elected register of wills in 1842, he accompanied him to the county seat, West Chester, as an aide. There he enrolled as a day student in Science Hill, a boarding school operated by Quaker educator Joshua Hoopes. Fixing his attention on the possibility of entering medical school, in 1843 Parke began the study of medicine in West Chester in the office of one of the state's most respected physicians, Dr. Wilmer Worthington. He then attended medical classes for three years at the University of Pennsylvania in Philadelphia, from which he graduated on April 3, 1847. His essay in medical school was titled "Scarlatina."[36]

Upon his graduation from medical school, Dr. Parke practiced for a year at Concordville in western Delaware County, Pennsylvania. In 1848 he came to Illinois to join his half-brothers, John, Samuel, and George, on the east bank of the Illinois River in Tazewell County, across from Peoria, where the three brothers ran a water-powered furniture factory. In the autumn of 1848, Dr. Parke moved to Como, a settlement on the north side of the Rock River in Whiteside County. Exactly what prompted him to move from his half-brothers northward to Whiteside County is not known, but in the township of Como and the surrounding area in Whiteside County were a number of households from Pennsylvania. Little is known about Parke's motivations, for no letters or other private papers written by him are known to exist, other than some items pertaining to his life in Bloomington years later. Not much is known of his life in Como, and his presence there did not manifest itself in existing county records. In any case, a desire to move to new locations (it would stay with him until he was well into his thirties) surfaced once again, and in April 1849 he became the surgeon for the Como Pioneer Company.

In significant ways, Parke's education and general background set him apart from most of his contemporaries, but in other ways his views and attitudes reflect much of the popular thinking of the era. As was true of many people who trekked overland in 1849, Parke is quick to see in some Indians lofty traits and in other Indians base qualities. Cautious curiosity perhaps best describes the basic attitude Parke and countless others displayed that summer toward most Indians. Some of his views probably reflected some reading he had done on the West, and other views were probably the products of conversations with other emigrants and his personal observations along the way.[37] His views of the Hispanic world were ambivalent. On the one hand, he was fascinated by the lovely scenery he found there, the pleasant people, various foods, flora and fauna, cities, and other aspects of life. On the other, he was shocked and repulsed by what he regarded as cruel brutality, corrupt church-state relationships, wasteful inefficiencies, violence, and sloth, to cite only some of the conditions that grated on him. A number of factors probably combined to shape his views of the Hispanic world: the course of the recent Mexican War; his Protestant background and brewing anti-Catholic nativism in Pennsylvania and else-where; his personal quest for education and his zeal for reform in society; a belief in republicanism and the institutions that reflect republican values; his strong work ethic; a perhaps somewhat prudish attitude; an abhorrence of military violence in politics; some unfortunate personal experiences; and perhaps a tendency to regard some groups of people prejudicially. His views of others, in short, appear to be products of his personal background, the social environment in which he matured, and his contact with others.

Parke's diary is the work of an inquisitive, intelligent, and energetic man who had strong opinions. He has an anthropologist's eye for Indians and their lifestyles, a young man's eye for the ladies, a sociologist's eye for the roles that various people play in their societies, and a politician's eye for the art of governance. He was interested in interpersonal relationships, friction between individuals, and many other aspects of social intercourse. He developed strong predispositions, even contempt, toward some people and certain lifestyles. There is irony in this, for often it is these people—the people for whom Parke has the strongest dislike—who are the subjects of his writing. Now and then humor surfaces, as it did when he described some poor fellow who simultaneously had seasickness and bowel difficulties. His diary indicates that he held some views that were deplorable yet probably reflected popular thought in contemporary society, but these very attitudes and others resulted in some memorable and valuable observations.

Unlike many gold-rush diarists, Parke did not flag near the end of the trail. His entries for western Nevada and the Sierra Nevada Range are vivid and vibrant. He did not miss a day. Another strength is the fact that he continued to write in California, although the entries become sporadic after mid-September. In the mining camps he was intrigued by the unusual roles of women, white-Indian contact and conflict, violence, sickness, inflated costs, and the kaleidoscopic, effervescent society. He and his mining associates must have found enough gold to eke out a living, but in the end Parke's enthusiasm ebbed, as did that of most other miners. He resolved to return to Illinois.

His choice of routes was fortunate because it gives his diary a rare quality. Of the overlanders who returned to the eastern states, perhaps some ninety thousand did so via Panama, but only a few hundred traversed Nicaragua and Mexico.[38] Parke returned through the young nation of Nicaragua and saw much, including turbulent politics that involved the Mosquito Indians and rivalry between international powers.

The diary is not free of weaknesses. It contains inaccuracies and there are omissions, as well as ambiguity. There are a couple of slips of the pen. One of the most bothersome characteristics, however, is Parke's tendency to refer to people on the trail and in California by surname only. This irritating habit made it impossible in many instances to identify people with any degree of certainty.

Even though it has faults and even though Parke's foibles were hardly minor, the diary is a fascinating account of life in the middle nineteenth century. Parke takes obvious delight in crafting his sentences and paragraphs, and his enthusiasm and interest in the world around him are catching. He and his diary exhibit many of the era's strengths and weaknesses by shedding light on motivation, personal interaction, national character, and other aspects of the human experience. Finally, the diary provides valuable assistance in helping America to understand its past.

Note on the Editing

The bibliography contains authors' full names, titles, and related information for all the works cited in this volume. Overland journals, diaries, and other accounts are cited by authors' surnames and pertinent dates or page numbers. In editing Dr. Charles Ross Parke's diary for publication, my purpose has been to retain as much of the original as possible, making changes and corrections only when failure to do so might produce misunderstanding or incomplete understanding. Care was exercised to preserve the flavor and flow of Parke's rich narrative. For ease of reading, however, Parke's spelling, including medical and geographical terms, has been modernized. For the same reason, it made no sense to retain his few slips of the pen, squiggles, or ambiguous marks, given the often trying conditions under which he wrote his diary. Errors of spelling by Parke and others that threatened understanding, clarity, or flow have been corrected, as have a few threatening lapses in punctuation. Excessive capitalization, employed during the era to indicate emphasis, has been modernized. Wherever necessary, reasonable paragraphing has been provided. In a few instances when sentences were deleterious to the flow of the narrative or to comprehension, the offending sentences were either slightly altered or deleted. Occasionally, Parke omitted a word; whenever possible, I have furnished by means of brackets the intended words. Even with these corrections and interpolations, however, the manuscript here is virtually identical to Parke's diary. At the end of most of Parke's daily entries, two mileage figures appear. The first figure is Parke's; the second figure, in brackets, is that of David Carnes, another member of the Como Pioneer Company. Excerpts from Carnes's diary augment Parke's entries, and these excerpts appear in brackets.

Whiteside County to Old Fort Kearny

April 8–May 17

☛*The Como Pioneer Company left home on April 7 for St. Joseph, Missouri, a key outfitting post. Traveling in a southwesterly direction from Whiteside County, the company ferried the Mississippi River just south of Burlington, Iowa, traversed southeastern Iowa, and entered Missouri by way of Scotland County. From this point it followed a westerly route before turning toward St. Joseph. Learning that cholera had reached St. Joseph via steamboats from St. Louis, the company veered away from that town and went up the east bank of the Missouri River, crossed the southwestern corner of Iowa, then ferried the Missouri River and camped just beyond Old Fort Kearny. ☛ This leg of the journey was a shakedown, a chance to test and learn and adjust. Members of the company coped with sickness, strayed animals, the need to forage, mechanical problems, failed logistics, discouraging counsel from people who had given up and were returning home, and general fatigue and tension. They grappled with the need to make crucial decisions on the basis of imperfect knowledge. They forded rivers, set up camp, admitted new members, and did such mundane things as "my own washing for the first time in my life." Their perception of conditions resulted in their avoiding St. Joseph, heading instead for Old Fort Kearny, a staging area used by few overlanders. On balance, members of the Como Company proved to be durable, resourceful, flexible, and adaptable. Things augured well for the remainder of the journey.*

APRIL 8—MAY 17

APRIL 8,
SUNDAY

Capt. Simeon Sampson of Como, Whiteside County, Illinois, organized the Como Pioneer Co., April 1, 1849. Object: crossing the plains to California in search of gold and sight seeing.

The Co. consisted of the following persons, with three wagons each drawn by three yokes of oxen:

1st team	Capt. Simeon Sampson
	David Carnes
	Daniel Brooks, Esq.
	Dr. Charles R. Parke, Surgeon
2nd wagon	Levi Strope
	William Cushing
	Frederick Stiman
3rd wagon	Robert Pollock
	George E. Kelsey[1]

We left home April 7, 1849 direct for St. Joseph, Mo. Arrived at Prophetstown. Called after Black Hawk's prophet, this being his home.[2] 12 miles. *[11 miles]*

APRIL 9,
MONDAY

[At] Geneseo, half past 2:00 p.m., where we will remain until morning.[3] We spent most of the afternoon practicing with our rifles, target shooting 138 yards. Bullseye 3 inches in diameter. My ball struck 4 inches from center and was awarded the best shot.

David Carnes taken with a chill.[4] *[9 miles]*

APRIL 10,
TUESDAY

Laid over on account of severe storm with big wind veering from S.W. to N.W. when it cleared off.

Gave Carnes grs. viii Quinine and grs. ii opium.[5] He is feeling better. William Cushing shot a wild goose, one of the fattest I ever saw. Acres of them in view. Sold out our flour on account of weight. All hands well and in good spirits.

APRIL 11,
WEDNESDAY

The first day out we drove 12 miles to Prophetstown; from there to Dutchman, 14 miles; then to Geneseo, 8 miles; from Geneseo this morning [to] Andover, 18 miles; and from Andover to private house, 6 miles. Met a Mr. Graham the afternoon we laid over at Geneseo. Said he was bound for California on a mule. Think he may need company before he reaches the "diggins." Saw five deer this afternoon.

All sorts of reports prevalent about crossing the different ferries on the Mississippi River.[6] Mr. Carnes missed his chill today. Has been on duty. Gave him quinine and capsicum last evening and this morning.[7]

The prairie has been on fire all day.[8] Some places we had to turn out of its way and "save our bacon."

APRIL 12,
THURSDAY

Drove 8 miles this morning and have decided to cross the Mississippi at New Boston. 18 miles.

APRIL 13,
FRIDAY

Drove 10 miles yesterday afternoon and camped all night at a mill.[9] Rained furiously all night.

We left this morning at 9:00 o'clock and traveled 16 miles on our way to New Boston. Weather clear and cold. Price of hay 12½ cents per yoke of cattle. Corn 18¾ cents per bushel. 16 miles.

APRIL 14,
SATURDAY

Traveled 11 miles today. Could not cross at New Boston on account of high water, so [we] determined to go up to Burlington, Iowa.[10] We have traveled through Whiteside and Henry counties, and are now in Mercer. All of us well, excepting my sore lips and ankle. This portion of the Mississippi valley is beautiful. 11 miles.

APRIL 15,
SUNDAY

Made 15 miles of a drive today. Saw one deer and one wolf. Some of the company thought there was a chance for fresh meat, but the smoke of the powder had hardly blown away before the meat was out of sight. We are now in camp on Henderson Creek, one mile from the Mississippi River and ½ mile below Oquawka.[11] Good weather, and all of us feeling fine. 15 miles.

APRIL 16,
MONDAY

Came to Shauka River this morning 6 miles below Burlington. Here we took the steam ferry and crossed over to Burlington, Iowa, and are now camped about one mile west of the city. We traveled in all 17 miles. River very high.

Burlington is a very pretty city, situated on an elevated piece of ground on the Iowa bank of the river. The wharf is rather confined, which will prevent the city from extending up and down the river.

We paid $2.00 per team to cross [the] ferry. 17 miles.

APRIL 17,
TUESDAY

Laid over at Major Smith's about 1½ miles west of Burlington. A very cold day with snow squalls. Smith was a Major in the Black Hawk War.[12]

Shipped all our meat and flour, also my books, to St. Joseph, Mo.

APRIL 18,
WEDNESDAY

Left Smith's camp this morning. Came 12 miles. Crossed Skunk River at Augusta, 9 miles west of Burlington. Augusta is quite a business place.

The river is dammed here, which runs a saw mill and carding machine. There is also a distillery in this place. One of Esq. Brooks' oxen jumped overboard while being ferried across the river. He swam to the other shore "right side up with care." Two boys were drowned this morning, carried over the dam in a skiff. The three men who accompanied them swam ashore. The boys were sons of a widow. Bodies not found yet.[13]

Two miles from Augusta is the town of Denmark, a very handsome little town, some brick houses.

The country through which we passed today is the prettiest I have seen in the West. We are now encamped on Lost Creek, named on account of its sinking and rising again some distance below. 12 miles.

APRIL 19,
THURSDAY

Left Lost Creek camp this morning at 8½ o'clock. Came through West Point, a very pleasant looking town.[14] Traveled 18 miles through a beautiful country. 18 miles.

APRIL 20,
FRIDAY

Broke up camp and traveled 16 miles, camping 5 miles from the river "Des Moins." We are now in Van Buren County. Oats in sheaf, 15 cents per dozen. Corn 15 cents per bushel. Eggs 3 to 4 cents a dozen, and you better believe we enjoyed them, "all fresh from the mint." This is a great chicken country, but being an inland town and no railroads eggs are a drug. All well with the exception of sore lips. 16 miles.

APRIL 21,
SATURDAY

Came 14 miles. Crossed the Des Moines River at Keosauqua, a very prosperous looking little town, the county seat of Van Buren County.[15] There is a fine brick court house, and the other buildings are in proportion handsome. The people are generally intelligent looking. While our company was being ferried across the river, I seated myself on a log and watched the performance. Soon I was accosted by an old farmer looking "josie."[16] "Which way are you traveling, mister?" I told him and changed the interrogatory, asking him where he came from and what was his name. He seemed very communicative. Possibly had not seen any strangers for a long time. He remarked his name was Pearson and years ago hailed from New London Cross Roads, Chester County, Pennsylvania, and was now living in Keosauqua.[17] Had two children.

I was thunder struck and remarked, "You from Chester County, Pa? That's where I was born and raised." Then I told him my name and it was his time to get a thunder clap. Said he knew all the Parkes, and of course he asked me many questions about all the people he left at his old home. And we parted *forever*.

The road from Keosauqua to Tippecanoe is through a broken country, moderately timbered. Fall wheat looks splendid. Saw a couple of deer, but did not get a shot at them.[18] 14 miles. *[16 miles]*

APRIL 22
SUNDAY

Came 14 miles today (Sunday), entered the state of Missouri. Scotland County. This part of the state is very sparsely settled and very broken. Camped on a small stream. Esq. Brooks shot the head off a grey squirrel with his rifle, which elated him very much. Suppose he will blow over it all the way to California. 14 miles. *[13 miles]*

APRIL 23,
MONDAY

After spending a very pleasant Sunday evening and night on ———— Creek, we left this morning, driving 15 miles and camping on ———— Creek. Six other teams in sight. All hands well. Strope threw up his supper last night, but is all right this morning. Cattle all doing well. Have been turned out on grass for last two nights and fed them corn.[19] 15 miles.

APRIL 24,
TUESDAY

We traveled 21 miles today and are now camped on "Grand Sharatan River."[20] There is quite an abundance of timber along this stream, mostly white oak. We passed through Lancaster, the county seat of Schuyler [County] Missouri. Tis a small town, but has a jail in which is confined a murderer, sentenced to streatch hemp shortly.[21]

The "divide"—as the Missourians call it—ridge, which leads from Lancaster to the Sharatan at Haregraves Mill, is well timbered. This is a ridge with spurs extending out about 50 yards on either side. These spurs are about 25 yards from each other and the ravines between are from 50 to 100 feet deep. Sides nearly perpendicular.

Good joke on Kelsey last night. He fed his horse all Mr. Strope's brewed coffee.[22] Two or three straggling teams came into camp this afternoon. One of the men had a wife. Scarce articles in this "neck of woods."

Esq. Brooks' imagination carried him back to the settlements as soon as he saw this female and suggested the idea of biscuits for supper. He accordingly broached the subject to her, and she consented, delighted to think she could add to our comfort. We too were happy in anticipation of *home* "doins." In due time the long looked for morsels appeared from the Dutch oven smoking hot, but the color was yellow and they could be scented afar off. Solid as lead. Oh, Lord, what a disappointment. Sorry for the poor woman. She thought they were splendid.

When we cross the Sharatan [we] will be in Putnam Co. 21 miles.

APRIL 25,
WEDNESDAY

Came from Haregraves Mill to Shoal creek 9 miles. Camped early to bake bread.

I strolled up the creek in search of game. Saw one wild turkey. Shot a fine fox squirrel. Saw 9 deer today. Brooks acted as nimrod but failed to get meat. Price of corn 30 cents. Plenty of grass on creek bottom for cattle. 9 miles.

APRIL 26,
THURSDAY

Came 18 miles through a very broken country. Passed through Winchester, the county seat of Putnam. It contained about *six* log houses with interstices filled with mud, and *not one pane of glass in the whole town*.[23]

William Cushing sick with bilious colic. All hands in good spirits. Oxen doing well on grass with some corn.[24] 18 miles.

APRIL 27,
FRIDAY

Drove 14 miles and camped on a small creek. Plenty of company today. Six wagons from Milwaukee. Deer and wild turkey plenty. Shot a fine turkey. Consequently, will feast tonight.[25] 14 miles.

APRIL 28,
SATURDAY

Came 20 miles. Parted with our company early in the morning and have not seen them since. We are camped 6 miles from Princeton, Mercer County.[26] We passed through Dodge County. Have now been out 3 weeks and are 100 miles from St. Joseph, Missouri. All hands well except Carnes, who feels a little chilly. Paid 40 cents for corn.[27] 20 miles.

APRIL 29,
SUNDAY

Came 11 miles. Camped about 5 miles west of Princeton. Carnes took some quinine and feels pretty well this morning.[28] Princeton is a small village on the East branch of Grand River. This branch is well timbered, chiefly elm, hickory, and white oak. We cannot find two citizens to agree on the distances from this place to the county seat of Harrison County.

The country is rather broken with some prairie. Red plum trees from 2 to 20 feet high, all out in full bloom— a beautiful sight—while the atmosphere is loaded with their fragrance. When in such spots, we always think of

"Those we left behind," and wish they could enjoy it with us. They always refresh the "weary traveller."

Corn 20 to 25 cents. I shot at a turkey today and Brooks at a duck, but alas the feathers carried them away. 11 miles.

APRIL 30,
MONDAY

Came 12 miles today and camped on Rock Creek in Harrison County. Crossed the middle branch of Grand River about noon. Swam the cattle across first, then unloaded all the goods that could be damaged by water. The wagons were then run into the river, a long rope extending across the river was attached to the end of the tongues and to this the cattle were attached and the wagons drawn over. Every thing was safely crossed but Brooks' wagon. The wagon bed floated above the standards. The top being very high and a severe gale of wind blowing, it capsized. The fun of it was Cushing was in the wagon when it capsized, which was lucky, for he jumped out and towed the bed ashore.[29]

The river is well timbered, chiefly elm and white oak. It is situated in a beautiful valley, which is now waving with prairie grass, the best I have seen since I left home. Corn 15 cents. 12 miles.

MAY 1,
TUESDAY

Came 20 miles and camped on a small stream 6 miles west of Bethany, the county seat of Harrison County.[30]

Last night the wolves kept up a constant howling round our camp. It blew up cold last night and this morning there is ice in the camp kettles ½ inch thick. The flowers all hung their heads, and I hope their lives will be saved by the clouds that still obscure the sun. Crossed "Big Creek," a very nice stream. Above the ford there are two mills—grist and saw mills—also a dam. Country generally broken. Some timber on the streams.

All hands and cattle well. 20 miles.

MAY 2,
WEDNESDAY

It being rumored there was small pox and cholera in St. Joseph, Capt. Sampson dispatched me to the city to ascertain the facts. I mounted the pony at 10 o'clock and left the company at Gray's Mills on the west fork on Grand River.[31] I reached St. Joseph at 12 midnight, a distance of 60 miles. 60 miles. *[14 miles.]*

MAY 3,
THURSDAY

I found St. Joe in an uproar. Men of all grades, classes and conditions striving to get away. Some selling out, others crossing the river—Missouri. There are quite a number of cholera cases on the St. Louis boats, and some in the town.

I agreed to meet our company at Rochester on the 3rd, but on account of losing some of their cattle [they] were detained.[32]

MAY 4,
FRIDAY

Met company 20 miles east of St. Joe. Boys all well and in fine spirits. I saw but one dead ox and one pony during my trip. The report was that 7,000 people had died from the two diseases.

MAY 5,
SATURDAY

Drove 11 miles. Crossed over both bridges on the North Platte and the hundred and two streams.[33] We are now 7 miles from St. Joseph, and have been out 4 weeks today, Saturday. 18 miles.

MAY 6,
SUNDAY

Came to St. Joseph this morning 5 miles. Camped half a mile north of town in company with Mr. Merrill's family and Capt. Woodburn.[34] All seem very quiet today, this being Sunday. On the bank of the Missouri north of town is a high mound where lies the remains of St. Joseph, a Catholic missionary. The spot is marked by a cross.[35] Mr. Whipple and the Misses Merrill are at present exercising their vocal organs.[36]

All sorts of rascals in town and as a matter of course carrying on a high game. Not many cases of cholera in town. Cattle all tied up to the corralled wagons, where they will remain all night. Danger of being stolen.[37] 5 miles. *[6 miles]*

MAY 7,
MONDAY

Left St. Joe at 3 p.m. and camped 5 miles out on the Savannah road. Strope's team stuck fast in the mud. The goods we shipped from Burlington, Iowa via St. Louis

3. Ferry of the Nodaway. Wash drawing by James F. Wilkins, traveling west in 1849. State Historical Society of Wisconsin.

arrived on boat today, but as they were not consigned to any particular house were carried back before we were aware of it.[38] 5 miles.

MAY 8,
TUESDAY

Came 8 miles to Savannah. Got some repairing done.[39] Bought side meat for 4½ cents. Camped a mile from town. 8 miles. *[9 miles.]*

MAY 9,
WEDNESDAY

Left Savannah this morning and traveled 15 miles, passing through Newark, Andrew County.[40]

Bought flour at Hollister's Mill on the Nodaway, a

10

4. Nodaway Mill. Wash drawing by James F. Wilkins, traveling west in 1849. State Historical Society of Wisconsin.

small stream emptying into the Missouri.[41] The country through which we passed today is beautiful. Wheat 18 inches high.

This country well settled up. All nature in full bloom. Strawberry vines in abundance. Crab apple trees in full bloom, scenting the atmosphere with their fragrance. Merrills' wagon came up today.[42] 15 miles.

MAY 10,
THURSDAY

Laid over all day. Merrills are camping with us. We are now in Holt County, Missouri and intend going through Oregon, the county seat, on our way to Iowa Point, where we will cross the Missouri and go to what is called "The Mission" in the Indian Territory.[43] Mr. Burt of Farming-

11

ton, Iowa, passed through our camp today. His teams are at Fort Kearny. Whichever company reaches Grand Island first will leave a note for the other.

MAY 11,
FRIDAY

Came 18 miles and camped on Tarkio. The most beautiful scenery I ever beheld. Grass in quantity.

Had quite a heavy thunderstorm today. Large hail stones fell in abundance and with great force.

D. Carnes is better today, having had intermittent fever with bilious complications.[44] 18 miles. *[20 miles]*

MAY 12,
SATURDAY

Traveled 18 miles today on the prairie and near a small stream. Bill Cushing shot a "Barr" so named by the emigrants. 18 miles. *[20 miles.]*

MAY 13,
SUNDAY

Camp 15 miles. Passed through London [Linden], the county seat of Atchison County.[45] All Well.

Capt. Woodburn met with a mishap. Ran into a rut and dished one wheel. Had to stop and have new spokes put into both hind wheels. 15 miles.

MAY 14,
MONDAY

Traveled 10 miles today. Crossed Nishanabottany [the Nishnabotna River]. The road is very low and flat, quite muddy.

Beautiful scenery in the distance. Carnes still sick but improving.[46] Bill Cushing shot a hog, so we lived high on Sunday. 10 miles.

MAY 15,
TUESDAY

Laid over until noon, then drove 5 miles and are now at Fort Kearny on Table Creek.[47]

Road through the timber and mud to any depth. Timber principally cottonwood of the finest kind.

The Virginia Company are here, newly rigged up and ready to start with mules.[48] Parakeets in abundance. Their plumage is beautiful, but their shrill cry anything but musical. 5 miles.

MAY 16,
WEDNESDAY

Crossed over the ferry at Fort Kearny this afternoon and came 3 miles, camping on the prairie. Merrills are within half a mile of the river.[49] The Knox County teams are coming up tomorrow.[50] Fort Kearny is quite a place. Lots of log houses and an eight square blockhouse in center.[51] There is a sergeant there to protect the U.S. Government property.

The parade grounds are beautiful. No one is allowed to camp on it. The country here is a beautifully rolling prairie. Timber scarce. All hands and cattle in good condition except the "old Red Cow." She has a sore foot. Saw a pelican. Shot at him across the Missouri, but could not strike him. Distance about 300 yards. There is one Chicago team in company.

[Carnes: Old Fort Kearny "is in a delapidated condition. It was constructed wholly of logs."]

MAY 17,
THURSDAY

Laid over all day. Did my own washing for the first time in my life. Wrapped our wagon bows and did some other necessary jobs. The weather has cleared off, still [from the] east.

Wrote a letter to Wm N. Worthington, West Chester, Pa.[52]

Merrill came up today. Wagons and teams in good condition and party all well.[53]

Old Fort Kearny
to Fort Laramie

May 18–June 16

☛*When they left Old Fort Kearny, Parke and his companions struck northwest until they reached the Platte River, then hugged its south bank past Fort Kearny into present-day western Nebraska where the Platte swells from the confluence of the North and South Platte rivers. The company crossed the South Platte and traveled the south bank of the North Platte to Ash Hollow, where it crossed the river and pushed on to Courthouse Rock, Chimney Rock, and Scott's Bluff. Following the North Platte into what is now Wyoming, the company crossed the Laramie River near its confluence with the North Platte and immediately came upon Fort Laramie, at that time still a privately owned trading post.* ☛ *The Platte River was the natural conduit for emigrants going to California and Oregon. The ascent was gentle, the footing generally firm, and there was sufficient grass, water, and fuel. The Pawnees, reeling from attacks by encroaching Sioux and suffering other difficulties, were in no position to bother emigrants. The trail along the river, the Great Platte River Road, led to new and marvelous sights: Indian villages, prairie-dog towns, savage storms, colorful trappers with Indian wives, striking geological formations, unusual flora and fauna, and voracious mosquitoes. Emigrants repeatedly expressed awe at the seemingly endless cavalcade of wagon trains, but there were problems, too: the death of people and animals, various kinds of accidents, discontent, the secession of individuals and groups from companies, the need to deal with outsiders wishing to unite with companies—which prompted some companies to halt, draft or redraft constitutions and bylaws, elect officers, and thrash out issues. Moreover, almost from the beginning the travelers realized they had packed too much, so they jettisoned belongings all along the way. When they arrived at Fort Laramie and saw the brooding Rocky Mountains to the west, they knew the easiest part of the journey was over.*

MAY 18–JUNE 16

Came 16 miles through a vast prairie. Not ten acres of timber within sight all afternoon. Had to gather "rosin-weed" to cook by, and the only water was dipped up from the slough. 16 miles.

Came 18 miles today and camped on the same prairie over which we started, and no signs of timber yet. Had quite a time gathering "rosinweed" for fuel.[1]

Was on guard last night from 11 until 1½ this morning, which reminded me of a soldier's life. Just as my time expired, there came up a violent thunderstorm during which electricity was used in profusion.

There is a peculiar sound made by thunder on these prairies. Tis sharp, like the crack of a rifle. The lightning flashes also appear more vivid. Our Dutchman yesterday strolled off from camp in search of game, but to his surprise saw a "Red Man" in the distance. The Indian made signs as though he was going to shoot, when Cushman beat a hasty retreat toward camp. He reported to the Capt. he was searching for one of his oxen. On being interrogated as to why he did not go up to the Indian and ask him if he saw his ox, he said, "No rifle, no pistol, no good." This is a very [desolate?] prairie. Water scarce and no wood of any account. Now and then you will see a tree or two scattered here and there, and a few shrubs in the distance. We saw one or two circles about ten yards in diameter, said to be made by the blind buffalo. They run round the ring until they die. *So they say, etc.,* but I doubt it.

There is a company of 24 Missourians about ten miles ahead. 18 miles. *[16 miles.]*

[Carnes: After supper we called a meeting of the company and elected a captain and such other officers as we thought proper to regulate matters, it being necessary to have some system. The Co. now consists of 11 teams and about 30 men. A

15

committee of 3 was appointed to draft laws and submit them on Monday evening.]

MAY 20,
SUNDAY

Came 18 miles. Crossed Cottonwood and Salt Creeks.[2] The former is a small stream with a few cottonwood trees scattered along its banks. Salt Creek is a larger stream and named from the brackishness of the water. 'Tis said by the Mormans, 40 miles above where we crossed, there are "large rocks of salt." This may be one of "Brigham's latest." Six or eight of us this morning thought we saw an elk or buffalo in the dim distance, and a hunt was proposed.

Our rifles and all the necessary apparatus were hurriedly gotten into proper shape, and off we went. Some on foot and some on horseback, but lo and behold when near enough to take in its dimensions, it had neither bones, muscles or blood. *It was a rock.*

Passed thr[ee] emigrant trains today. One of 24 wagons, and one of 8 from Mo. Also 17 Mormon wagons. Camped out on the prairie once more, where there is not a tree or bush to be seen, and water as scarce as hail in Pluto's regions. Man is always learning something from those more ignorant than himself on many subjects. Hunters and frontiersmen have a novel way of utilizing all the heat produced by even a few rosinweeds, especially on a windy day.

An oblong hole is dug in the ground, say 18 inches long 8 inches wide and 6 inches deep. The sides are banked up with sod, about 4 inches. The kettle or frying pan is placed on top. The fuel, rosinweed, "buffalo chips"—dried manure—or wood, is placed in the open oven and lighted.[3] The end of the oven is always facing to wind, consequently a fine draft is created. Simple, economical, and yet so perfect and practical. Better than a stove for a frontiersman. 'Tis always on hand and doesn't have to be transported.

Wind still south, and showery, but not enough to make roads muddy. Country still broken prairie, with very little water and that in the slough after rain. 18 miles. *[21 miles.]*

16

MAY 21,
MONDAY

Came 16 miles to day and camped on the prairie 8 miles west of Elk Creek. Crossed Little Muddy, Big Muddy, and Modest Muddy, then Elk Creek.[4] The country over which we passed to day is quite broken and *rocky*.

Elk Creek is well supplied with fish, principally suckers. Some of our men speared a few, and had them fried for supper. Such breaks in our regular "hard tack" and "side meat" supplies are quite enjoyable.

Caught up with another emigrant company. Their camp is in sight. I stood "on guard" for the first time last night. My "chums" were Capt. Sampson, Esquire Brooks, and Capt. Woodburn. Quite a rain today. Wind west this evening. 16 miles.

MAY 22,
TUESDAY

Came 17 miles. Loaded on wood along the road and camped on the prairie. Grass good but water scarce. Mr. Fields of Adams County, Ill., taken last night with diarrhoea, symptoms of cholera.[5] I prescribed a pill of opium every hour which quieted the gripping but did not stop the diarrhoea. I next ordered hyd. chlorite grs. viii, capsicum grs. iii, and camphor, but it has not had the desired effect yet. This evening he has been vomiting, which he says is caused by the capsicum, it always serving him so. *It may be*. I have now given him 5 grs and in an hour will give him two grains more. Has run down very much. Has a poor constitution.

Took two more teams into our company today. They are from Wisconsin.

Met a company of Mormons on pack mules direct from Salt Lake. They left the latter place April 17. They report roads good and South Platte fordable. 17 miles.

[Carnes: One man very sick with diarrhoea.]

MAY 23,
WEDNESDAY

Wednesday. Came 15 miles today and camped on the Platte bottom, near the junction of the latter with Silver Creek. The valley of the Platte is beautiful. Very little timber.[6]

Quantities of antelope. One of our company and myself mounted our horses and tried for "fresh meat," but could not get a shot at them. Capt. Sampson and some others are now trying what they can do. Antelope are very shy as well as fleet on foot. One would think they were all females or does on account of their *curiosity*, but that cannot be. You cannot slip up on an antelope, but you can excite their curiosity, entice them up to you, and shoot them. This is a simple procedure. All that is necessary is to hide behind a "sage bush," draw your ramrod from the rifle, and fasten a *red* handkerchief or shirt on the end of it, and move the red object back and forth. As soon as it is seen by the antelope, he will circle round it gradually approaching nearer and nearer until within good shooting range. 15 miles.

[Carnes: After writing in the morning, "Sick man no better. A confirmed case of cholera," Carnes noted in the evening, "This evening patient much better. Miller had slight attack of diarrhoea."]

MAY 24,
THURSDAY

Traveled 18 miles today and camped on the bottom near the river.

Mr. Fields' attack developed into a case of *cholera*, a very bad case, but he is convalescing. Mr. Miller has diarrhoea tending toward cholera. He is also better. Both slightly salivated, but that is better than death. I postponed giving a laxative to carry off calomel for fear the bowels would get too loose again, so chose the risk of salivation to excessive purging. Saw plenty of antelope but could not get a shot. Had a grand hunt today after a wolf, which two horsemen ran down and then shot. It was a splendid sight on the level prairie and very exciting. We could see the race three or four miles distant.

The Platte River is quite a rapid stream at this point, and in some places a mile wide. The water is quite riley, nearly the color of red clay. More so than the Missouri.

Timber is very scarce. What there is, is cottonwood and red cedar and it generally on north bank.

The mail carrier from the Fort is with us tonight and tells doleful stories about the scarcity of grass in and about "Grand Island." 18 miles.

Came 14 miles and camped as usual on the river bottom. Last night was one of the stormiest I ever experienced.[7] The rain descended in torrents and the wind howled through and around our wagons and tent poles. Although our tents had ditches cut round upper and end sides, yet we were literally washed out before morning.

The greatest and most interesting sight I have seen since leaving the frontier is the village of the once powerful tribe of Indians known as "Pawnees."[8] It is on the right bank of the Platte. This Pawnee village contains 95 wigwams. The main or central wigwam is much larger than the balance. The structure shows considerable ingenuity and at a distance reminds one of an eastern coal pit or mound.

In the first place, round poles are set up about 3 inches apart all round the circle according to size of wigwam desired, and about 7 feet high. These poles are all united by small brush and strips of bark woven in and out between alternate poles like basket work. Forked poles or posts are next planted in a circle about five feet from the first mentioned or outer circle. These forks are about ten feet high and from the tops or forks of these poles, or rafters you might call them, are laid to the top of the outer circle. These rafters are again bound together like the perpendicular side walls. Other poles are then planted near the center on which rafters are laid and tied together as above described. These are then covered with grass, leaves, and dirt sufficiently thick to turn both water and cold.

In the center of top is a hole or chimney, as it were, through which the smoke passes.

The fire in a wigwam is always in the center. Near the fire is planted a crooked stick in an inclined position and on this is a fork. The inclination is such as to make the fork directly over the center of the fire. On this fork the Indians hang their meat to cook and smoke it.

On one side of the base of this wigwam is an opening about 4 feet square. From the sides of this opening, sticks are driven into the ground and extending out about 12 feet. Other sticks are crossed on top and woven together as in the main building. Covered with grass and earth. To enter, you must get down on hands and knees and crawl in. The earth in center of wigwam is removed to the depth of about 18 inches out to near the middle tier of posts, leaving a bench of six feet all round the outer circle. On this they sleep. All the wigwams are constructed after the same plan, only some are larger than others. Each wig-wam has a *vault* or *caske*. These vaults are about 8 x 10 feet and reach within 4 feet of surface. You enter from a small opening at the top.

The bottoms of these vaults are covered with small bundles of grass about six inches in diameter.

These underground caves are for the purpose of stor-ing their corn and meat for the winter. There is also a subterranean passage said to be ½ mile long extending from the village and on either side of this [a] branch passage. The purpose of this underground passage we could not divine, unless the squaws were secreted here during their tribal wars.

There were only 4 Indians (Pawnees) in the village and they sick, they said, with "small pox." I suppose they reported this in order to have us leave, and it had the desired effect. I did not venture in to investigate. Why the village was deserted we know not, but rumor said they were at war with the Sioux on the other side of [the] river.

Some of our company broke one of the 10 command-ments and appropriated some of the grass matting—4 x 6—found in the wigwams.

When the report spread that the Indians had deserted the town on account of the small pox, the grass matting was tumbled out of the waggons in a hurry, and several persons [were] very uneasy for a couple of weeks there-after.[9]

Near the village is a grave surrounded by 62 horse heads or skulls. Suppose it marked the last resting place of some celebrated chief. The symbols would suggest *many horses*. 14 miles.

[Carnes: Started 10:00. In about 5 miles came to Pawnee village. But 4 or 5 Indians here and them sick. The government has caused them to evacuate this town. The village is constructed of poles shaped like a cone, thatched with long grass and then covered with earth. The entrance is on the east side. An opening is left in the top to let the smoke excape. Near this town we saw what was supposed to be the grave of some distinguished chief. There were 62 skulls of horses arranged in a circle with jaws pointing to the center which was the grave. Hundreds of emigrants have written their names on those skulls. This curious sepulcher is visited by all who pass this [way]. Numerous patches of corn stalks show that a crop was grown here last season, but now all is silent. The inhabitants have been removed to insure protection to the hardy pioneer.]

MAY 26,
SATURDAY

Came 18 miles and as usual camped in the valley. 18 miles. *[17 miles.]*

MAY 27,
SUNDAY

Laid over today. Some washed their shirts, some wrote letters, some repaired their wagons, while some played cards and shot at marks. One, more refined than the others, played the fiddle.

A Lieut. from the Fort says 2400 teams have passed the Fort this spring. Mosquitoes beat "Old Scratch" along this river.

MAY 28,
MONDAY

Came 20 miles up the river and camped in the valley. No wood on this side [of] the river. Saw two wolves today. Mr. Wood of Quincy, Ill. shot an antelope, which we are now preparing for the pot, with increasing appetites.[10]

Some of our teams stuck fast in a slough. 20 miles. *[18 miles.]*

[Carnes: Bad and wet traveling.]

MAY 29,
TUESDAY

Came 20 miles and camped near the junction of the Old Fort Kearny and Fort Jessup roads.[11] Passed the grave of Dr. David Harris, buried April 12, 1849 on the bank of the Platte near this place.[12] There are any quantity of teams in sight. Grass very short.[13]

5. Pawnee Village. Wash drawing by James F. Wilkins, traveling west in 1849. State Historical Society of Wisconsin.

A man has just arrived from St. Joseph, Mo. May 13 reports a great many graves along the route caused from cholera.[14] We have some visitors this evening, a team from Putnam Co., Ill. and a mule team from Georgia. Weather fine, wind from the southeast. Grass poor as a general thing.

Brooks complaining bowels rather loose. 20 miles. *[19 miles.]*

MAY 30, WEDNESDAY   Traveled 3 miles to Fort Kearny and 14 miles west.[15] Our camp is surrounded by emigrants from various states.

Quite a heavy rain this morning which delays our usual early start.[16] Passed yesterday and today 200 teams. The report at Fort is that 3500 teams have passed up to yesterday.

Fort Kearny is a poor looking place. Houses all made of *sod*. They are now building a frame house. The troops here are preparing to start for Oregon.[17] They are a fine-looking set of men, especially the officers. Met three men returning home to Louisiana.[18] Mules run down and some of their wagons broken. Wind S. W. this morning. Wood scarce. River bottom 2 miles wide. 17 miles.

6. Fort Childs or New Fort Kearney, June 3rd. Drawing by James F. Wilkins, traveling west in 1849. State Historical Society of Wisconsin.

[Carnes: This fort is constructed of sods, contains about 20 buildings, and is garrisoned by 200 troops. [It] is situated on the naked bottom of the Platte River at the head of Grand Island. No timber except on the islands in the river.]

MAY 31,
THURSDAY

Traveled 15 miles and camped in a splendid place on the second table of the Platte bottom. Teams are quite numerous and the cry is "still they come." We passed nearly 200 teams today. The Buffalo Company from Springfield, Ill. is ten miles behind. Andrew Merrill is two days behind.[19] Grass good here, and wood enough, there being

24

some seven scattering trees on the banks of sloughs and ravines.

Wind has been S.W. all day, with some showers. Rather cold. An encampment has been seen on the north side [of the] Platte on Council Bluff road. Quite a number of persons are selling their interests in companies and returning to the *States*. Satisfied with this kind of life. It is a little rough, but 'shaw, "When you are into a scrape, go through, be a man or a mouse or a long tailed rat." Meat, corn meal, pilot bread and beans are distributed profusely along the roads. All hands seem to be "lightening up" their loads.[20] Last evening our company adopted a Constitution and bylaws.[21]

Not a buffalo seen since we left the States. Game of all kinds scarce. Don't see how a poor lazy Indian can live here.

500 Cavalry expected at Fort Kearny on their way to Oregon. We passed the Badger Company from Wisconsin today. The Louisiana Enterprise Co. a mile ahead. 15 miles.

[Carnes: Five hundred teams are in sight, and the "whole prairie [is] alive with cattle, etc."]

JUNE 1,
FRIDAY

Came 20 miles and camped on the bank of [the] Platte. Grass scarce. No wood and only river water. Members of company all well. Day very warm and clear. Some of the company met old acquaintances to day, an oasis in the desert. I was called in to see a Mr. Livermore from Galena, Ill. Has flux, buried his daughter this morning, rather sad.[22] Passed 171 teams today from various parts of the United States. 20 miles.

JUNE 2,
SATURDAY

Came 15 miles and camped. Grass scarce, no wood. Used "buffalo chips" for cooking. There is timber on an island opposite our camp. The bluffs on either side of the river, or rather river valley, are very high and abrupt, presenting a rather picturesque appearance.[23]

Weather clear, wind S.W., and all hands well.

Heard from Mr. Livermore. He was doing as well as could be expected. 15 miles.

JUNE 3,
SUNDAY

Came 20 miles and camped on the river bottom. Grass of the best kind and plenty of water. Timber scarce except on the islands. Will lay over tomorrow and have some washing done. In company with one of our men, I climbed the highest bluffs near camp. The country beyond is very rough, with numerous ravines. Saw "buffalo chips" and tracks on highest peaks. Saw also what we called "Old Man" in Pa. and a plant with long spicated leaves and stem up the center resembling the aloe plant except in color, being pale green or yellowish. We found black currants in the ravines, quite large.

Passed through a "Dog town" today. *Prairie Dogs.* They resemble a "Ground Hog" somewhat, only the head is that of a puppy two months old.

There is a mound at each hole and these are from 10 to 20 feet apart, sometimes extending over 20 or 30 acres. On entering one of these dogtowns, you will see any quantity of the little rascals, sitting up like a squirrel, on top of the mound, barking for good life until you approach within 50 yards of them, when as if by magic they disappear. Tis said rattle and other snakes are frequently found occupying the same nest in these holes, dwelling together in perfect harmony, but I doubt if there is much actual love and good will in the matter.[24] My notion is the dog digs the hole and makes the nest to protect himself from the cold and outside enemies, while the snake is looking out for himself and the *young dogs* as soon as born—snake like.

[Carnes: The company voted it expedient to move on today where fuel and water could be obtained and lie by tomorrow. 20 miles.]

JUNE 4, MONDAY

Laid over all day for Mrs. Merrill to wash, but the D—l got into her as large as an ox and she left. She was continually dictating to the company what we should do and how to do it, as would a Lieut. General. Mr. Merrill and Mr. Whipple wanted to remain, but the old lady put her foot down and "Dad" had to obey and Whipple followed the pretty daughter. Joy be with them.[25]

There is a lovely little creek near camp, and full of fish. I caught some cat, suckers and "Hickory Shad" which broke in on the usual monotony of our tea table on the ground. Wind E.N.E. and cloudy. All Well.

JUNE 5, TUESDAY

Came 20 miles and camped on the north side of the South Fork of the Platte, about 3 miles above the ford.[26] Roads have been good all day but very dusty. The ford was a good one, the water not crossing higher than the axletree. Bottom sand.

The ford was about ¾ mile wide, the water running swiftly. The company crossed safely, not an accident to man or beast. Have not heard of Merrills since they left. One of the Indiana company and some Indians killed 2 buffalo here this afternoon.[27] The Indians are very friendly and intelligent looking. 20 miles.

JUNE 6,
WEDNESDAY

Traveled 20 miles today. Broke camp this morning at 6:00 o'clock and traveled up South Fork about 6 miles, then crossed over the bluffs to the valley of the North Fork of [the] Platte where we are now encamped. Rain commenced falling last evening and continued all night.

There was the sharpest kind of lightning and heavy thunder.[28] About noon today it cleared away. Mr. Fields and myself went hunting this morning, but came back to camp hungry and without meat.[29]

We passed through a Sioux village this morning on the bank of the South Fork numbering some hundred wigwams and from 500 to 1000 souls. They are a very intelligent looking tribe, and quite friendly.[30]

We made them many presents of small value which they thankfully received.

Six buffalo were killed on the road before us today, but we did not see any of the fun. We caught up with and passed Merrill's teams today. They had joined the Oswego Company. All things were working finely. New broom, etc. 20 miles.

[*Carnes commented on the Sioux village, noting that it "contained about 100 lodges, and a thousand persons. The lodges are built by buffalo skins stretched on poles in the shape of a cone, with an aparture in the top for the smoke to escape. The men are athletic and large and the women from appearances pay some attention to cleanliness of person."*]

JUNE 7,
THURSDAY

Came 22 miles over good roads, some bottom and some bluff, and camped on the river bottom. Grass scarce. Fields and myself went out on another hunt today. Saw some antelope, wolves, and two prairie hens, sagehens. Hares three times [the] size of a common rabbit. The speed of the hare surpasses anything of the quadruped kind I ever saw. They travel as though shot out of a cannon. Of course, we did not shoot any. Not a buffalo or Indian to be seen.

Saw what some call a "cockspur" in bloom, the prettiest flower I have seen for some time. I suppose it is a cactus. The flower around the edge of the circle is a beautiful pink.

Wind north and a severe electric storm approaching. 22 miles.

[Carnes: We usually start at about 6½ or 7 a.m. Half an hour at noon to lunch and water the stock. Camp at 5 p.m.]

JUNE 8,
FRIDAY

Traveled 25 miles today and camped on the Platte bottom, opposite to what we suppose to be "Castle Rock" of Fremont.[31] Our course lay up the valley nearly all the way, having to ascend the bluffs only once, which led us into "Ash Hollow," where I was disappointed, seeing so little timber. But my disappointment was counterbalanced by the charming spring of pure, cool, sparkling water that gushed from the hillside. Oh, what a treat to the tired thirsty emigrant this warm day. We all enjoyed the treat hugely.[32] At the mouth or outlet of "Ash Hollow" there are some wigwams belonging to the Sioux. Amongst these Indians was a white man, who had a squaw wife and lots of pretty "little halfbreeds." He had been with the Indians 16 years; followed trapping, etc.[33]

One of our Wagons met with an accident today— Cooks. Cracked a tongue.

The valley up which we passed today is narrow, the bluffs high, presenting a washed appearance. As to resembling "Castles," that is all in my eye.

Brooks and Miller both taken with diarrhoea.

Gave a teaspoon of liquid opium laudanum at a dose. Took two more wagons into our company this morning, with six men. One team from Aurora, Ill. and one from Wisconsin. At present writing, train after train are pouring into this valley.[34]

One young man shot himself in the leg today. An

accident. Was on his way to Oregon. Doing well.[35]
25 miles. *[22 miles.]*

[Carnes: Noon halted at a grove of ash and cedar [which] fringed the bold and craggy precipices. After dinner we ascended the bluffs and by a winding road of 5 miles descended into Ash Hollow, down which the road from the upper crossing of the south fork also descends. Here is some springs of good water and [an] abundance of wood. Seven miles brings you to Castle Bluffs at which we encamped.]

JUNE 9,
SATURDAY

Struck our tents at 8:00 a.m. and traveled 18 miles, camping on Spring Creek.[36]

We passed what are called "Castle Bluffs" by a happy streak of somebody's imagination. I can see a little something that resembles the ruins of an old castle, but tis at best a strain. Possibly it looked more like a castle than anything else when General Fremont gazed at it with his architectural eye.[37]

Capt. Sampson and I scaled the heights of one of the best, and was well paid for our trouble. From the top, the scenery surrounding [us] was very beautiful. Emigrant teams, oxen and mules, could be seen for miles, with their white covers wending their way up the valley.

The side of one of the bluffs was upward of 200 feet high, and almost perpendicular.

Away up high on this cliff, the little swallow had stuck her frail nest, in perfect confidence that all would be well with her little ones.

This peculiar habit is called instinct by man because he does not like to acknowledge that so small a creature could *think* and *plan something* better than he, but so it is. Why did the little mechanic gather his mud and grass and systematically stick fast one with the other against the rocks, hundreds of feet from the ground? To get beyond the reach of certain enemies of course. This art of nest building is handed down from one generation to another. No doubt some are better builders than others, like men, but all can do it. They seem happy, yea are happy, while training the little ones how to fly from home and back again, singing and chirping as they go.

These "Castles" cannot be called rock, for they are not, but made up of gravel and yellow clay cemented together as though at one time the whole valley was made up of this formation and in time washed away, leaving these monuments of its history. Great masses are constantly crumbling and falling to the bottom from the effects of wind and rain. On the lower side of this "Castle" we found the remains of a buffalo and a great many black currant bushes, loaded with green fruit and very large. The wild rose is here also, perfuming the air and adding to the beauty of the scenery.

Roads very heavy, sand six inches deep. Grass rather poor.[38] Brooks and Miller attacked with diarrhoea again. Sent a letter home by a Mormon.[39] 18 miles.

[Carnes: A crowd of wagons as usual. The bottom was literally alive with cattle. . . . The bluffs here assume all kinds of fantastic shapes. The imagination can fancy almost anything in the shape of a castle.]

JUNE 10, SUNDAY

Laid over all day today. We had [a] violent storm last night. Thunder, lightning, and rain in torrents.[40]

[Carnes: Last night had very heavy thunder shower. The peals of thunder boom heavy and the lightning more vivid than I have ever witnessed.]

JUNE 11, MONDAY

Raised camp this morning at 6:30 and traveled 20 miles. Off to the left could be seen "Pine Bluffs." Today we passed one of the finest kinds of springs, resembling the old sandstone springs of my childhood home in the keystone state. Last night was another stormy one. Never saw a worse one. The flashes of electricity were almost continuous and of the most vivid kind, while the thunder never stopped rolling, apparently shaking both heaven and earth. An explosion here and there immediately on our heads, while the rain fell in sheets and the wind blew with such force that every man had to grapple with the tent poles and cords and make himself generally useful. During the flashes we could see the stampeded cattle of another camp under full run and making for our corral.[41] Three of the men in close pursuit, as there was no use in

31

trying to stop them until the cattle became exhausted. Our wagons were corralled and the cattle all tied to the inner wagon wheels or possibly we would have been minus motive power also. A horse was killed by lightning in a camp close by.

Today we passed through more mosquitoes than ever lived in a Louisiana swamp.[42] We are now in sight of what we suppose to be "Solitary Tower." Wind N.E. Roads moderate. Grass good. We passed the grave of a man from Michigan and also that of Wm. P. Stevens of Boone City, Mo. The latter died of consumption [and] was traveling for his *health*. Poor soul; it proved to be for his *death*. Both were buried on the 6th inst.[43]

How the sick grasp at straws! How poor their judgment seems to be, which by the way is not astonishing, but we should expect better advice from *friends* and *relatives*. *Home* is the place, of all places, to die. It matters not how horrible it is. I have seen enough persons die to satisfy me that even the presence of a friend at that time is comforting, but oh what a thought to be buried here, in this sand, away from home, and an hour after the last clod is placed upon your blanket—no coffin here—your companions march off and leave you alone forever!! 20 miles. [*22 miles.*]

JUNE 12, TUESDAY

Traveled 16 miles. Had to camp early on account of rain. The rain last night was about as usual. The high wind drove it into our tents. This morning I left the train in company with Messrs. Boil and Corrington to visit "Castle Rock" or "Solitary Tower," which was some distance ahead and 7 miles from our road.[44] After traveling 8 or 9 miles obliquely from our road, we reached "Solitary Tower" or "Church."[45]

We found two large columns, the east or smaller one being about 150 feet high and about 100 feet in diameter near top and 150 at base, which was oval or egg-shaped, egg on side with larger end to the east. It is composed of rock, sand, and clay, just sufficient of the latter to cement the other together, but as there was no way to reach its top I could not ascertain its composition exactly. The sides of

[the] tower looked as though the heavy rains and wind of this region [had] washed and changed the original shape. In fact, I have no doubt but what the church and tower at one time were all one high eminence worn by time and [weather] to its present form.

The main "Church" or "Tower" is about 300 feet high and on the south side, nearly perpendicular. On the north tis about 250 feet [high] and length 300 x 100 feet. On the north side, the ascent is gradual up about 50 feet, where we assumed the ascent proper. Our course was then east along the side of the "Tower" ascending between rocks and the main body of [the] tower up to the first bench. After resting a few minutes, we commenced climbing to the second bench by steps or holes in the side of the tower and almost perpendicular. At this point many of our associates faltered and finally turned back.

This second bench gained, we took a good rest. This 2nd bench is about 20 feet wide.

The remaining 10 feet was perpendicular, with only small holes for the toes of your boots and nothing to hold to with your hands save a few round projections made by the constant wear of wind, weather, and feet. The wind was blowing very hard from the south, which made the ascent more difficult. This last ten feet overcome, the difficulty was over, and few of us reached the "promised land" 800 feet above the level of the river. On the top in this hard clay, we found many names carved. I undertook the job of carving mine, but gave it up as too much of a job for so little pay. Many of the names were nearly washed out. About 200 yards from the south side runs a fine stream of water. The view of the surrounding country from the top of this tower is simply sublime. Altitude above Gulf of Mexico 3350 feet. 16 miles. *[18 miles]*

JUNE 13, WEDNESDAY

Raised camp at 6:00 a.m. and commenced our march westward, making 19 miles, and camped about 5 miles east of Scott's Bluff. Wood and water scarce.

Capt. Sampson and I walked to Chimney Rock about three (3) miles from the road.

This rock has been noted by all travelers through this

country as one of the great curiosities of the western plains.[46] I was therefore very anxious to visit it. Upon reaching it, I found it to resemble in form a hay stack with a long pole sticking from the top.

It is about 300 feet high. The central [part] or top is about 150 feet or half the whole height. Base, 200 yards, while lower portion of perpendicular portion is about 70 feet and well carved up to top. It leans slightly to the east, with a large crack extending down some distance from the top.

The composition and makeup of Chimney Rock is the same as that of Solitary Tower, as are also all the neighboring bluffs.[47]

Upon the sides of the base grew the same aloe-like plant already described. Altitude, 3350 [above] Gulf of Mexico. 19 miles. *[20 miles]*

JUNE 14, THURSDAY

Came 20 miles and camped on a small stream within two miles of Horse Creek.[48] We found a beautiful and refreshing spring at the base of Scott's Bluff from which our water casks were filled.[49] Near this spring was a fresh grave, made this morning. Dunn was the name. Died of cholera.[50]

From the top of Scott's Bluff can be seen many peaks of the Rockies, especially Laramie Peak. Rained some this evening.

Saw by the roadside the skull of a Rocky Mountain goat. Base of horns 2½ x 3 inches. 20 miles.

JUNE 15, FRIDAY

Traveled 16 miles, roads good. Crossed Horse Creek and Ten Mile Spring. Saw many cards on trees, but none for us.[51]

Camped near the Platte River. Feed poor. Passed many large sand hills which are quite common in this country.

Black currant bushes, wild mustard, lilies, and roses are abundant. Also a species of cactus.

Wind S.W. A light shower this evening. Camped in a dog town. Well settled, but the inhabitants all quiet. 16 miles.

JUNE 16,
SATURDAY

Came 15 miles and are now camped two miles above Fort Laramie on the Platte.[52] We crossed the Laramie River this afternoon safely with one exception.

The water at the ford is about 3½ feet deep and very swift, making it necessary to block up our wagon beds about 6 inches.

By some mishap Mr. Fields' wagon on descending the river bank broke the standards and capsized, damaging some provisions and wetting his bedding. The wagon body was towed ashore.[53]

Fort Laramie is situated on the north bank of Laramie river, thus [Parke has made a drawing at this point]. The parade grounds are beautifully situated. Weather very warm, causing our cattle to protrude their tongues and breathe by the mouth. 15 miles. *[16 miles.]*

[Carnes: Fort Laramie is a trading station of the North American Fur Company. Today the Government train arrived with troops to establish a military post at or near this place under the command of Major Sanderson. The post is built of sods as [is] the post at Fort Kearny, and is situated at the confluence of the Laramie River.]

Fort Laramie to
South Pass

June 17–July 5

☛ *Glistening snow on Laramie Peak symbolized the higher elevations west of Fort Laramie. The terrain became more rugged, fording operations more dangerous, feed less certain, and in the parched region beyond, where the trail veered from the North Platte, the water became deadly. Sickness and putrefying carcasses greeted Parke and his associates as they crossed this region to the life-sustaining waters of the Sweetwater River, a tributary of the North Platte. Following the Sweetwater upstream and fording it repeatedly, the party passed Independence Rock and Devil's Gate before ascending the almost imperceptible incline to South Pass, a watershed on the Continental Divide. Few emigrants lingered long at wind-swept and arid South Pass, however, most preferring to push on to Pacific Spring or to other sources of water farther on.*

☛ *Fort Laramie was a transition point in several ways. Emigrants littered the plains near the fort with still more surplus possessions, something they continued to do all the way to South Pass and beyond. They also discarded their tendency to use firearms promiscuously, and in many cases weapons themselves were abandoned near the fort. Mercifully, Fort Laramie marked the point on the trail at which cholera ceased to plague overlanders. Even so, problems abounded. Diseases associated with inadequate diet and wretched water thinned the ranks, and drownings marred fording activities in the thirty-mile stretch of the North Platte beyond Deer Creek. Swarms of grasshoppers added to the woes of the Whiteside County forty-niners. Parke's company took time to celebrate the Fourth of July and the next day crossed the Continental Divide at South Pass, an act of much symbolic and emotional importance that was noted by virtually all diarists. Parke and his friends were now in the drainage basin of the Colorado River.*

JUNE 17–JULY 5

JUNE 17,
SUNDAY

Laid over in camp 3 miles above the fort until 3:00 p.m., when we raised camp and drove 7 miles, camping near where the road leaves the bottom. While in camp at Fort Laramie we cut off our wagon beds and coupled up the wagons preparatory to entering the Black Hills.[1] The idea being, to make it as light as possible for our stock, enabling them to do the hard work before them and keep in good condition, for without them we can do nothing. 7 miles. *[8 miles]*

JUNE 18,
MONDAY

Came 17 miles and watered our stock at Warm Spring.[2] This beautiful spring is at the foot of a hill and from its clear sparkling appearance the thirsty traveller would think he would have a refreshing drink. We were all very much disappointed to find [it] unpleasantly warm. It boils up so rapidly it carries the sand up from the bottom. It produces a stream about six inches in diameter. Our next water was Bitter Creek, a beautiful clear stream, rather warm. Here we watered our stock and rested an hour, some of [us] paddling in the water like in our boyhood.

Our next spring was one of the finest I ever saw. It is about 3 miles up Bitter Creek in the direction of Laramie Peak.[3] Timber more plentiful than for some time. Mostly cottonwood and elm. We found the horn of a mountain goat or sheep which measured three (3) feet in length and 15 inches in circumfrence at the base. He would have been a good fellow to have used against the walls of Jerico. 17 miles. *[18 miles]*

JUNE 19,
TUESDAY

Came 15 miles over the worst kind of a gravel road, amongst what we called the "Black Hills." We crossed several streams fed by delightful springs bursting forth from the hill side, clear as crystal. We are now camped on Horseshoe Creek, a very fine stream.[4] There is a smaller creek between camp and Horseshoe Creek, the water of which is of the best quality and of course refreshing to both man and beast. Timber along these streams mostly willow.

Near the ford on Horseshoe Creek is a beautiful spring of clear cool water around which are camped several companies.

Daniel Brooks shot an antelope this evening, which made quite an agreeable change in our bill of fare this evening. The salt side meat, or anti-Jew flesh, was allowed to rest and our stomachs met with an agreeable surprise.[5]

The Black Hills so far are not as bad as I anticipated, there being more grass and the roads better than one would expect from reading the published accounts of explorers, many of which write for buncomb[e]. I may change my mind after a few days more travel.

On these hills I find some fair pine timber. In fact, there is no other kind on the bluffs. Along the streams we find willow and cottonwood. Laramie's Peak is still seen and appears at about the same distance as when first seen. I should estimate the distance at about 25 miles.[6] There is something shining or glistening on its top. Some of our men call it snow, but to me it looks more like flint rocks such as we have seen along our road through this part of the country.[7] 15 miles.

[Carnes: Emigrants continue to throw out provisions and goods to lighten up which lie scattered along the road.]

JUNE 20, WEDNESDAY

Came 17 miles over one of the hilliest kinds of roads. Passed several beautiful springs on the road side, always welcome, and are now camped one mile west of La Bonte River.[8]

There is some timber on this stream, nearly all willow. The water is clear. Saw some very large elk horn along the road. One would measure 3 to 4 feet in length. We met some U.S. soldiers who were returning from the Platte with an emigrant who had stolen a horse from the fort.[9] They report feed scarce and plenty of buffalo. I doubt it.[10]

Most of those we meet have some doleful tale to tell.
17 miles.

JUNE 21,
THURSDAY

Raised camp early this morning and traveled 16 miles and
camped on La Prele River in a small grove of timber. Box
elder, willow, and cottonwood.[11] Were favored with
good roads today considering the face of the country. In
some places the dust is red, resembling iron rust. On the
sides of the different hills can be seen the strata of red and
pale-colored clay.[12] The rocks are more or less porous and
presenting the same color.

Grass has been and is poor. Weather dry and oxen feet
tender. Have been applying boiled tar and rosin to them,
hot as possible. This fills up the cracks and forms a coating
over the hoofs, protecting them from the sand. The sand
here grinds like emery.

Tis 8 miles from La Prele river to Fourche Bois river.[13]
16 miles. *[15 miles]*

JUNE 22,
FRIDAY

Came 17 miles, which brought us over the Black Hills to
the Platte. We are now camped about half a mile from the
Platte on Deer Creek.[14] The country through which we
passed today was quite rough and hilly, but better roads
than for the last few days.

On arriving at the Platte, we found its bottom covered
with emigrant wagons and cattle, most of them anxious to
cross and many crossing on a flatboat made by lashing
three canoes together and cross tying with logs.[15] The
cattle were unyoked and made to swim across.

Deer Creek is a very handsome stream, clear as a crystal
and full of fish, principally suckers. One of our hunters
brought in a saddle of a blacktail deer and one of an
antelope. Consequently, we expect to live high for a few
brief hours. There are two blacksmith shops here—Mormons, I think—shoeing horses and oxen.[16]

There is stone coal here in the banks of the stream.
Some of the emigrants have been burning it. Weather dry
and warm. Grass rather poor. 17 miles.

[Writing on June 23, Carnes observes: "The blacksmith's hammer may be heard at all hours. About 80 yards up the creek is plenty of coal. As a specimen of charges for blacksmithing, $1 is charged for setting a shoe on a horse, all formed. All other work in proportion."]

JUNE 23,
SATURDAY

Laid over on Deer Creek until half past 2:00 p.m., when we raised camp and traveled 8 miles up the valley.[17] Three Wisconsin teams camped with us, also some pack mules. Shope doing some needle work on his underwear.[18] Shows what a man can do when he is compelled by time or nakedness!!

Grass poor, and wood sufficient for our purpose. Weather warm. Roads dry and dusty.

The ferry here (Platte) is doing a good business, charging three dollars ($3) a team.[19] Brooks badly alarmed last night. Lost one of the oxen. Thought the Indians had its scalp sure, but this morning he found him. 8 miles.

JUNE 24,
SUNDAY

Laid over until noon, when we raised camp and drove ten (10) miles to the ferry, which we expect to cross in the morning.[20]

One of Mr. Fields' steers taken sick this morning. I think he drank too much muddy water. We dosed him on soap, lard, and new milk. Since then he is some better.

Warm breeze blowing from noon to evening, which seems to be common in this country. 10 miles.

JUNE 25,
MONDAY

Last night we camped on the east bank of the river, opposite the ferry. This morning early we commenced crossing on a boat swung across the river on two ropes.

Two yoke of cattle were attached to the end of the ropes on either side, one towing the boat over there. The other cattle would tow it back. We were all across safely by 9:30 a.m. Our oxen swam across beautifully.

A pack of mules tried it this morning, but one of them got his head under, missed the landing, and drowned.[21] Roads sandy and heavy.

Traveled 14 miles and camped on the Platte. This is my 26th birthday, which I celebrated by losing my sack coat.

Most people expect their wardrobe to be replenished about this time, when all is joy and gladness. My loss will make some other fellow glad. 14 miles. [15 miles]

[Carnes writes: "The boats are 3 canoes lashed so as to admit the wheels in the two outside ones, making a safe boat for a heavy loaded team, excluding the cattle which are forced into the stream and compelled to swim. The ferry is worked by oxen. A long line is fastened on the boat on either side, sufficiently long to reach across the river, which is about 300 feet. Cattle are hitched on to the line opposite from the boat, and by driving off directly from the shore the boat is hauled across, and by holding the opposite end taut, the boat heads the current, and thereby prevents the liability of filling, etc. The charge is $2." He then mentions that his company had 17 teams.]

JUNE 26, TUESDAY

Raised camp this morning at 6:00 o'clock and traveled 20 miles. Very warm and dusty during the forenoon. An electric storm came up at noon and lasted all afternoon. Mr. Van Ness and myself left camp at noon to visit Mineral Lake and spring to the south of our road. The country through which we passed today is of a volcanic character and highly charged with alkali, the water in some instances poisoning the cattle when drunk.[22]

We passed many dead cattle today and quite a number of sick ones. During the storm today 4 yoke of cattle were killed by one bolt of electricity. The drivers, fearing a severe blow, turned the rear of the wagon to the approaching storm and took the cattle from the tongue, leaving them all stand chained together. The lightning seemed to strike the hindmost yoke first, passing along the central chain. Killed all 4 yoke instantly. The team belonged to Mr. Jones of Harrison City, Mo. A Mr. Robinson, standing near the wagon with a rifle on his shoulder, was considerably stunned, causing headache and a blue spot under right eye.[23]

Today we encountered millions on millions of large

grasshoppers. In fact, they had eaten all green leaves and vegetable matter within reach and were devouring each other. The ground was literally covered for acres. The wagon ruts were full of what looked like molasses and grasshoppers mashed or mixed together. Such a sight ought to cure a man from eating bread and molasses.[24]

While out, Van Ness and I found a boggy place, with tufts of grass here and there 6 inches high on a tough sod. By jumping on this sod we could shake the surface for 20 feet round, and by pressing we could force from its top a peculiar looking substance resembling black lead and whitewash, emitting a very fetid odor. I ran a stick down 3 feet without touching bottom. What is below the Lord only knows, and I will not attempt to guess. Sure tis not Illinois soil, but may be the outcropping of some valuable mineral hid away in the earth below.

We are now camped near a spring on the south of the road and near the bluffs after crossing the Alkaline bottom.[25]

[Carnes: The camp was one and a half miles from the road and had "cool water and good grass." He also lamented: "We find the feed very poor over the road, from being feed down, and are obliged to often go as far as 3 miles to find sufficient [grass] for the stock. This day we had no water for the oxen till we camped."]

JUNE 27, WEDNESDAY

Traveled 20 miles today through volcanic country, passing Willow Springs. The latter is a fine spring of good cool water on the little stream we are now camped on.[26] This is the *second* stream entering into [the] Sweetwater.

There is good grass and water in this place, a blessing long and devoutly looked for.

The country here is generally rough, though this is a splendid valley but small. Plenty of game. One of D. Brooks oxen died with murrain today. Dead cattle are strewn all along the road, poisoned we think by drinking the alkaline water.

We had a slight shower this evening from the west. Wind cooler. More cattle sick. 20 miles.

[Carnes: I think we have seen 50 head of oxen dead by the road side today, from drinking alkaline water. Our team lost one. Several oxen sick in the train.]

JUNE 28, THURSDAY

Raised camp and traveled ten miles, camping at the celebrated Independence Rock.[27]

The Sweetwater is a narrow beautiful stream of clear cool water with low banks as a general thing, and swiftly running, as are all the mountain streams.[28] Fish plenty, suckers.

Independence Rock is an isolated, hard granite rock, about 300 yards long and 75 feet high, rounded top like a tortoise but crossed by fissures.[29] The top can be reached by a gradual ascent in the center on east side. The rock is well covered with names of former travellers, some of which are nearly effaced from the effects of the weather. We painted Como Company Ill. on it, and gave it a long, everlasting farewell.[30]

How this large granite rock came to be left out here all alone, miles from those of its kind, wise men may attempt to explain. At any rate here it is, defying wind and weather, a permanent land mark for the weary traveler. 10 miles.

JUNE 29, FRIDAY

Came 18 miles up Sweetwater valley and camped where the stream emerges from the mountains. Five miles from Independence Rock we came to Devil's Gate, a gap or canyon through a rock or spur of the mountain.

The stream and opening through the mountain is about 100 feet wide, and I should judge 3 or 4 feet deep. Quite rocky bottom, and runs very rapidly, cool and clear as a crystal. The almost perpendicular ragged opening through the solid rock is about 400 feet high at one point.[31]

Length about 300 yards from entrance to the crevice and its outlet to the valley below. I should judge in this 300 yards there is about 30 feet fall, making one of the finest water powers I ever saw. The stream is about the size of the Brandywine near West Chester, Pa. These mountains are well-named, being nothing but the rock, with here and there a small shrub of cedar, or *scrub,* I should say.

The roads today were heavy. Water good, also grass.

Here, again, the traveler is at his wit's end: why and when this break through solid rock 400 feet high and 100 feet wide when the water could have easily gone round the point of mountain only a few hundred yards distance. Possibly one day it did, while there was fire below, but when the fire went out, the crust cooled so rapidly this mountain rib contracted and cracked in twain, allowing the stream a shorter cut to the valley below. 18 miles.

[Carnes: "Saw several trains breaking up to pack. Wagons, provisions, &c., scattered along the road in profusion." He also saw twelve dead oxen this day.]

JUNE 30,
SATURDAY

Came 18 miles over a very heavy road, sometimes on the river bottom and then again divided from it by a ridge of mountains.[32] This valley is on an average about ten miles wide. Sometimes it is quite narrow between two rocky ridges about 300 yards distant from each other.

Upon raising the ascent and turning the point of the first spur of mountains, we got our first view of the Wind River Mountains, with their peaks covered with the white eternal snow, which, glistening under the bright sun presented a grand and picturesque appearance. When we gaze on such a sight, the 30th day of June, it almost makes one feel chilly.

One of our company visited the mountain about 10 miles distant on our left where he found *ice* three hundred yards in length and 40 yards wide in ravines. Pine trees about 40 feet high, 4 to 6 inches in diameter, cover the hills.

Grass today fairly good.

Mr. Fields' team nearly broken down. He is lightening up, after wearing his oxen out hauling oats to feed them.[33] We frequently see *two extra axles* strapped under a wagon. Wearing one out prematurely by carrying two others may be wise, but I doubt it. 18 miles.

JULY 1,
SUNDAY

Raised camp and traveled up the river 10 miles. After crossing Sweetwater twice, we laid over to unload and lighten up. Our last river crossing was a bad one. Water came into our wagon boxes and wet some of our goods.

We cut our supply of bacon down to 360 pounds for our mess (6 persons) and threw out beans, etc.[34]

We left camp about 4:00 p.m. and came to this, the third ford on the Sweetwater after entering the narrow valley.

The Wind River Mountains are again in view with their silvery tops of snow. 10 miles.

[Referring to the overland migration in general terms, Carnes writes, "I am surprised that there is no more difficulties, considering the multitudes of emigration, and among all general good order prevails."]

JULY 2,
MONDAY

Came 19 miles and again camped on Sweetwater. After leaving the ford this morning, we traveled 16 miles before coming to the river again, which we immediately crossed and traveled 3 miles over a sandy road to our present camp.

The wind has been high all day and the dust at times almost intolerable, so you could hardly see the cattle.

Quantities of dead cattle strewn along the road. Wind River Mountains still in view, looking more beautiful as we approach them. This is not one of the cases where "distance lends enchantment to the view."

There is a man to be tried for murder tomorrow. Of course "Judge Lynch" holds the Court out here. I do not know the particulars. The murdered man's name was Read ———.[35]

Grass and water good at this point. 19 miles.

JULY 3,
TUESDAY

Came 15 miles and camped on Strawberry Creek.[36] After traveling 6 miles up Sweetwater, we [left] it for the bluffs, where we found rough rocky roads. Wind as high as usual and dust flying.

This is a beautiful little stream and running east. Water good and grass scarce.

Within half a mile of us there are large banks of snow. Air quite cool. Wore my cloth coat all day and felt comfortable.

There are quite many fish in this little stream. A long sucker with reddish sides.

We are now entering what is known as the South Pass of the Rockies, but a stranger would not know it as a pass if he had not read a description of it.[37] A beautiful ascent up a narrow valley. 15 miles.

JULY 4, 1849, After crossing Sweetwater for the last time, we traveled up
WEDNESDAY the valley 10 miles and camped on a small brook, arriving at 1:00 p.m., where we laid over all afternoon.

This being the nation's birthday and our under clothing not as clean as we could wish, we commenced our celebration by "washing dirty linen" or rather woolens, as we all wore woolen shirts. Washing done and shirts hung out to dry—we never iron—all hands set about enjoying themselves as best they could. Some visited two large banks of snow about half a mile from the ford on Sweetwater.

Having plenty of milk from two cows we had with us, I determined to [do] something no other living man ever did in this place and on this sacred day of the year, and that was to make *Ice Cream at the South Pass of the Rockies.*

Mr. Pollock of Whiteside Co., Ill. and cousin of Gov. Pollock of Penn. assisted me.[38]

I procured a small tin bucket which held about 2 quarts. This I sweetened and flavored with peppermint—had nothing else. This bucket was placed inside a wooden bucket, or Yankee Pale, and the top put on.

Nature had supplied a huge bank of coarse snow, or hail, nearby, which was just the thing for this new factory. With alternate layers of this, and salt between the two buckets and the aid of a *clean* stick to stir with, I soon produced the most delicious ice cream tasted in this place. In fact, the whole company so decided, and as a compliment drew up in front of our tent and fired a salute, bursting one gun but injuring no one.[39]

This morning we found ice in our buckets 1½ inches thick. Fire is quite a treat and cloth coats are not any too comfortable. The snow bank from which I procured my ice was several feet deep, and the most singular part is, about 15 feet from its edge is *green grass* 3 inches high. 10 miles. *[12 miles.]*

Traveled 23 miles and camped on Dry Sandy.[40] While crossing the Pass, all eyes were anxious to know when we arrived at the summit, so gradual is the ascent up the valley. All anxiety satisfied by finding Pacific Spring about three miles west of the supposed summit.[41] This spring is the first water running *west* and of course decided the matter. It is a beautiful spring of clear pure cold water, boiling up three inches high. After running about two miles, it sinks into the ground and is lost.

Dry Sandy has but little water in it and that is decidedly brackish. Grass poor.[42] Roads sandy and dusty.

Distance from Como, Ill: 1269 miles.
Distance from St. Joe, Mo: 859 miles.
Distance from Fort Laramie: 231 miles.

23 miles.

[Carnes: It is almost impossible to tell where the precise summit is. The point of culmination is between two low hills and disappoints the expectations very generally of the traveler whose imagination is formed to see something remarkable of a gorge-like appearance.]

South Pass to the Humboldt River

☞ *After attaining South Pass and pushing beyond, Parke's company decided to strike straight west to the Green River via Sublette's (or Greenwood's) Cutoff rather than head southwest to Fort Bridger. The route they chose was arduous, taking them into an unexpectedly lengthy stretch of desert before they finally arrived at the salving waters of the Green River. This waterway was an obstacle, necessitating delay and expense for the ferry, but it enabled emigrants to refresh and refit before entering the mountains to the west. After entering the mountains and negotiating rushing streams and precipices, the company emerged into the relative lushness of the Bear River Valley, where the legendary Thomas L. ("Pegleg") Smith held forth. The trail then took emigrants northwest to Soda Springs, past extinct volcanoes, and on to Hudspeth's Cutoff, which was opened July 19, the day Parke and his companions used it. This cutoff eventually saved travelers time and labor, but the first groups using it found the going rough. The route then crossed Raft River, passed through the jumbled City of Rocks, cut through to Thousand Spring Valley in northwestern Nevada, and finally reached the headwaters of the Humboldt River.* ☞ *Variety and the unexpected were constants along this portion of the trail. Some of the trail passed through the drainage basin formed by the Colorado River, some through the region of the Great Basin, and some through the watershed of the Columbia River. Some of the fords were difficult, some easy. Days were often searing, and nights brought bitter cold. Feed was uncertain, terrain was varied, springs were alternately hot and cold, and discomfort was produced by both dust and snow; denizens of the region included trappers, Shoshoni Indians, half-bloods, some Mormons, and others.*

JULY 6–AUGUST 3

JULY 6,
FRIDAY

Traveled 16 miles and camped on Big Sandy. Ten miles after leaving our camp yesterday on Dry Sandy, we reached
what is called Little Sandy River.[1] The latter is a beautiful
stream about 2 feet deep and thirty feet wide, running
swiftly, both muddy and cold. Six miles brought us to Big
Sandy, where we are now camped.[2] Big Sandy is quite a
large stream about 20 yards wide and 18 inches deep. Swift
current and muddy, but not so cold as Little Sandy.

The valleys through which these streams flow are very
narrow and the grass is poor. Grass is always inferior
where the wild sage bush is abundant.

I took my gun yesterday and in company with Mr.
Brooks started in search of antelope. After traveling two
or three miles we separated. When I saw several antelope
in the distance, I crept slowly toward one of them, keeping a wild sage bush constantly in front of me until within
160 yards, when luckily I planted a bullet in his temple,
which told me the tale. I was now in a sorry plight; plenty
of good fresh meat, but all alone and my company at least
a mile ahead. There was but one thing to do, and that was
to cut off what I could pack. So with a heart alternating
between joy and sorrow, I cut off the saddle, tied the feet
together, ran my head between the legs, and started for
camp. Providence finally came to my relief. A "lonely
horseman" as the nomads say came riding by and carried it
to camp for me after—as the Darkies say—I had "toated"
it six miles. It was the heaviest piece of meat I ever packed,
especially the last mile, but it set well on the stomach
when properly prepared.

We are now preparing for Subletts Cut-off, which we
will undertake tomorrow night.[3]

Roads dusty and weather cold. 16 miles.

JULY 7,
SATURDAY

Laid over on Big Sandy until 15 minutes after 4:00 p.m.
Feed scarce.

49

JULY 8,
SUNDAY

We left camp quarter after 4:00 p.m. last evening and drove all night and today until 3:00 p.m., expecting every hour to reach Green River, which according to Ware's Guide was only 35 miles.[4] A grand mistake, it being at least 50 miles of terrible barren desert. The first 25 miles were of the prettiest kind, level and soft for the cattle's feet, being a clay dust. But the western 25 miles made up in vileness, the dusty hills being nearly perpendicular in some places.[5] We saw quantities of dead cattle strewn along the roadside, caused no doubt from the excessive dust and fatigue. No wonder, just think of the poor dumb beasts dragging these heavy wagons all night and nearly all the following day 50 miles without a particle of food or water through alkaline dust that took all the skin off my lips, compelling me to wear an oiled cloth constantly between them.

There is a fair quantity of grass over the river. We had to lead our cattle to the river and water them with much care as they were crazy for water. Will have to rest them on this side.[6] 50 miles. *[52 miles.]*

JULY 9,
MONDAY

Laid over all day to recruit our cattle. We crossed Green River at the Mormon Ferry. Our cattle we swam and all were safely landed on the other side. Six dollars is all he charged us for each wagon.[7] Some others he charged $7.00.

Green River at this point is a beautiful valley about half a mile wide, and as a general thing the grass on the west side is good.[8] Water good, though there are some alkaline ponds.

The surrounding country quite bluffy. There are some French trappers here with their squaw wives. Also, two halfbreeds.[9] They are of the Snake and Crow nations, are darker than the Sioux, short and heavy. Not nearly so fine-looking as Sioux.

We had a treat today in the shape of mountain trout, which I caught out of Green River. They were excellent, especially to those who are fish hungry.

[Carnes: There are several ferries kept here by Mormans . . . and they charge the exorbitant price of $6 for crossing each wagon. Have plenty of business. . . . There are several

Mormans at this place for the purpose of speculating off the emigrants and to gather up what they leave . . . wagons, lame stock, baggage, cooking utensils, etc., etc.]

JULY 10,
TUESDAY

Laid over all day at Ferry. I was called to see one of Capt. Hawkins' men who was sick. Took the Captain's horse and rode 12 miles.[10] 12 miles. *[0 miles.]*

[After noting that it was necessary to drive cattle four miles to get grass, Carnes wrote, "hundreds of wagons arrived today." On the previous day he thought there were twenty-five hundred teams ahead of them and five thousand behind.]

JULY 11,
WEDNESDAY

I remained at this camp all day. Our wagons came up today [at] noon and laid over. My patient is from Kentucky, has a bilious attack, will soon be well.

There is a fine stream near and good grass. Some fine fish and plenty of antelope.

The surrounding country is quite rough and bluffy. Some Indians and halfbreed trappers are camped near us. All quite friendly. There are several newly-made graves at this place, which speak of sorrow and sadness at some once-happy home.[11]

Snow is seen on the mountains west of us. The days are fairly warm while the evenings are cold. Roads dusty as usual, six inches deep, and very light. 0 miles. *[14 miles.]*

JULY 12,
THURSDAY

Traveled 17 miles through a barren hilly country. We crossed many delightful streams fed by the mountain snow drifts, and that packed in the ravines to almost any depth. Lovely springs of pure crystal liquid pour out here and there on nearly every mountain side. The only useful thing visible in this country. We passed any quantity of snow. I climbed over drifts 20 feet deep from which flowed the best of water over the clean washed rocks.

We camped on a small stream about half a mile from the road. Here we found the best of grass for our cattle and horses.[12] 17 miles.

JULY 13,
FRIDAY

Traveled 18 miles over one of the roughest countries we have yet met with.

51

Ten miles from our morning camp brought us to what I suppose is Thomas' Fork of Bear River.[13] It is a fine stream of water about 2 feet deep by 50 feet wide, running swiftly. Eight miles farther over a very high mountain brought us to this camp, near a fine spring flowing from the ridge which bounds the Bear River Valley.

Nearby is a quakenasp grove which is very beautiful, standing alone in this Godforsaken country where the springs are taken out. Under the quivering leaves of these beautiful trees are lovely springs fed by mountain snow nearby.

Wild flax and grass have been abundant since leaving Thomas Fork. Wild sage scarce.

Snow, grass, heat, cold, and mosquitoes, combined with rock and dust, make up the most interesting part of this country.[14] Our Government would do well to trade the Indians out of their good land and force them on to a "reservation" such as this and then proclaim to the world what a Christian people we are.

At present a small rainbow graces the eastern sky. Nearly all nature is quiet. Naught to be heard save the sound of the ox bell as its sturdy bearer plucks the green grass, and with this sound of civilization comes the "buzz" of the much dreaded mosquito. The Lord only knows what the latter are good for. It may be the little active fluid they manufacture is a connecting link that makes the world move. I know it makes me move. 18 miles. *[16 miles.]*

JULY 14,
SATURDAY

Traveled 18 miles over one of the finest mountain countries we have yet seen. Grass abundant and a beautiful spring of clear cool water gushing from every ravine. Banks of snow are also scattered along the northern slopes of the mountains and hills.

Today we passed through several beautiful little groves of quakenasp and fir trees, the first timber of any account we have passed through since we left the States. Every tree nearby had a name cut on it. We passed up and down some very steep mountains before we arrived at Bear River Valley. The scenery here is indescribably beautiful. Nothing heretofore so grand and picturesque. From the high mountain the beautiful Bear River Valley looks but a short distance below, but as we descended we found many smaller hills and valleys intervening between us and the main valley.

Bear River Valley is walled in on either side by high bluffs. Grass is very abundant and of several varieties to me unknown.

This river is rather sluggish at this point. We traveled up the river three miles and camped on a small tributary stream. This may be Thomas' Fork instead of the one mentioned yesterday as we have no certain way of finding out.[15] Our guide book does not mention all the streams. 18 miles.

JULY 15,
SUNDAY

Laid over until noon, when we crossed a very bad ford and traveled eleven miles over a good road and camped near a fine spring. We had to cross the creek twice, then over a very rocky road opposite a high mountain, the end of which looked like scenery I have seen in theaters. Is said to be 1500 feet high. Rained some little today. 11 miles.
[10 miles.]

JULY 16,
MONDAY

Left camp early this morning and traveled twenty miles following up the river some distance over good road when we came to a sudden bend to the west in the river, where we were compelled to travel round some sloughs above the bend. Here we ascended the high bluffs again and passed into another valley, small but beautiful, where the grass was *two feet high*. We then ascended one of the longest hills we have yet met, and descended one equally bad when we came to the river bottom again.[16] Here we found an Indian trading Post. Snakes.[17] 20 miles.
[16 miles.]

[Carnes: Everything new. All the vegetation is unlike anything in the States. You will see many new varieties of animals, fowls, and fish. This is the most wild and romantic country that the imagination could picture.]

JULY 17,
TUESDAY

Traveled 20 miles and camped in a small ravine leading to the river. Ten miles of the first part of our road was as level as a floor, the remainder more rolling.

Grass good. We crossed many fine streams of pure water running from the mountains. Still some snow visible on the mountain sides, [even] if it is *July*. I visited a sick man today, a Missourian.[18] Has typhoid fever, but doing well.

Last evening we visited "Fort Smith" to see the Indians. This is a trading post at Big Timber. The squaws were a dirty looking set, short and heavy in build and quite dark brown in color. Like the mosquito, Lord only knows what they were made for. 20 miles.

JULY 18,
WEDNESDAY

Left camp early in the morning and traveled 16 miles. We traveled ten miles and nooned near a spring boiling out of a rock made of the sediment. At this spring were two Snake Indians who had been trading with the emigrants. When we called on them they were preparing their dinner. Four ground gray squirrels was their stock of provisions and yet they seemed happy!! Is ignorance bliss? It was very interesting as well as amusing to watch them prepare their food, not for the table, not they, but for their stomach, to satisfy hunger. They first prepared a fire with plenty of live coals into which the 4 squirrels were buried just as caught, hair, entrails, and all!!!

Every now and then a squirrel would be dragged out with a small stick and into it would be thrust a stiff weed or splinter to ascertain whether it was cooked enough or not. When satisfied the fire had done its work, the squirrels were all drawn out and as soon as possible thereafter, without stopping to offer up grace, they swallowed the quadrupeds, hides, entrails, and most of the bones, apparently happy, although not knowing where the next meal would come from.

These squirrels are gray in color, with flat short tails, quite fat, and very good eating, even to a man from the States.

Six miles brought us to "Soda" or "Beer" Spring, one of the greatest curiosities we have yet seen.[19] The water is said to contain carb. lime, carb. magnesia, iron, and c. sodium.

These springs flow from the top of a cone made by the deposits of sediment from the water. Some of these mounds or cones are from 30 to 80 feet high. There are quite a number of them, and many have ceased to discharge water from the top. The water is rather warm. By the addition of a little sugar and lactanic acid we made quite a palatable drink. The road today [is] good, also grass. Went fishing today. Caught a speckled trout 15 inches long. Mr. Fields shot a badger today, which from a culinary standpoint was a treat. Tastes very much [like] young shoat.

We have two Indians and a squaw with us tonight. They are very friendly, and gave us some information relative to the country. 16 miles.

[Carnes, writing on the next day: "Indians visit our camp every night. Appear friendly. Go away satisfied after we give them something to eat."]

JULY 19,
THURSDAY

We left camp early this morning and traveled 18 miles, passing any number of springs, the most interesting of which was Steamboat Spring. We found the best spring about two miles from camp, at the edge of a small stream. The carbonic acid gas was so strong it was impossible to breathe over it for any length of time. The Steamboat Spring is a curiosity. The water is forced up through an artificial rock or encrustation to the height of 3 feet, with a puff of noise like a steamboat. About 11 feet from the aforementioned jet, on the same level rock, is a small opening acting as an escape pipe, through which a small quantity of water is forced up a few inches, beating in unison with the larger one. These springs continue to deposit sediment and enlargen the area. The water seems to be well charged with iron, coloring the deposit [with] a reddish color.

All this country or basin (which has a diameter of about 4 miles) seems hollow, as we drive over it. Similar to driving over a bridge.

We next visited an old crater which was also quite interesting.[20] It was about 70 feet deep by 100 in diameter. The sides present a charred appearance where the combustible material has melted or burned out.

We left the main road at the bend of the river and bore off to the S.W. following Myers and Hudspeth. The former was a mountain guide, the latter captain of the Company—Missouri company. Both have been through to California before.[21]

We are now camped on a beautiful creek 15 miles from the Old Road.[22] Water cool and clear, running swiftly. Grass good. 18 miles. *[17 miles.]*

[Carnes: About four miles on the plain west of the river stands an old crater. It is about 150 feet high and near a mile in circumference at the base. The top is concave. The crater is about 80 feet deep and 100 in diameter. The rocks here resemble the cinders of a blacksmith's fire. The rocks appear to have been in a state of fusion, and on the plain for miles distant are rent in innumerable fragments. In some places they have the appearance of having been belched up and are full of deep dangerous fissures.]

JULY 20,
FRIDAY

Left camp early this morning and traveled 18 miles. We ascended a hill after leaving camp and in about 2½ miles we came to a small stream. Three miles more brought us to another small branch and after winding through the valleys we came to a large stream at the foot of a hill three miles from [the] last.[23] Here we nooned. Grass has been good all along our route today.

This stream we think is the Pannock River. Below where our camp is, is a natural breastwork making a dam some 8 feet deep. Below this dam the bank is perpendicular rock. The stream and banks well-supplied with willows. We left this camp at noon and traveled over hills and through narrow valleys a distance of 10 miles to this creek in a fine valley some two miles wide. Road good.[24] Also grass quite abundant. Stream rather sluggish. 18 miles.
[17 miles]

[Carnes: Broke up camp early. Ascended a hill and in 4 miles came to the Pannack River, and in 3 miles further came to another considerable stream on which we made our noon

56

halt. Small parties of Indians visit us on every stream. They are all of the Snake tribe.]

JULY 21,
SATURDAY

Left Pannock early this morning and traveled 18 miles. Our road lay up a long hill for seven miles in one stretch and then descended two miles to a branch of Pannock Creek, where we camped for noon.[25] Here we found a lovely spring boiling out from under some willows, and after traveling down the hill half a mile farther to the left of the road we found another of those ever-welcome, refreshing springs. Grass very good.

At 1:00 p.m. we raised camp and traveled through numerous ravines in the mountains until we reached the headwaters of "Roseaux" or "Reed Creek," which runs south, showing us we are in the Great Basin.[26] This stream is nine miles from Pannock. The road today is of the best kind. Water good, and grass fine, mixed with some wild flax. Indians plenty. Cloudy today. 18 miles. *[17 miles.]*

JULY 22,
SUNDAY

Left camp like good Christians this morning and traveled 16 miles over good road.

Six miles from camp we discovered another beautiful spring some 50 feet in diameter with good gravel bottom. Nobody but a weary traveler can appreciate such a spring. The common loafer that whittles in front of a neighboring grocery store until noon or evening then manages to drag himself home in time for a dinner or supper prepared by the hands and muscles of a feeble old Mother has no idea of the sweetness of pure spring water when quaffed by a weary traveler, a man who has walked miles up hill and down, under a July sun until his muscles almost refuse to contract at his bidding. We California Pioneers could just now appreciate the good things we years ago received from the old table at home sweet home. What is a loafer, male or female? A *barnacle,* a useless attachment, a nuisance, and should be ashamed of himself.

This is a beautiful country, made up of fine mountains, which with few exceptions are covered with green grass, and lovely fertile valleys growing wild wheat in abundance, six feet high. Also, some wild flax.

We left our noon camp about 4:00 p.m. and traveled ten miles, crossing a high range of mountains. The ascent was gradual and we accomplished it with ease, gaining the summit by dusk.[27] We then commenced the descent on the western slope down a ravine, which was both dangerous and difficult, but by great care or good luck we arrived at the bottom safely where we camped for the night, fifteen miles from water. 16 miles. [15 miles.]

[Carnes: Two teams "split off this morning, leaving our number just 10."]

JULY 23,
MONDAY

We left camp this morning at the foot of Big Hill and traveled 24 miles. The first 16 miles was over a rolling country, when we came to a fine spring which both man and beast enjoyed as much as any "old toper" ever did his toddy. The grass here being so tramped up—or down— we raised camp at 4:00 p.m. and moved to the next spring 8 miles distant.[28]

This spring is in a mountain gorge some distance from the entrance. Grass has not been so good today as usual. Part of the Alton, Ill. Company and two other camped here. One of our company shot an antelope this morning and another a sage hen. So we are rather set up this evening and will surprise our stomachs by giving them fresh meat instead of the slabs from an old sow.

While in camp we were visited by a dozen Indians of the Shoshone. They were a dirty-looking set.[29] Not energy enough to take a good bath. I often think of the amount of money spent, and wind exhausted in prayer, over the degraded state of these poor d——ls and how little they appreciate it, for they have all heard of it. Catholic priests have spent years and years trying to improve the different tribes in this country. Protestants have also tried their hand on them, but all to no purpose. The only way to improve this people is to take all their children away from them and educate them, never allowing the child to go back until the old cusses have all passed "over the river." 24 miles.

JULY 24,
TUESDAY

Left camp this morning by sunrise and traveled 3 miles, when we came to a fine spring. Four miles further brought us to another one the left of the road under some willows. We followed this spring branch 2 miles down the bottom, where we camped midst plenty of good grass. This road passes up the mountain gorge to the summit, which lies between the springs.

Left our noon camp at 1:00 p.m. and traveled 6 miles down the branch where it sinks into the ground and goes Lord only knows where. From this sink we traveled 12 miles down a gradual descent until we reached Raft River, some 50 miles from Fort Hall. Grass scarce between here and the mountains over which we passed. An abundance of detestable wild sage. Grass at our present camp good, wood scarce. Nothing but sage to burn.[30]

These mountain streams are full of speckled trout. Mr. Carnes baited his hook with grasshoppers and caught a fine lot. Threw them out as fast as he could bait his hook. The stream is only about 2 feet wide, runs swiftly, and in places is nearly covered by the long grass growing from the banks. *Where did* these beautiful fish come from? They must come up through some subterranean passageway from the Columbia River or Raft River, a tributary. 27 miles. *[28 miles.]*

[Carnes: "Here is an encampment of some 200 wagons and they made a splendid appearance when all the camp fires were lighted." He also mentions some Indians who wanted to trade, but "at best they are a trecherous set, not to be trusted." Moreover, he added, "they subsist on whatever comes their way. Even grasshoppers are devoured greedily just as they are caught."]

JULY 25,
WEDNESDAY

Laid over to rest until 1:00 p.m. when we moved forward 5 miles to the Fort Hall road, which comes down Raft River and opposite this place turns into the canyon going westward or S. West.[31]

We crossed two small streams on this bottom and are now camped on the third. Grass good on all these small streams.

Capts. Hedgepeth of Missouri and Hawkins of Illinois

are camped 1½ miles ahead of us with Myers as their guide. We are now 123 miles west of Sublettes Cutoff. 5 miles.

[Carnes: We are up with Hawkins and Hedgpeth's trains and will probably travel in company.]

JULY 26,
THURSDAY

Left camp early this morning and came into the Old Road from Fort Hall.[32] Here we met many trains that had gone round by the Fort. They report many families branching off to Oregon from the latter Fort.

The distance from here to Fort Hall is said to be 75 miles and 60 miles from there to the bend of Bear River or Soda Springs, where we branched off to the S. W. leaving the Old Road. We traveled 8 miles up the north fork of Raft River where we cut good grass for our stock.[33] We left camp at 2:30 p.m. and traveled 4 miles farther to where the road leaves the stream to the right in the mountains. The creek here divides into three and forms a fine bottom covered with the most delicious grass. At least I should judge so from the manner in which it is devoured by our stock.[34]

Snow is still to be seen on the various mountain peaks. Wild currants and gooseberries are quite plentiful in places. There is also a small shrub 5 inches high with a leaf resembling that of the apple tree, and on its top bears a small blue berry resembling the chicken grape with a somewhat similar taste, or like the sour cherry. I don't know what it is. 12 miles.

JULY 27,
FRIDAY

Left camp early this morning, traveling 11 miles in S. W. direction up the valley. Eight miles brought us to a creek and in two miles we came to another, where we nooned. This latter creek no doubt is fed by the melting snow and in due time will dry up.

We left camp at 1:30 p.m. and after traveling 3 miles reached some Warm Springs on the right of the road. They were warm enough to cook an egg in 3 minutes.

Grass growing luxuriantly for 30 yards all around the spring. From the springs we traveled 4 miles, passing into the mountains where we are now camped near another spring of lovely water.[35] Isolated rocks are scattered all around us in the valley as though the work of art. Some are 50, 75, and 100 feet high by 60 at base and of greyish appearance. Granite, I think. Grass and water good. 18 miles.

JULY 28,
SATURDAY

Left camp early this morning bound for Goose Creek 20 miles distant.[36]

The early part of the road and country through which we passed was one of magnificent grandeur, the country being dotted over as it were with granite pyramids. In our travels today, we crossed the new Mormon road from Salt Lake.[37] Here we met some teams, etc., that took the Old Road at Sublette's Cutoff two days before we started in. Two miles west of the Mormon road we passed several small spring streams which I suppose are fed by the mountain snow. For ten miles until we reached Goose Creek Valley our road was terrible for both man and beast. We had to descend about 900 feet through ravines and hills to the river bottom.[38]

The creek bottom is about half a mile wide. Grass fairly good near the road, but much better farther down the stream. Caught some speckled trout in this creek.

The Salt Lake emigrants report fair crops where they come from. They report sugar 50 cents a pint and flour very high. The money they used was *gold dust* wrapped up in paper with value marked on it by their head man. Of course, it was not worth the face of it, as this people are always on the make. 20 miles.

JULY 29,
SATURDAY[39]

Left camp early this morning and traveled 10 miles up Goose Creek over a fine bottom road, camping for the noon at some hot springs on the right of the road. After an hour's rest, we broke camp again and traveled 7 miles to the end of the valley or where the road enters the canyon by the side of a small stream while Goose Creek turns off to the right.

We traveled up this creek through several rocky canyons for 3 miles to where the road leaves the creek. Here we took supper—not tea—and had a good drink of *water* from a spring under a rock at the bluff. After supper, *each man licked his tin dish.* Don't wash dishes in this country. Even squaws don't wash. We proceeded on our weary way 5 miles up the bluffs, where we camped for the night amongst the wild sage with its delightful odor. Smells like a crushed bedbug. Sorry so few civilized [people] are acquainted with the odor. Think they could better appreciate its fragrance, which is all lost on the desert air.

No water and but little grass.[40] In fact, more scarcity since leaving Goose Creek Valley, the country being mountainous and barren. 25 miles. *[26 miles.]*

JULY 30, MONDAY

Left camp early this morning and traveled 8 miles when we came to a small creek with plenty of springs along its banks.[41] Five miles further brought us to Well Springs, where we camped for noon. Grass very good at these springs.

We next traveled 9 miles down the valley and over a point of the bluffs into the valley again below, where we are camped. Grass here very good of its kind.[42] The water sinks in the bed of the creek. Can get plenty of it by digging two feet. The country has been quite hilly for two thirds of our way. 22 miles. *[20 miles.]*

JULY 31, TUESDAY

Left camp 7:00 a.m., being detained by the loss of some of our stock, and traveled 9 miles down the valley to another set of well springs resembling those where we nooned yesterday. Although the water was not so cold, it was good. Grass also good. Left noon camp at 3:00 p.m. and traveled 9 miles down the valley to warm or hot springs, where we are camped.[43]

These springs are a real curiosity. Quite numerous and occupying half an acre of ground, forming numerous streams which finally unite forming one main stream about 16 inches deep and 8 feet wide. These springs are hot enough to boil an egg in 5 minutes, at the least calculation, and are constantly sending up a vapour which can frequently be seen ½ a mile distant, especially at or before sunrise.

About 200 yards below these hot springs there empties into the creek a small stream of cold water. The hot water smells strongly of sulphur. At the junction of the hot and cold streams, I had the pleasure of a good bath, which was quite a treat. The hot water being on top and the cold in the bottom, I was compelled to bestir myself in order to restore the equilibrium, or be uncomfortably warm above and rather cold below.[44]

While thus enjoying my first warm bath since leaving the States, I was astonished to see a beautiful wild duck sail down and light in the hot water nearby. The heat did not disturb it in the least. 18 miles.

AUGUST 1,
WEDNESDAY

Left camp this morning early and passed the warm springs near which we found a large cold spring 3 feet deep and 5 feet wide and the best kind of soft water. Wending our way on down the valley 8 miles brought us to a small stream at the bluff. After resting a short time and watering our stock we moved on 6 miles over the bluffs, where we nooned at a well on the right of the road.

We raised noon camp at 2:00 p.m. and traveled 6 miles down a valley through which runs a small stream, rising and again sinking every two or three hundred yards. Along this stream we found some grass. 20 miles.

AUGUST 2,
THURSDAY

Raised camp early this morning and traveled over the ridge to the next valley, a distance of 6 miles, to more well-springs of good water. Grass good. We continued our course down the valley for 3 miles, passing another fine well of water on the right of the road.[45]

We left the valley at this last well, and passed over some small hills covered with sage bushes into another valley. Here we found a fine stream of water about 6 miles from the well. Here we halted and rested our stock, as well as surprised our stomachs with hardtack and side of hog cooked on a spit. At 5:00 p.m. we took up our line of march down the stream, a distance of three miles, where we are now camped.

This is one of the most beautiful valleys I ever beheld. [It is] nearly as level as a floor, and two miles wide, gradually spreading for some distance between two lofty mountains on the tops of which are large quantities of snow. This valley is covered with fine grass, some of which is wild redtop clover.

In the valley above this one were numerous alkaline springs, around which were plenty of dead cattle. 18 miles. *[19 miles.]*

AUGUST 3, FRIDAY

Raised camp at 5:30 a.m. and traveled down the valley 4 miles, where we came to a small branch or headwater of Humboldt River. About 3 miles farther down the stream comes in another branch from the Humboldt range of mountains.[46] At this point we named it Humboldt River as a venture. Four miles farther down the river brought us to our noon halt.

Raised camp at 4:00 p.m. after resting 3½ hours and traveled 9 miles down the river, where we have camped for the night. Plenty of good grass all the way down the valley with some wild redtop clover.[47] Game is beginning to appear again, which for some reason has been quite scarce.

Today we passed a fresh grave. Poor soul died of consumption away from friends and home. Tis the same old story. Consumptives going from the comforts of home and friends to seek health. Bad judgment, nay nonsense!!! 20 miles.

Humboldt River to the Truckee River

☛ *Landmarks along the Humboldt River were less distinct and less identifiable than those on other portions of the trail, but emigrants were aware of significant junctures as they followed the river's three-hundred-mile course. They passed Lassen Cutoff, which soon siphoned off large numbers of emigrants, taking most of them on a memorable odyssey through the trackless mountains of northern California. Farther to the south, Parke and other emigrants faced the choice of taking either the Carson River route or going by way of the Truckee River (also known as the Salmon Trout River). Parke and his party elected to do the latter. After struggling across the cruel desert south of Humboldt Sink, he and his fellow sojourners reached the verdant banks of the sparkling Truckee.* ☛ *Certain aspects of travel along the Humboldt and overland to the Truckee were unavoidable. One unpleasant reality centered on the fact that as travelers approached Humboldt Sink, the water quality deteriorated markedly. Furthermore, grass was heavily impregnated with salt and the sun blistered man and animal. Deep sand, sharp volcanic cinders, and choking dust exacted their toll. Nights were often cold, and of course the Digger Indians were active then. For these reasons and others, the Humboldt River—a vital ribbon of sustenance in a caldron—was lined with the bloated carcasses of animals and was the final resting place of many emigrants. These severe strains had heavy physical and emotional effects, and many companies suffered death, crippling defections, and even complete disintegration. Conditions along the winding river frequently produced faulty thinking, and even when decisions were sound the means of carrying them out were often lacking. The trek along the Humboldt was an ordeal long remembered.*

Humboldt River to the Truckee River

AUGUST 4,
SATURDAY

Left camp at 5:00 a.m. and traveled 3 miles down the valley, where we crossed a branch coming in from the north.[1] Here we ascended the bluffs, the river passing through a canyon. We passed through several small valleys when we touched the river again 3 times and camped for noon, 8 miles from where we started over the bluffs.

Left our noon camp at 2:00 p.m. and traveled 8 miles down the valley. The valley is about 5 miles wide here and covered with good grasses. No timber.[2] Today we covered in all, 19 miles. 19 miles. *[21 miles.]*

[Carnes: At 6 A.M. the company caught up with an army detachment: "Lt. Pleasanton of the U.S.A. with an escort of 10 dragoons and as many mountaineers, all on mules, passed us this morning on their way to San Francisco from Santa Fe."]

AUGUST 5,
SUNDAY

Raised camp early this morning and traveled down the Humboldt Valley 11 miles, where the road led over the bluffs, the river passing through a canyon. Here we camped and rested our stock until nearly dark, when we drove three miles farther, crossing the river once, then we passed into the canyon and camped at the second crossing of the river.[3]

This morning we passed one of the finest boiling springs yet seen. The temperature was so high I could not bear my fingers in it a minute. There were several springs gushing out of rock made from the sediment deposited by the water. The water is not bad tasting and will thoroughly cook meat in a reasonable time. 14 miles. *[13 miles.]*

[Carnes wrote of "hot springs of temperature sufficiently high for cooking purposes. They are situated on the east side of the river and can be recognized by the steam rising from them."]

AUGUST 6,
MONDAY

Left camp early this morning, traveling down the river through the canyon, crossing the river three times—fording—making 7 miles.

The mountains on either side are very rocky and some 400 feet high. They are continually crumbling down, being made up as it were of small squares sticking loosely together.

Laid over here until 3:00 p.m. when we moved on down the river to where the road ascends the bluffs, a distance of 5 miles. About half a mile above this place a small stream comes in from the N. West, the water of which is pure.[4] Our distance today was 12 miles. 12 miles. *[13 miles.]*

AUGUST 7,
TUESDAY

Left camp early this morning and ascended the bluffs 8 miles to the top. We passed two fine springs, one on the right and one on the left of the road.

There is a well on the top of this bluff where we nooned and then descended into the valley, a distance of 10 miles, where we again reached the Humboldt.[5] We passed several springs as we passed down the ravines. The road was very rocky and dusty all the way down.

Feed poor at this camp. No timber, only a few willow bushes on the banks of the river. 18 miles. *[19 miles.]*

AUGUST 8,
WEDNESDAY

Raised camp at 6:00 a.m. and traveled 8 miles down the river, crossing it once. Here we nooned. Grass poor. At 2:00 p.m. our march was continued down the river 8 miles further, crossing the river once more.

Two companies of emigrants who camped near us last night had several of their cattle driven off by the Indians, while others had arrows shot into them. One had the arrow still hanging into him, the point of which pulled off while trying to extract it.

One Indian was found in the grass amongst our cattle while we were driving them up to camp. He seemed very friendly and assisted in driving the stock to camp, but as soon as he got something to eat he left in a hurry. No doubt the cuss intended playing the same game on our stock but was detected in the grass before his hellish work was accomplished. We had [not] learned the bad news from the other companies before he left, which was the only thing that saved him. By wounding the stock so they could not travel they would necessarily fall into the hands of the Indians, enabling them to live high for a few days at least.[6]

Grass down the river rather poor. No spring water. Mountains on either side of the valley barren.

It has been our regular custom from the time we first entered the Indian country to send a guard out with our stock every night. Consequently, we have not lost one ox. How this "red cuss" slipped in amongst our cattle, in such short grass too, without the guard seeing them is a mystery. I think they must have been sleeping.

Cattle have a regular habit in feeding. They will feed early in the evening for about two hours, or so, according to the supply of grass, when they will lie down and rest, chewing the cud. About 10:00 p.m. they will get up again and feed a short time, then lie down together and remain until daylight. So the herders can sleep after the cattle lie down the second time, and in all possibility this was the fact and the Indian was a little late reaching our feeding ground. 16 miles.

[Carnes: The "Diggers" have commenced. This morning almost every train here had some cattle missing, some with arrows shot into them. This is a common practice to wound and maim cattle so that the emigrants will be obliged to leave them behind.]

AUGUST 9, THURSDAY

Left camp 6:30 this morning and traveled down the river 6 miles where we camped for the noon. Nothing of any note on this part of our journey.

Left noon camp at 1:00 p.m. traveling down the valley 8 miles until we passed around the point of the north range of mountains.[7] Here the road turned down another valley in a N.W. direction. Here we camped. 14 miles. *[16 miles.]*

AUGUST 10, FRIDAY

Left camp at saleratus bottom this morning as the sun commenced peeping over the eastern mountains and traveled ten miles down the river in a northwesterly direction. Grass poor on the N.E. side of river. Willows along the river banks.[8] Capt. Sampson shot a beautiful waterfowl this morning. The plumage was a grayish color bill painted and feet webbed. It looked somewhat like a gull in makeup.

The Indians stole 5 head of horses from emigrants a few nights ago while camped at Saleratus bottom.[9] They were followed several miles into the mountains but escaped with their booty, the owners thinking it not prudent to follow them farther.

There are quite a number of wild duck on this stream.

Broke up camp at 1:00 p.m. and drove down the river ten miles farther, making 20 miles in all today.

The valley at this point has spread out to 10 or 15 miles in width. There is grass on the south side of river, while quite barren on the north side.

Humboldt River at this point is not over 100 feet wide, low banks, and not over 3 feet deep. 20 miles.

AUGUST 11, SATURDAY

Left camp again with the rising sun and traveled 4 miles down the river to where it enters a canyon when we left it and traveled round the point of a hill, striking the river again in 6 miles. After passing down the river 2 miles farther, we camped for noon on the bank of river. Grass here becoming very dry. Everything of the vegetable kind in this portion of the valley is strongly impregnated with salt.

Left noon camp at 1:00 p.m. and traveled down the river 8 miles in a westerly direction to where the river seems to enter the mountains. Feed poor. 20 miles.
[18 miles.]

AUGUST 12, SUNDAY

Laid over until 2:00 p.m. when we broke up camp and traveled 10 miles, crossing over low hills. Road very heavy with sand. There was another road passing down the river through the canyon, but we feared to attempt it.

Grass at this point very poor.

Samuel Beck overtook us today. He came through from Salt Lake on pack mules.[10] 10 miles.

AUGUST 13, MONDAY

Left camp early this morning and traveled 9 miles down the river in a northwesterly direction.

Last evening I could see in the distance a smoky mountain which I took to be the Sierra Nevada.

Left camp at 2:00 p.m. and traveled down the river over low sand hills 9 miles past a long, low piece of ground of many acres full of sloughs and bushes. Here we found quantities of fine grass.[11]

The ground here is covered with a white salty deposit, and all the grass and vegetable matter is impregnated with it.

Nothing but willow brush for fuel. 18 miles. *[19 miles.]*

[Carnes: We find this stream rather too deep to ford. In many places it is a sluggish deep river.]

AUGUST 14,
TUESDAY

Left camp at 7:00 a.m. and traveled 8 miles down the river. The latter part of the road was very heavy-wheeling over low sand hills.[12]

This has been one of the warmest days experienced since we left home.

Left noon camp at 3:00 p.m. and traveled down the river 8 miles to where we are now camped for the night. 16 miles.

[Carnes: The best road is on the south side of the river, but the water being up in (the) river, making the fords too deep, the main travel has been on the north side.]

AUGUST 15,
WEDNESDAY

Raised camp at 7:00 a.m., traveling 4 hours and only making 8 miles. We camped for noon. After traveling down the river 4 miles this morning, we had to ascend the bluffs. Sand 8 inches deep. We traveled 4 miles on the bluffs through heavy sand, making it very hard on our stock.[13] When we reached the river again, we forded to the opposite side, where the feed for cattle is better.

Left the noon camp at 3:00 p.m. and traveled 6 miles down the river, crossing once and camped on the bottom, where the road takes to the bluffs.

Most of the time our route has been on the north side of Humboldt River. 14 miles.

AUGUST 16,
THURSDAY

Left camp early this morning and ascended the bluffs, traveling 14 miles over the sandy miserable road until we reached the river again, where we camped for noon. Grass scarce.

Broke up our noon camp at 3:30 p.m. and traveled down the river over a low sand bluff, a distance of 4 miles, when we came to what is called the "Cutoff" or the "South Oregon Trail."[14]

Dr. Swain informed me that his company found a portion of a mastodon skeleton near Fort Laramie, one 3 feet 9 inches long [and] another 3 feet 8 inches.[15] The circumference of the socket not given, but diameter 9 inches. 18 miles.

[Carnes, commenting on the decision not to take the cutoff: "May take this road (the Cutoff), but nothing is known about its termination as yet. Left hand road leads to the sink." An entry from later in the day: "There is a desert of some 60 miles either way with little or no feed. We decide in favor of the old road."]

AUGUST 17,
FRIDAY

Laid over until 2:00 p.m., when we traveled down the old road to the Sink, a distance of 7 miles, and camped at the edge of a desert which is said to be 15 miles across. Rained a little all day today.[16] 7 miles.

[Carnes: The grass in some places is so salty that the cattle will not eat it.]

AUGUST 18,
SATURDAY

Raised camp at sunrise this morning and moved one mile down the river, where we ascended the bluffs again and traveled 14 miles across a desert where we reached the river again. Here we nooned, letting our cattle browse on the willows, there being but little grass.

The river banks all the way down are of barren clay, 20 to 30 feet high.[17] We crossed two deep ravines. Left noon camp 6:00 p.m. and traveled until 10:00 p.m., making 12 miles. Here we turned out our cattle to again browse on the willows.

This afternoon's travel lay across a barren place.[18] Not vegetation enough to keep a grasshopper alive. Our day's drive [was] 27 miles. Terrible on stock, to say nothing about ourselves. 27 miles. *[26 miles.]*

AUGUST 19,
SUNDAY

Left camp early this morning and traveled 14 miles over another barren plain to the slough.

We traveled down along the right spur of the mountain, around an old dried-up slough, grown up with wild cane.[19] In many places the roots had burned about 16 inches down into the ground. The ground was all cracked in three feet squares, to the depth of 6 feet.

The grass here at the slough is very fine. Indians are seen skulking round and several head of stock have been lost by other companies. 14 miles. *[15 miles.]*

[On August 22, Carnes referred to vegetation, "the roots of which form a thick turf and in the dry season take fire and burn off thousands of acres, often 3 or 4 feet deep. The unsuspecting traveler is often suddenly precipitated through the thin crust covering a bed of burning embers."]

AUGUST 20,
MONDAY

Left camp early this morning and traveled down the slough 7 miles, where we found the best grass, and camped for noon. Here we cut grass to feed our stock while crossing the desert.[20]

This slough or sink is said to be about 3 miles wide and at least 20 in length, all covered with fine grass and wild cane. This slough is made by [the] Humboldt River spreading. The water sinks under the desert said to be ahead of us.[21]

There [are] some Indians here at present. They are hired to pack grass or hay across the slough. Some Indians [are] from California. Here we met a Mormon train from California. 7 miles.

[Carnes: Indians visit our camp today and make demonstrations of friendship and at the same time commit depredations by stealing cattle, etc.]

AUGUST 21,
TUESDAY

Laid over all day preparing hay and provisions for the desert or sink.

In the evening we moved camp down the slough 2 miles where the grass is 18 inches high. This is a glorious place for recruiting our cattle.

Messrs. Woodworth of Stirling, Ill. came up today.[22]

The mountains on either side of this place are perfectly barren. Indian fires are seen burning at the base of the mountains on the south side of the slough. 2 miles. *[1 mile.]*

AUGUST 22,
WEDNESDAY

Left camp at the usual time in the morning and traveled down the Sink of Humboldt River a distance of 10 miles. Five miles more brought us to Sulphur Springs, where we fed our hay and laid over until 10:00 p.m. when we started across the desert, preferring night in order to avoid the hot sun.

These springs are very strongly impregnated, and the water hardly fit to drink.[23]

Part of the country passed over today resembles a brickyard.[24] 15 miles. *[17 miles.]*

AUGUST 23,
THURSDAY

After traveling all night last night, excepting an hour at midnight, we reached this place, Boiling Springs, at 10:00 a.m., a distance of 20 miles.[25]

The country over which we traveled is volcanic in character. The springs are truly a curiosity. There is one 5 feet by 10 feet and 5 feet deep. Here we made tea out of the already boiled water. We also boiled a whole ham of a hog, cooking it through and through in two hours. A tent pole was laid across the spring and the ham suspended from it. Those of our men who drank the water after simply cooling it and without the tea suffered terribly from strangury, while the tea did not produce that effect.

There is also what is called a "Steamboat Spring" nearby, which is much more grand and impressing than that at Soda Springs. The water in this boiling steamboat spring is forced through an opening in the rock or crust about 8 inches in diameter and thrown most of the time to a height of 3 feet. One peculiarity about this spring: its action is not constant. Sometimes there will be a constant flow for 30 minutes to an hour or two, then it will quiet down for several hours, or a less time. Knowing the uncertainty of the flow, we caught as much water as possible in large tin pans and as soon as cool enough allowed our cattle to drink it without any bad effect. No [unintelligible] in them.

One of our company thought this would be a good place to wash his shirts, so [he] consigned a couple of them to the boiling column, and for a time was delighted to see them tossed up and down, when he almost imagined he could see the dirt fly. But suddenly, to his utter amazement, water and shirts failed to appear and all was quiet. Of course he was the butt of many a joke. After an hour or so a great rumbling was heard and all hands rushed to the hole in the ground awaiting developments, when with the first gush of the scalding fluid my friend beheld his shirts, and with the aid of a cane fished them out.

Who knows? There may be a celestial laundry down there.

Left Hot Springs at 4:30 p.m. for Truckee or Salmon Trout River.[26] 20 miles. [Carnes gives no mileage figure.]

AUGUST 24,
FRIDAY

Traveled all night over the desert, a distance of 14 miles, which brought us to the sand bank over which we traveled 6 miles and reached Truckee at sun rise this morning. Here we found some willow bushes and cottonwood which was an agreeable sight, not having seen a tree for some 800 miles.[27] We will spend the day here, resting up our stock as they are in great need of it. 20 miles. [Carnes gives no mileage figure.]

[Carnes: The desert just passed over presents a grand scene of destruction. The road for 60 miles is literally stewn with cattle, horses, mules, waggons, etc., etc. The last 8 miles of the road before striking this water is a very heavy loose sand, and many are obliged to leave their wagons at the commencement of this sand, drive the cattle to the river, and return and get the wagon. The stench of the dead carcasses is offensive in the extreme.]

Truckee River to Bidwell's Bar

August 25–September 20

☛ *Parke and his company pushed up the Truckee River, passing through Muddy Basin and fording the waterway dozens of times. They manhandled their wagons up and down rock walls, overcoming the granite palisades of the Sierra Nevada Range, the most formidable obstacle to date. They paused at the site of the Donner Party disaster, then pushed on to the Bear River and entered mining country. Parke and his friends made their way to Deer Creek, visited Sacramento briefly, and then turned north to the Middle Fork of Feather River. There, five miles upstream from Bidwell's Bar, they began serious mining.* ☛ *By the time forty-niners reached the eastern slope of the towering Sierra Nevada, their ranks were thinned, their draft animals decimated, their strength sapped, and their morale low. The soothing waters and shade of the Truckee River and the knowledge that only the Sierra Nevada stood between them and the gold fields provided the extra resolve to enable them to clamber over the boulder-strewn route and endure the thin, cold air. Fatigue, despair, and social disintegration were rampant, as was sickness, and they admitted that they had seen the elephant. Once over the rugged mountains, emigrants scattered to various nooks of the gold fields. Having suffered dreadfully in getting there, they were in no mood to tolerate anyone who tried to deprive them of their meager possessions. Consequently, the laws the miners created in the absence of effective law, not in opposition to it, were exceedingly severe, swift-acting, highly popular, and very effective in the short run. These men had sacrificed much and were dead serious about their security and well-being.*

AUGUST 25,
SATURDAY

Remained in camp all day yesterday and last night. Broke up camp 8:30 a.m. and traveled up Truckee River 9 miles, crossing 7 times—fording—camping under the shade of some fine cottonwood trees.[1]

This is a beautiful swift-running stream of clear snow water. At this season of the year about 2½ and 3 feet deep, with very rocky bottom. The valley is very narrow, being walled in on either side by high rugged mountains perfectly barren. One would suppose this was a very crooked river, on account of having to cross it 7 times in 9 miles, but such is not the case. The trouble is the bluffs butt out against the stream every now and then, compelling us to cross over. 9 miles. *[10 miles.]*

AUGUST 26,
SUNDAY

Left camp this morning at 6 o'clock and traveled up the river 10 miles, fording it 6 times, water up to our waists and running so swiftly we could barely keep our feet under us.[2]

Grass good at this place, so will remain until tomorrow as our drive today was a hard one on both man and beast. While on the march yesterday and today, we forded the river so often we were compelled to let our clothes dry on us. The stream ran so swiftly cattle would not cross, but allow the current to turn them down stream. This made it necessary for one of us to be on the lower side of each yoke to probe them up and strike the opposite bank at the proper place. The sun is warm but the water thundering cool.

The mountains on either side not quite so high as those of yesterday. 10 miles. *[9 miles.]*

AUGUST 27,
MONDAY

Left camp with the rising sun and traveled nine miles up the river where we camped for noon. Crossed the river 7 times.[3] Fords fairly good for this country and about 3 feet deep.

Left noon camp at 2:30 p.m. and traveled 7 miles up the river to Muddy Valley or the Basin. We crossed the river twice this afternoon [and] one ford, a very bad one. The road this afternoon was bad. We came down two very steep mountains, the one at the second ford being very rocky. This is quite a basin, averaging 10 miles in width and covered with splendid grass.[4]

The river banks here are studded with willows as usual. Here and there the mountains are spotted with scattering pine. On the left of our entrance into the valley is a slough or bog quite difficult to cross on account of miring. 16 miles. *[17 miles.]*

AUGUST 28,
TUESDAY

Left camp at 6:00 a.m. and traveled 16 miles up the river to the foot of the mountains, crossing the river 5 times. At our first ford today, there was a small mountain branch emptying, making it the most difficult crossing yet encountered on this stream.[5]

We climbed up the mountains rapidly and soon came to the beautiful pines which cover the Sierra Nevada Mountains.[6] A short distance ahead can be seen through the smoke still higher mountains covered with pine. The river here is as beautiful as ever. 16 miles. *[17 miles.]*

[Carnes, writing in the evening in camp: "We are now in the forest of the most majestic pines I ever beheld. Great numbers of trees are 4 to 6 feet (in) diameter and of towering heights."]

AUGUST 29,
WEDNESDAY

Left camp quite early this morning and traveled over the first mountain range. We found the mountains very steep and high, but not so bad as we had anticipated. They were covered with pine and balsam fir and some white cedar.

After reaching the highest point of this range of mountains, we descended the western slope, which was very steep, into a valley, a basin where we found a small spring and rather good grass.[7] At this point our road bore to the west and up the valley where the latter contracted to narrow dimensions and then spread out again at this place where we are now camped. There is good grass here and some standing water. Will remain here all afternoon and night. 10 miles. *[12 miles.]*

AUGUST 30,
THURSDAY

Left camp this morning with the rising sun and traveled 4 miles when we came to a stream, which we suppose is Salmon Trout or a tributary. We soon left S. T. Valley and traveled 4 miles over a rolling country into another valley where we nooned. Here we found fairly good feed and plenty of good standing water.[8]

The second range of Sierra Nevada Mountains are in view, covered with snow, a strange sight in August. The question naturally suggests itself: Does this snow ever disappear, or are these mountain peaks eternally snow-clad?

Traveled 10 miles this afternoon, crossed another tributary, and reached S. T. in 9 miles, when we again left the valley, driving over a spur and returning in one mile, where we are now camped. 18 miles. *[19 miles.]*

AUGUST 31,
FRIDAY

Left camp at sunrise and traveled 5 miles to the foot of the mountain, passing one of the houses built by the unfortunate Donner party, 40 or 50 of whom perished during the winter from cold and starvation.[9] This house is built of logs and divided into apartments, showing there were two sexes in the unfortunate company.[10] It is built on a low piece of ground in a thicket of small fir trees. Around the house there are plenty of bones, they having eaten their cattle, and rumor says some of their *own company*.[11]

The stumps around the house are 15 feet high, showing the depth of the snow at the time they were cut.[12] It would be a cold-hearted cuss that could stand on this sorrowful spot without showing some feeling for his unfortunate fellow emigrants who perished here in 1846. There were several other houses, but they were ordered to be destroyed by General Kearny on his return from California in 1847 in order to keep the Indians from living in them. Five miles farther brought us within ½ mile of the summit, where we in fact found "the Elephant." At this place there is a small area of level ground where we rested our cattle for the ascent.

We reached this point at noon and watered our stock at a little brook by the roadside, fed by the melting snow which covered the mountain sides. Karr's Missouri train being in front of us, we were detained somewhat, but after dinner we [made] the ascent. There are two of these about ½ a mile in length, the first being a little the longest and lands you on a table about 80 yards in length. The second ascent starts from this table and lands you on the summit of the Sierra Nevada over a terrible road. Steep 45° and winding.

This road is over a material comprised of clay, and small rolling stones, which roll under the feet of the cattle, making it almost impossible to get up themselves let alone draw the wagons.[13]

Some of Capt. Karr's wagons had 15 yoke of cattle attached at one time, and even then stuck fast at times. We drew our wagons part way up the mountain with 4 yoke of cattle and the aid of a long rope round the end of the wagon, extending up by the side of the oxen and beyond. The men pulled on the rope and aided materially not only in the ascent but in keeping the oxen in line until we arrived at the most difficult point of ascent. Here we were obliged to double teams, putting 8 yoke on the wagon and two yokes to the end of the rope that was continued on up to the table above. In this way we were enabled to get all our wagons on the summit an hour by sun and without a single mishap. After giving three cheers, we started for the valley on the west side, all delighted with our success. Three miles and a half brought us into the valley where we are now camped. Grass and water good. Timber nearly all fir.[14]

Left the great basin on the last day of summer. Last day of August and it was our last day in the basin. Don't think any one of the Como Company would care to take the back track. As for me and my house, we will go home by *water* even if we turn Missourian and puke.[15] 15 miles.

SEPTEMBER 1, SATURDAY Left camp this morning at 8:00 o'clock and traveled over one of the most terrible of all roads. In fact, no road at all until we reached Fremont's Peak, where we camped for the day.[16]

We passed several lakes, some covering 20, 30, and 40 acres. An old grizzly left an impress of his beautiful foot in the sandy road last night. I am satisfied his forefathers had never heard of the Chinese idea of pretty feet.

There are plenty of blacktail deer in the mountains. We had one for dinner today.

Lieut. Thompson and wife of the U.S. Navy camped with us last night. He is ordered to join the Pacific Squadron.[17] 9 miles.

SEPTEMBER 2,
SUNDAY

Left "Camp Fremont"—Fremont's Peak—on headwaters of American Fork at sunrise this morning and traveled 6 miles, when we reached the Yuba River. Two miles more brought us to a terrible rocky "jump off" in the road, where we were compelled to unyoke our cattle and drive them round and through a narrow path. We let our wagons down over the rocks by tying a rope to the hind axle and taking a turn of the former round a pine tree while four men managed the tongue, guiding as seemed necessary. The tongue—like some other tongues—at times was quite unruly, not being particular where it struck.

After getting all our wagons over the rocks safely and our oxen harnessed up again and on the tongues, we started on our journey two miles more, bringing us to our present camp. I protest against calling our route a road.[18] Tis nothing but a miserable trail such as a snake might choose. 10 miles *[11 miles.]*

[Carnes: At this place we had to take the cattle from the wagons and lower them by manual labor over steep precipices, and in fact the road for the most part of the way has been almost impassable for wagons.]

SEPTEMBER 3,
MONDAY

Left camp early this morning and traveled 6 miles to Capt. Greenwood's camp over rocks and hills of the vilest kind, arriving safely at 1:00 p.m., where we have camped for the day.[19]

We passed two beautiful lakes on the top of the mountains and surrounded by solid granite of the most beautiful kind.

Today was the first time we have seen oak trees for many a day. 6 miles.

SEPTEMBER 4,
TUESDAY

Left camp this morning at 6 o'clock and traveled 6 miles over a good road, but dusty, until we reached the foot of Bear River Mountain.[20]

These mountains are amongst the worst we have met, being both steep and long. Here it became necessary to "rough lock" our wheels, which was done by wrapping log-chains around the fellows.[21] Some of our company adopted the novel idea of cutting down small trees and trimming them up so as to leave the stump of the limb project about 12 inches. The top of the tree was fastened to the hind axletree and as it dragged the projecting stumps of limbs plowed through the ground, filling the bill nicely. Mr. Clark was not so fortunate as the rest of our company. His chain was torn loose from the side of [the] wagon box, and the whole wagon rolled down the mountain side, scattering flour, bacon, blankets, tinware, and wagon wheels to the four winds.

Fortunately, there was only one yoke of cattle on the tongue. When the staples drew out of the wagon's bed, the cattle were making a sudden turn, in order to angle down the side of the mountain. At this moment, the rear end of the wagon rose heavenward in the twinkling of an eye. The rear ox fortunately threw his rear end in the same direction, allowing a large pine tree to come between him and the wagon tongue, snapping the latter off like a pipe stem. It was a sad sight to the owner, but laughable at the same time to see so perfect a wreck in so short a time. The wheels were picked up and a cart made of the hind axle. At this place we met a Mr. Woodworth from the "diggings."[22]

Today we were first introduced to the celebrated soap-plant. It resembles an onion wrapped up in the outer rind of a coconut. Mowed grass here for our oxen. From the top of the mountain we traveled two miles down into the valley. 8 miles.

[Carnes: The Como Company "had the misfortune to have one of the wagons of the train to break the lock, and it was

precipitated over the deep descent, rolling down, and was too much damaged as to render it useless as a wagon. The hind wheels (were) used as a cart."]

SEPTEMBER 5, WEDNESDAY

Left camp at 8:00 a.m. and traveled down the valley a short distance, when we crossed Bear River and entered the timber. The headwaters of Bear River here is quite a small creek. For five miles we had rocky roads and some bad hills after crossing Bear River until we reached it again. Two miles more brought us to our noon camp, at a lovely spring on the top of the mountain which we commenced ascending after leaving Bear River.

At one point on the mountain, we were compelled to double team, in order to climb it. After resting our stock and feeding them the grass cut at yesterday's camp, we commenced our descent on the west side, over a very dusty road for four miles.[23] No rocks. This brought us to a beautiful spring on the left of the road, where we are now camped.

From the fact there is not grass here, we are compelled to browse our cattle by cutting down small oak trees, the tops of which they devour eagerly. We have some of our cut grass left yet. Some cattle have been poisoned here by eating laurel.[24]

We are now emphatically in the "diggings," having seen some men come out of a canyon with their wash pans and spades.[25]

The dust in this part of the country, being mixed with charcoal from the pine leaves, etc., [blackens] our faces so completely all we need is the kinky hair to make us resemble a full-blooded African.

Timber here oak, pine, and cedar. Traveled twelve miles today. 12 miles.

SEPTEMBER 6, THURSDAY

Left camp before sunrise and traveled 8 miles to "Steep Hollow."[26]

The country over which we passed this morning [is] quite hilly but not rocky. The hill or mountain side down into "Steep Hallow" was one of the worst yet. We were compelled to put our oxen behind the wagon, but the tree top made the best brake.

Our descent here landed us amongst the miners. Tin-pans, cradles, picks, and shovels were all in motion.[27] This stream is a branch of Bear River.

Some miners were doing well, and others poorly. After gathering all the information we could, we continued our course over a very steep mountain, striking Bear River again. Here we met miners in profusion, all of one mind, while the knowledge possessed by all regarding the object sought, like our own, was *nil*. As "Onward Over the Hills" was our motto, we ascended another steep mountain side, taking the main road to this valley, where the grass is good.[28] Last night we had to browse our cattle.

There is a spring or two at this place. We traveled altogether 16 miles today. 16 miles. *[18 miles.]*

[Carnes: Steep Hollow is about the steepest descent on the whole road, but there are no rocks. The best way to get the wagons down is to attach a small tree under the hind axletree, and with one yoke you can manage the tongue.]

SEPTEMBER 7, FRIDAY
Left camp early this morning and traveled in a western direction across the timber to Woodworth's camp 4 miles from last night's camping ground.[29]

Here we found good grass and excellent water. Some more of our wagons came in today. Others were abandoned and the oxen packed.[30] 4 miles.

SEPTEMBER 8, SATURDAY
Laid over all day recruiting. Three of our men started out prospecting this morning, their first experience, and returned with about $5.00 worth of dust.

Found some old friends from Wayne County, Ind. Capt. David Wood from Centerville and his Father.[31] Also made the acquaintance of Mr. Beesely of New Jersey.[32] Weather fine and all of us enjoying ourselves.

SEPTEMBER 9, SUNDAY
Still in camp resting up, and prospecting for the "filthy lucre."

SEPTEMBER 10, MONDAY
Made two cradles today, and struck out prospecting. Our success was not very flattering, but every "young mother" has to learn how to rock the cradle and keep hunger from the door.

SEPTEMBER 11,   Spent another day prospecting over a big, rough country,
TUESDAY   for small scales and "nuggets," badly scattered.

SEPTEMBER 12,   Moved our camp over to Deer Creek, a distance of 4
WEDNESDAY   miles. This is a fork of the Yuba River.

     We arrived here at 10:00 a.m. and worked our cradles
all afternoon, collecting an ounce of dust. 4 miles.

[Carnes: Lay at camp Woodworth till Sept. 12, recruiting the stock, making gold washing, etc., . . . but emigrants are crowding in so fast that we think it prudent to move out, as we are doing nothing here.]

SEPTEMBER 13,   Spent the day in prospecting, with but poor success.
THURSDAY   Collected about 6 ounces. 1=$16.00. With flour at $40.00 per hundred and every other article of provision in proportion there is but slim prospect of getting rich in a few days. I preserved a beautiful specimen of horned toad.

SEPTEMBER 14,   Moved forward toward Sacramento City, traveling 8
FRIDAY   miles.[33]

     Camped 4 miles from "South Yuba." Saw some nuggets of gold picked up in Spanish Slough by an old miner and weighing four ounces (&1/10). Such "slugs" are exciting to say the least.

SEPTEMBER 15,   We reached Sutter's Fort on the American Fork, and soon
SATURDAY   after the City of Sacramento on the river of the same name and just below the mouth of the American.[34]

     Sacramento is a city of tents with a few plank houses, mostly one story, with plank perpendicular.[35] Boarding houses and provision stores do all the business.

     We soon found it to our decided advantage to procure what provisions we needed and get back to the "diggings" as soon as possible. One thousand dollars soon left our wallets in exchange for flour at $40.00 per hundred pounds, and bacon and sugar in same ratio.

SEPTEMBER 16,   Capt. Sampson, David Carnes, John McWhirter and my-
SUNDAY   self started north for Feather River.[36]

Our course lay up the east bank of Sacramento River over a beautiful prairie covered with wild grass and wilder cattle.

Camped for the night near a landing called Fremont, after the famous "Pathfinder" of that name.

SEPTEMBER 17, MONDAY
Destination: Bidwell's Bar, on Feather River at foot of hills.

Forded Yuba River a short distance above an old adobe ranch house, where another stretch of level prairie lay before us.[37]

SEPTEMBER 18, TUESDAY
Arrived at Bidwell's Bar this evening. Here we found saint and sinner—especially the latter—rich and poor, educated and ignorant, well-disposed and vicious. In short, all sorts of people, and no law but that of the miner to govern them.

"Self protection" is a necessary law, and amongst well-disposed people, a good law. Poor, well-disposed people have no time to fool away on those known to be vicious and give them a chance to escape their just rewards in shape of punishment.

Consequently, the "miners' laws" are swift and certain in their execution. Men seldom steal even a pick or shovel here, the penalty being death without delay, with priest and preacher many miles away and no disposition to hunt him up. No "great criminal lawyer" is allowed to humbug twelve dough men in this country, thereby creating a hope of escape in some would-be assassin. When caught in the act, *up they go,* and that's the end of it.[38]

Life in the Mines and Cities

September 20, 1849–September 18, 1850

☛ *Although he was an active member of the Union Bar Company, Parke managed to travel a bit and observe conditions in the emerging society. One incident caused him to go into the mountains for a while. When some provisions were stolen in December, suspicion fell on some Indians and a punitive expedition was launched. Parke and seventeen others tracked the Indians, engaged them in a bloodless skirmish, and returned to camp. Occasionally, short trips were made to nearby camps and towns for supplies. In late August 1850, he, Captain Sampson, and William B. Lorton terminated their affiliation with the Union Bar Company and went to Sacramento, where Parke engaged in a little medicine and retailing. After staying in that town for about two weeks, he and Sampson decided to return to Illinois, so they left for San Francisco to arrange passage to Central America.* ☛ *Parke's accounts of his stay in California reveal much about society there. Now and then in observing the scene, he passed judgment on the attributes of various women, and he commented extensively on Indian-white relations. Observing or hearing about attempted claim jumping, drunkards, criminals, gamblers, fallen clergy, spats between people, mob action, and general social decline during the course of a year, he opined that large segments of humanity were really quite base. Seeing sickness, hardship, and death around him and having limited success in mining, he became discouraged. While in San Francisco, he saw the flotsam and jetsam of the gold rush—hundreds of abandoned ships rotting in the harbor, their crews having jumped ship for the gold fields—and observed feverish attempts to make the city more habitable. Society was in flux, and before California became a state in September 1850, Parke had penned his impressions of it.*

SEPTEMBER 20, 1849–SEPTEMBER 18, 1850

SEPTEMBER 20, We made a claim 5 miles above Bidwell's Bar and half a
THURSDAY mile above Oregon Bar.[1]
    The following compose our mining company and pro-
pose to turn the channel of the river this coming winter.
And in the Spring when the Oregon Bar is worked out,
we will take out the dam so as to drain the lower part of
our bar.

Names of Members of the
Union Bar Co., Feather River, Cal.[2]

Capt. Simeon Sampson of Como, Ill.	
David Carnes	" "
James W. Whipple	" "
Charles R. Parke, M. D.	"
Robert Terrell	Philadelphia, Missouri
George Terrell	" "
Nathaniel Dunn	" "
H. C. Smith	" "
Fred Smith	" "
Wm. Yates	" "
——— Thornton	" "
Randal Rice	Fairfield, Iowa
Isaac Boyle	" "
John Boyle	" "
Quincy Thompson	" "
Thomas Thompson	" "
Asa Daniel	" "
John M. McQuarter	" "
John Kenyon	" "
——— McCutchin	" "

OCTOBER 1, Cabins all built and work commenced on race to turn the
MONDAY water from the riverbed. At times some of the company

are out prospecting and collecting sufficient "dust" to keep us in bread and butter, while the rest work on the race.

DECEMBER 1, SATURDAY

Water so high since the rainy season set in we cannot work on race, but the high water floods the race and helps by washing it out.[3] Much of our time is spent prospecting and hunting deer, as meat is an object now.

Deer are quite numerous in this part of the country and of the "blacktail" variety. Their flesh is quite palatable, especially to men who have been living on salt pork for the last six months.

JANUARY 1, TUESDAY

So far this has been a rather monotonous winter—rain, rain, rain, at least half the time. Tremendous floods, caused by the melting snows far up on the mountain tops, bringing down large pine logs pitching headlong over the granite rocks, threatening death and destruction to everything in their way.[4]

Prospecting, hunting game, cooking, eating, reading, sleeping, and wishing for letters from the "dear ones at home" has been the order of the day for the last month.

Target shooting and spinning yarns were not omitted, especially the former when the Indians visited us. These Digger Indians seem to be the lowest of all God's creation. They still use the old bow and arrow. Consequently, [they] have great respect for the white man who can send a leaden bullet through a "Bull's-Eye" one hundred yards distant. He thinks there is a poor chance for him in case we want him. They never bring their squaws with them when they visit, which is not very complimentary to either squaw or white man. A great want of confidence. When the various bands go to war—which, by the way, is an everyday affair—the victorious band always take their enemies' squaws, the latter being all they have that is worth anything. In most cases, bow, arrows, and a very poor "britch-cleat" being all left after the squaws have departed. Tis no wonder then these bands are continually at war. What man would not fight for a woman, and a buck Digger Indian is partly man and partly beast. The man part fights for the women, while the beast part makes her do all the work.

Some of the young squaws are fairly good-looking—about the color of a new saddle—with raven black hair and black eyes, but they seem to fade early. I remember seeing but one very old woman amongst the Indians. She appeared to be over one hundred. She was small in stature and quite shriveled. In fact, nothing but skin and bone, entirely toothless and barely able to walk by the aid of two canes. She was evidently quite a charge to the band.

The finding of this old mother squaw was a mere accident. One evening after returning to camp, some of our neighboring miners reported their cabin had been broken into in their absence, and quite a quantity of flour and bacon stolen. As a matter of course, Indians were suspected and a company of 18 men enlisted to follow the trail and if possible recover the flour and bacon as well as chastise the thieves. We struck their trail early in the morning. A little flour here and there along the trail told the story as we ascended the steep mountain side covered mostly with pine and oak. An old Texas Ranger led off cautiously with one other while the balance of us followed nearby so as to prevent an ambush. After one of the hardest day's march[es] I ever made, we reached near the mountain summit amongst the clouds.

Here our scouts discovered the Indians' village very peculiarly located. Two steep mountain spurs ran nearly parallel to the summit, with deep ravines between most of the distance. The ravines gave way to a narrow valley on top of the ridge, thus [Parke has made a drawing at this point]. The village was built in this valley designated by X. Beyond this village the mountain was just as steep as the south side we had climbed, enabling the Indians when pursued to make rapid exit on either side.

When we arrived at no. 1 on the diagram, our company was divided equally. I took eight men and started up the mountain in the direction of no. 2, while an old Texas ranger took the remaining 8. When he thought we had time enough to get in the rear of the village, he was to march directly on the village up the ravine.

Our march was a much more difficult one than anticipated, the mountain being very steep. When we arrived at no. 2, we were amongst the clouds. Every few minutes the clouds would brush by. When we could [see] the Indian town distinctly, I would then order our men to fall on their faces and remain perfectly quiet until another cloud hid us from view. Then we would hasten our march until it swept by. When we arrived at no. 3 on the summit, a protecting cloud swept by and I saw our comrades just in the edge of the village. There was no time to be lost, as there were but nine of them and we knew not the numerical strength of the Indians. I ordered a charge down the mountain, and as much *noise* as we were capable of making, in order to terrify the "redskins" and make them believe we were quite numerous. It had the desired effect, for you could see the red blankets flying in every direction, and in a few minutes not an Indian could be seen but the chief and the old squaw above mentioned.

The barbarous old chief tried to make us believe it was this old squaw who had stolen all the meat and flour. It was hard to keep our men from shooting him on the spot, but better council prevailed, and he finally gave the guard the dodge and made his escape. We wound our way home, neither succeeding in recovering our provisions or drawing blood.[5]

A buck while in camp the other day was greatly amused and puzzled. One of our company had occasion to use an auger. As the instrument buried itself into log with every turn of the handle, and the chips dropped out, the old savage looked thunderstruck. He gently folded his legs under him like a tailor and watched every chip drop. Of course, that night the auger was safely stored away, our experience being that all *wild* Indians are natural thieves and liars.

APRIL 25, [THURSDAY]   Expressions of Missourians. "Nigh upon had you." "Bless Becky." "Dog on."

McCabe's darkey on a stiff today. White pants, with *butternut* colored coat, cigar in mouth, and tin pan. Starts out to prospect.[6]

Another strange sight happened today in this civilized Christian land. One Doctor Blake, an Irishman late of Missouri, loaded up with booze down at the ranch below Dutch Charlie's, took upon himself to rob the squaws of their already scant attire. He ran them into the wigwams and pulled off several "fantails," then left in haste. He was one of Smith O'Brien's men who fled his country a few years since.[7]

On one of my trips to Sacramento after provisions, while passing through Marysville, my attention was called to a young lady resident. She changes her dress several times a day, and sometimes appears in *pants* and woolen shirt, red sash around her waist. Hair short round her neck and a Spanish sombrero on her head. She bets freely on horse races, talks much with the miners, and finally gets drunk. Very pretty, and only sweet *sixteen*. How is that for young America? Call home the foreign missionaries. Said to have been brought from Boston to San Francisco by her Father, whom she left in the latter city and strayed off with a gambler. Of course she deals monte nicely, swears, and smokes cigarettes.[8]

Some bilious fever and diarrhoea in camp, also scurvy.

APRIL 29,
[MONDAY]

Weather extremely warm in the middle of the day. Nights cool and pleasant with heavy dew.

Heard from home yesterday through W. C. Miller who had received a letter from Dr. Murphy of Parkesburgh stating Father and family were all well and had received the gold dust I sent last December.[9]

APRIL 30,
[TUESDAY]

A certain Mr. Dixon of Illinois jumped a small claim of ours up in the canyon the other day. We notified him last Sunday he must leave it. Capt. S. Sampson did most of the talking for our company. He became somewhat excited, telling Dixon (who is very much disfigured in the face from a burn) all the men on Feather River could not drive him from his rights. Dixon then became courageous, and with a squeaking voice I shall never forget, said, when he knew he was right, "he would stand up to the cannon's mouth." After blowing off, both cooled down and the Captain held the diggings.[10]

MAY 1,
[WEDNESDAY]

David Carnes, Ike Boyles, and some others went out the other day to hunt "dry diggins." Some Indians would molest them. One night, while asleep in the tent, the Indians came to the rear, pulled up the pins, and took from under their heads a gun and axe without wakening them. In the morning the discovery was made, and the tracks of an Indian were left in the sand, three feet from the sleeping guard, who was inside the front of [the] tent. So much for certainty in an Indian country.

To add to the intensity of their injured feelings, their morning lunch had hardly made the acquaintance of the gastric juice before they heard the crack of the stolen rifle. An Indian village was supposed to be nearby, and the boys thought it prudent on their part to retreat toward camp, hoping the accidental discharge of the gun had ripped up the liver of the thief and sent him to the "happy hunting ground."

This is a beautiful day, though quite warm. Nature is clothed with her most beautiful garment, the brilliancy of which was never equalled in the states. The wild flowers here are coarser, but the colors are much brighter than amongst cultivated flowers.

Went up the river to Evans Bar after beef.[11] Saw Mrs. ———, a *beautiful little woman* of fairy form, which is a rare sight in this country, and when seen animates the most depressed of men. She and husband are late from Chicago, Ill.

MAY 3,
[TUESDAY]

Just finished reading *A Life in the Far West* by Lieut. Ruxton in which the "far west" and all its savage hordes, etc, are faithfully portrayed, especially the Mormons.[12] He tells a good story about the Prophet Joe Smith, who being called upon to perform some great miracle in order to reconcile some who were weakening in the faith, called the brethren together on the banks of the Missouri on a certain day and in the announcement stated he would walk across the river on the water as did Christ at one time. The day came and Joseph was on the ground bright and early, surrounded by an anxious crowd of saints.

When the hour arrived, Joe pulled off his boots and stockings and boldly walked to the water's edge, where he addressed the sisters and brethren as follows:

"Brethren, this is a great day for us. Shall it be seen that I am truly a prophet, etc." But he added, "You must believe I can do it, and I must also believe, which I do." He then asked, "Do you believe?" to which all responded, "Yea." He then said as he also believed, consequently it was not necessary for him to do it. He then drew on his stockings and boots, turned on his heel, and walked away, as though he had done wonders. There are very many adherents in other associations who display an equal amount of blind devotion and ignorance, following the lead of demagogues and deceivers.

This is another very warm day. River rising rapidly.

MAY 4,
SATURDAY

Nothing doing as usual. Heat more oppressive than heretofore.

Received the N. Y. *Tribune* of March 13th, which contains the important and gratifying news that Congress was becoming more *sober* and acting somewhat like statesmen.

MAY 8,
[WEDNESDAY]

Finished packing up our provisions today. No mail from home yet.

Dave Carnes accidentally met his cousin today. He left Illinois last year in the Holt County train. Arrived in Salt Lake last summer, where they spent six weeks, sold their oxen, and bought mules and horses, and with a *guide* took the South Trail for California with one hundred horses.[13]

After traveling some time, they determined to take a cut-off, or rather discover a new road. Unfortunately, after a few days they came to a desert, across which they were five days traveling without one drop of water. But one horse out of the hundred was able to stand the trip. The men ate the mules and horses as they died, and finally five of the men died of starvation and thirst. They arrived in California about six weeks since, having traveled or wandered all winter amongst the mountains—so he says.

There is nothing like practical knowledge in this world. I may not make a fortune this trip, but the knowledge I gain of human nature, both savage and Christian, will well repay me for all the privations and hardships incident to such an undertaking.

I have *deliberately* come to the conclusion that hardly 5 per cent of the human family—or more properly speaking—adult male portion, are reliable under all circumstances. I mean, when danger, hard work, or starvation is imminent, they will shirk or act the hog.

Many instances might be cited to prove the truth of what I say. *Man is selfish.* For instance, on July 19th, 1849 we left the main Fort Hall road, with the view of making a cut-off of 60 miles from the latter Fort. The matter was discussed while in camp near the Old Crater, and many of the emigrants learned our views and when we expected to start. Our first ten miles was across a sandy, barren desert. Three Missourians, dressed in "Butternut britches," concluding to take advantage of our knowledge, started in advance of us, and after traveling five miles camped on the dry sand, waiting our arrival. Capt. Hedgepeth started our Como Co. in ahead, his mule teams following in 6 hours. Capt. Sampson, the guide, Carnes, and myself started on foot, in advance of our teams. The walking was simply terrible, dry hot sand two or three inches deep slipping out from under your feet at every step, while the hot sun poured its rays down upon our unprotected heads. When we arrived at the camp of the three Missourians, we were nearly exhausted and very, very thirsty.

The three "Butternuts" were under their wagon, protecting themselves from the sun and awaiting our guide's arrival, so as to be able to proceed when our teams came up. They had a keg of water from which they were satisfying their thirst, while lunching. Capt. Sampson after passing the compliments of the morning, asked for a drink for us, when to our astonishment we were informed they had barely sufficient for themselves. The Captain, having followed the seas in his time, *pronounced a benediction* on the "Butternut brethern" for their selfishness, being willing to avail themselves of the benefits of our knowledge to shorten the route to California, but would not in return give us a drink of cool water.

Ten miles farther brought us to a beautiful stream of spring water flowing along under scrub willows, the surface being only a few inches below the bank. Here we lay on our faces and drank and blessed the Missouri butternut trio alternately. This is only one of our test cases of "man's inhumanity to man."

MAY 9,
[THURSDAY]

Went out hunting today. Saw one deer, several jack rabbits, squirrels and pigeons, but only captured one mountain grey squirrel, the tail of which measured 15 inches.

Thermometer today stands 90° in the shade.

Was called across the river to see a young German who was scorbutic. The old Father was very much broken down over his son's sickness and the probability of losing him. He and his two sons, 18 and 5 respectively, lived in a little log cabin and prospecting up and down the river. Their diet was quite simple: bread of their own making and bacon. Consequently, [they] were soon attacked with scurvy.

The poor old man told me the story of his trials and sorrows across the plains. The cholera broke up their company soon after leaving the States, two of his six children dying. With his 3 yoke of oxen, wife and 4 children, he followed along in the wake of large companies so as to be protected from the Indians.

From time to time he would lose one of his oxen until but one yoke remained. Then one by one he lost two more children, and buried them by the roadside. He finally cut his wagon down and made a cart of it so as to travel lighter and faster before the early snow caught him on the mountains. Finally, to cap the climax of his sorrow his wife sickened and died as they toiled through the snow. He and his sons dug the fond wife and Mother's grave and laid her to rest forever, after which they hurried down the western slope of the Sierra Nevada to the land of gold, wiser but sadder. The ridiculous part of the old man's story was, while the great tears rolled down his cheeks as he narrated each sad incident, he finished by saying, "I would not care a tarn fur all dat, if my big boy would only get well." He got well.

MAY 15,
[WEDNESDAY]

Mr. Lorton (Carnes' cousin) entertained us today with many anecdotes about the Mormons. He said Brigham Young was a very large man and quite "starchy." Rides in his carriage with *one wife* and coachman. Has complete control over all his subjects. They promptly obey all his orders. When a public meeting is called to raise funds for any particular purpose, he nominates all the committees and then says, "Now I nominate *myself treasurer*. All in favor say, 'aye,'" when all with one voice will respond in the affirmative. Then he will say, "Now brethren, I want you all to speak out, vote as you please, don't let me influence you. All opposed to me being treasurer, make it known by 'nay'". Not a voice was heard but a poor wicked emigrant, who shouted, "A Mormon vote, by G–d."

Upon seeing some Mormans lying round the emigrant wagons neglecting their work, he accosted them as follows: "You lazy, dirty D——s, clear out from here and get to work on the farms. You will lie round these emigrants all summer, and next winter, d—n you, you will come to me for something to eat. Gentlemen, you must excuse me for swearing, but it makes me so d——d mad I can't help it."

I record the story as I heard it.

MAY 20,
[MONDAY]

Just heard of the death of Hon. John C. Calhoun of S. C.[14] Peace to his ashes. Brains will tell.

Clay Smith and George Terrell went down to Bidwell's Bar to write letters to their girls.

Water falling slowly. Had a shower last night—scarcely laid the dust. Cool this morning.

MAY 21,
[TUESDAY]

Received a letter from Evan Jones today dated February 13th. Pretty old news. Said Wilson Strode was about starting for California, also that Henry McClellan and Benjamin Everhardt were dead.[15]

MAY 27,
SUNDAY
[MONDAY]

Warm day, water still falling. Mr. Fry of St. Louis was drowned two days since in the canyon above our dam.

JUNE 7,
[FRIDAY]

Mail just received for our Company, but none for me. Col. Heely, Mr. Carry, and Dr. Powel of Bidwell's Bar are all said to be *defunct Methodist preachers*. They don't deny it.[16] The first is a gambler by profession, while the second keeps a boarding house and gambling house combined. The third is a quack doctor, trifling with men's lives for a few paltry dollars.

Speculating in claims and preaching by turns as occasion offers to get into the good graces and confidence of the new-comers—beautiful characters for this country. No wonder I have lost confidence in most of the human family.

Dr. Jackson of Boston, a confirmed drunkard, died of appoplexy on [the] 5th. The evening of the 4th he made a speech after which the above mentioned characters made him drunk, lassoed and otherwise abused him, when on the morning of the 5th he was taken with spasms, which continued all day, he dying in the evening. None of his drunken companions visited him while he lay suffering from his debauche.[17]

JUNE 8,
[SATURDAY]

Had some fine vocal music last night from Mr. Lorton, reminding me of home. River falling slowly.

JUNE 9,
[SUNDAY]

Dunn put on a "biled shirt" today and started for Bidwell's Bar, having cast off his Bay pants. We conclude he is visiting the Misses McCabe on South Fork.

JUNE 18,
[TUESDAY]

Great excitement prevails along the river regarding the discovery of a certain "gold lake" on the headwaters of North Yuba river. Every pan of dirt is said to yield from

97

$32.00 to $200.00 Six of our Company have packed the mules and gone in search of the hidden treasure.

Received two letters today, one from Father and two from Dick Jefferies. Father's mailed in March and Dick's April 1st and 16th. One from Jones December 8, '49, and one from my Brothers from Little Detroit of same date.[18] Mailbag is a slow coach.

JUNE 24, [MONDAY]	Commenced digging a new race from our dam, along side of old one.
JUNE 26, [WEDNESDAY]	Men returned from their search after "gold lake." The lake could not be found, but "Nelson Creek" was found and three claims made.[19] On the bank opposite upper claim, [they] took out in an hour or two over one hundred dollars in very coarse gold—nuggets.
JUNE 27, [THURSDAY]	Some of our Company preparing to leave for Nelson's Creek tomorrow, which will leave but 11 at this bar.
JULY 1, [MONDAY]	Thermometer 115°.
JULY 4, [THURSDAY]	Worked on Bensley Bar today, raising dam. Some of the boys on opposite side went up to the Fairfield Bar to attend a celebration.[20] Did not find an extra dinner as in the States.

We turned the water in our new race yesterday and will commence our dam tomorrow. Weather still warm—100°. I worked with a long drill nearly all day yesterday, with the view of blasting a large granite rock in our new race. Two of us alternate with drill. While one drills, the other slides off the rock into the water, cools off, and comes up on the opposite side and takes the drill. |
| JULY 7, SUNDAY | Yesterday and day before, we worked on our dam, making good headway against the current.

On the 3rd, a band of 18 "Mo" Indians crossed the river here on the warpath. Their object was to fight the "Pikes." They returned in the evening, not having met the enemy.[21] |

JULY 27,
[SATURDAY]

Have been down with "mountain fever" for three weeks, but quite well again.

Was down at Bidwell's Bar yesterday. Saw many long faces on account of the failure of so many "bars." Weather very warm. Received a letter from Julia and Florence Sampson, Como, Illinois.[22] T'was quite a treat. Saw the "Old Oak Tree" where poor Pollock died and nearby his lonely grave, where wrapped in a woollen blanket he sleeps his last sleep, far from relatives and friends.

[Parke made a drawing at this point.]

This rude sketch will give an idea of Pollock's tent under the live oak. Under this, I found him sick unto death. I crept in beside him, streatched on a blanket, dark a midnight ever was, and with hand on his breast listened to his breathing, while the wind moaned and whistled through the branches above, until he died. Here I kept my lonely watch until morning.

AUGUST 13,
[TUESDAY]

As yet very little gold taken out of the river bed.

Thornton has had rheumatism and is very "old womanish." He is very partial to clover tea, which he says "quiets the nervous parts." He ate some stewed hawk last evening, but it did not set well on his stomach. After grunting all night, he restored to his favorite tea, which in a few minutes went to his feet, he said, and quieted his "nervous parts."

AUGUST 20,
[TUESDAY]

Prospects for working out our river bed claim this year poor. Have concluded to sell out and to try city life.

AUGUST 25,
[SUNDAY]

Capt. Sampson, Carnes, and myself wound up our connection with Union Bar Company today and make our first step toward *home*.

Sacramento City

SEPTEMBER 6,
[FRIDAY]

Left Feather River in August in Company with Capt. Sampson and Wm. B. Lorton and came to this city, where I have been loafing until a few days ago, when I went in partnership with Dr. Greenman of Illinois, practicing medicine and merchandising in a small way.[23] Selling pies and other necessaries of life. Must do something to live.

There was a mock funeral here yesterday, General Zach. Taylor being the supposed corpse. It was quite a failure, as everybody had to attend to his store, etc.[24]

Mail just arrived from the States via Panama on steamship *Tennessee*. Hope to hear from home.

The squatters and speculators have had a fight about two weeks since in which several on both sides were killed.[25] Amongst the killed were sheriff McKenny and the leader of the squatters, Mr. Malone. Mayor Bigelow was severely wounded and had his right arm amputated. There is some hope he will recover.

Laborers are engaged throwing up a levee round the city as contracted for.

This is called a city, but it don't look much like one at present. No telling what it may be, as all cities must have a start.

Sacramento City is on the east bank of Sacramento River a short distance below the mouth of the American Fork. The river banks are low, especially the west. Consequently, subject to overflow during the winter or rainy season, especially toward spring when the mountain snow commences melting. The mountains back of the valley are so high and steep and the quantity of snow so great that the warm spring rains cause terrible floods in the valley below.

There are no substantial houses here. The best are constructed of plank, set up on end, and cracks battened. A few are two story, but most of them only one, quite long and used for saloons and gambling houses. A majority of the inhabitants live in tents, such as they brought with them from the plains. Early last spring the whole city was submerged. The water broke over the levee or artificial bank of the American river, and covered the face of the whole valley from Sutter's Fort down. The citizens who were so fortunate as to have two-story houses were compelled to move upstairs, going out the upper windows and about in skiffs, while those dwelling in tents and sheds had to flee back toward the base of the mountains for protection. Here on these mounds all were collected, all sorts of living creatures. Even the Norway rat, heretofore unknown in this country, brought here on Eastern ships, had to associate with his numerous enemies. It looked as though Noah had dumped his old ark on this mound, the only difference being, in place of two of a kind, they seemed to be more prolific than Noah, for the mound was literally covered with the good-for-nothing little cusses.

If the good old saintly people of the States could only look in on these gambling dens for a minute or two, I know they would feel like calling home all *foreign* missionaries and turning them loose on this God-forsaken people. And this too would be a dangerous experiment, for madam rumor says—and there is no doubt but that she's correct—many of these dealers in Monte passed at home as missionaries, exhorters, etc., etc.

Many human beings, like dogs, are mere followers. They lack the disposition to lead. They imitate. Such men are Christians, pagans, or devils according to their surroundings. Step by step, they go one way or the other.

Some of these resorts are long one-story plank buildings, say 24 x 100 feet. Down the center of this room are placed small tables about 8 feet apart. At every table there is a man dealing Monte and surrounded by a crowd, some betting and some looking on. At the far end of the hall is a bar, where all fashionable drinks are dealt out for *one dollar* a drink. There is also a good band of music to enliven the crowd. I have stood by and watched these crowds many times with amazement at their perfect recklessness in staking their all on the draw of a single card. Of course, the dealer has the advantage every time. Frequent glasses of "toddie" are indulged in, increasing the recklessness of those engaged in the game.

At times those little tables are literally covered with buckskin bags filled with gold dust. Thousands and thousands of dollars changing hands every hour from morning until late in the night.

During all this excitement and apparent chance to get rich, I never made a single bet or took a chance. I know a Monte dealer has the advantage all the time. Besides, I prefer to make my living in an honorable way, so I can call it my own.

SEPTEMBER 15, [SUNDAY] Letters from home and no paying business here have been instrumental in causing Capt. Sampson to think seriously of turning his face homeward toward wife and interesting family. Not being blessed with wife or children, but very much attached to the Captain—having been with him since we left the States—I leave all to him, whether and when we shall return. We left Como, Illinois, April 7, 1849, since which time we have been constantly together. Slept in the same tent, bunked in the same cabin, cooked for each other, and ate of the same board, etc., and strange to say in all our dealings we never had the slightest misunderstanding, although he is considered a very austere, positive man, but just to a farthing.

San Francisco

SEPTEMBER 17, [TUESDAY] Yesterday we left the City of Sacramento and arrived here today bound for *home*.

This bay is full of craft of all kinds deserted by their crews almost as soon as they cast anchor. And here they lie rotting, it being impossible to obtain sailors. Every newcomer is suddenly taken with the "gold fever" and off he goes to the mines. Some of the vessels do not even have a Capt. or watchman to take care of them.[26]

This is one of the most beautiful harbors in the world, perfectly protected from the ocean by the high coast range of mountains.

[Parke made a drawing at this point.]

In general appearance, San Francisco is like all other Spanish towns or Mexican, but the day is soon coming when it will be Americanized. The diagram above will give an idea of location and entrance.

102

Laborers are actively engaged in scraping down sand from the hillside, filling up the streets out in [the] bay where the piles are driven.

Frame houses are being built on the piles. It may be a long time before the owner can boast of a dry cellar.[27]

The weather here is quite warm up to noon. A person is uncomfortably warm with a thin coat on until noon. About this time the sea breeze sets in, when an overcoat is quite comfortable.

The velocity of the wind is great as frequently to drive clouds of sand from the mountain side back of the city down through the streets, making it very disagreeable for pedestrians.

There is one advantage over an inland breeze in the country. This ocean breeze seldom induces cold or catarrhal trouble. No doubt on account of the salt in the moist atmosphere, as well as iodine, etc.[28]

Poverty and homesickness seem to be epidemic here.

We have made the acquaintance of quite a number of old "salts" since arriving in the city, amongst them several captains of old whalers from New Bedford, Maine. Like ourselves, they are all anxious to start home.

Capt. Sampson left this morning with the other captains to look up a ship and make arrangements to continue our course toward the States.

SEPTEMBER 18, [WEDNESDAY] The Captain has engaged passage on a small centerboard schooner for Acapulco, Mexico, or Panama.[29] We will sail in a few days.

The Captain of our schooner is a Spanish, or some yellow, mongrel. He will have about 20 passengers, mostly Americans.

Voyage to
Central America

September 20–November 7

☛ *Sailing for Panama from San Francisco in a centerboard schooner, Parke and his shipmates rounded Cape St. Lucas and stopped at Mazatlán, Mexico. Instead of proceeding to Panama, however, they made for the harbor of Realejo on the northwest coast of Nicaragua.* ☛ *The trip from San Francisco to Realejo was not pleasant for Parke. From the moment they set sail, the ship was mismanaged and badly handled. Storms, seasickness, leaks, oppressive heat, and inferior provisions and water compounded problems caused by the captain. Despite the fact that the captain managed to avoid damage from furious storms, mutinous sentiment bubbled, which probably did much to encourage him to put into Realejo instead of trying to reach Panama. The voyage was not without interesting episodes, however. Parke attended a grotesque bullfight in Mazatlán and was totally nauseated by it. In keeping with enlightened liberal thinking in the mid-1800s, he found much fault with Mexico's elites, some of that nation's values and institutions, and what he thought were sure signs of social and moral degeneracy. The only truly bright spots in the voyage were the opportunities for swimming and watching whales and sharks.*

Voyage to Nicaragua

SEPTEMBER 20, [FRIDAY] Bag and baggage all aboard the little craft and our bow beckoning and bowing to the Pacific swells as they meet us.

A little incident occurred today which gives us some insight into the character of our Captain.

Our schooner was anchored up one of the new streets that is to be. As she was being towed out by a tug, some of her rigging caught on the scaffolding of a new house that is being built out on the piles over the water.

How much damage was done I do not know, but the Captain agreed to go on shore and adjust the matter to the satisfaction of all.

Our ship proceeded out to sea in charge of a pilot, after which the first mate took charge of her. Our Captain soon made his appearance in a small boat, having dodged the officers and saved his fine or damages.

SEPTEMBER 25, [WEDNESDAY] Have had a rather monotonous passage so far. Sea very smooth and weather warm.

I have been about half seasick since leaving San Francisco. This is my first experience out of sight of land, and from what I now know I would not select the life of a sailor. Hope to reach Cape St. Lucas tomorrow.

Our Captain is not first class, as he ran by San Diego and other points along the coast of California.

SEPTEMBER 26, [THURSDAY] Reached Cape St. Lucas today. Quite a gale blowing and Captain has concluded to run into Mazatlan, Mexico for safety.

SEPTEMBER 27, [FRIDAY] Mazatlan, Mexico. Ran into this port just before dark last evening, making a lucky escape, as we learn nearly every ship outside this bay is more or less damaged while some are total wrecks. At least such are the reports.

The entrance to this harbor is very narrow, so very narrow that vessels outside in such a storm as we had last night were afraid to venture in, there being steep rocks on either side. This harbor is very much like that of San Francisco, only smaller.

As soon as we cast anchor, our little dusky Captain took a boat and ran ashore, leaving the ship in charge of the 1st Mate.

There is a banana schooner and a brig in the bay beside our schooner. Sea terribly rough and my stomach sympathizing in the repand motion.

SEPTEMBER 28, [SATURDAY] Last night was a frightful one. At daybreak it seemed to me we would be thrown upon the rocks and dashed to pieces.

In the night the wind veered round to the N. W. and all three vessels swung round on their cables a short distance from the overhanging rocks to the north of the landing.

Unfortunately, we dragged our anchor several feet, and—our cable being longer than that of the banana schooner—we came in contact with it. Every time the stern of our vessel rose up on a sea, the side of the little schooner would drop under us in the trough, receiving the whole weight of our ship's stern. As soon as the seas quieted down some, a line was thrown from the brig to the fruit schooner, and she was towed beyond our reach, but badly damaged.

As soon as it was safe, we all took to the boats and went ashore for the day, glad to rest on terra firma once more, although pretty "groggy."

OCTOBER 3, [THURSDAY] Raised anchor today and again started out on the dark blue sea.

Our stay in Mazatlán was quite pleasant, and long enough to get a good insight into Mexican life and customs.[1]

While in the city our meals were taken at a Chinese restaurant, and we spent the nights on board the ship. Our cook was called "John" of course. He spoke English very well. Said he was picked up from a wreck by a Philadelphia tea ship and taken to the latter city. Had worked his way this far back toward home. He was very friendly, indeed no doubt on account of the good treatment he had received in Philadelphia.

We spent one Sunday in Mazatlán and attended a bullfight in the afternoon. The whole performance was *very elevating* and exciting. Seven bulls were killed and quite a number of Mexicans injured, but what of that, they all were only animals.

The Governor of the state presided. No doubt he and all, but us American sinners, had attended "divine services" in the morning.

The enclosed ring was about 150 feet in diameter, with elevated seats in [the] form of a crescent on one side and half way round. In the center of this crescent was the Governor's stand, and opposite on the other side of the enclosure was the bullpen or stall, closed with double door opening out into the amphitheatre.

The subject of torture was driven into this stall from the outside. The top of the stall was open, so that when the proper time came Mexicans with their long spears could reach down and probe the animal until he came perfectly furious.

Six men, picadors, dressed like our American clowns, entered the arena, four on foot and two on horseback, the latter armed with long spears while the horses were covered with brightly colored trappings. Each footman had a red flag, 14 x 24 inches, which he held in his left hand, while in his right hand he grasped a long, slender sword.

Everything being ready, the Governor ordered the bull probed until he became desperate. Two men mounted the pen and commenced piercing the bull with long-handled spears. In a few moments we could hear the poor dumb brute bellow, when suddenly the doors flew open and the infuriated animal dashed out into [the] ring. For a moment he stood and gazed at the crowd, but particularly at the gaudy men and horses before him, when he made a dash for one of the red flags. The Mexican—who by the way was a convict—held the red flag under his right arm, in which hand he held his sword.

As the animal passed under his right arm with head down, he made a thrust at the neck, with the view of reaching the heart by way of inner side of scapula or shoulder blade, but missing his mark was compelled to jump to one side and let the bull pass. At this moment another Mexican ran up and planted a barbed torpedo into his hide. These torpedoes are passed through red paper, about 6 inches in diameter, and contain generally three charges, which explode in rapid succession, causing the animal to kick up his heels and bellow at each discharge, making him perfectly desperate. Sometimes half a dozen of these torpedoes will be hanging all over the bull at one time, exploding like a pistol. While in this terrible condition, he dashed at one of the horsemen, but the long spear of the rider caught him in the neck, changing his course, when he madly rushed at one of the footmen who, more skilled with the sword than his companions, struck the exact spot and thrust the long blade down through the heart of the animal, causing almost instant death. This caused great rejoicing. Ladies waved their handkerchiefs, and all clapped their hands and shouted, "Bravo!! Bravo!!"

The convict of course felt elated over his success. The second bull met a similar fate in the same manner.

Before the third animal was turned in, the Governor promised a convict his freedom provided he would kill a bull, while on stilts. This was a terrible undertaking, but the offer was gladly accepted. The stilts raised him about two feet from the ground. Sword in hand and a red flag under his right arm, he planted himself in the center of the arena, when the furious bull was turned in. The animal after being literally covered with torpedoes rushed wildly at him. The poor fellow missed the vital spot and fell headlong to one side, the bull passing by under his arm. The brave fellow was picked up and carried out of the ring, while his companions occupied the attention of the bull with their terrible torpedoes. After being rubbed down and duly stimulated with restoratives, he was given another chance for freedom, but with the same result. A third time he was brought in, and a third time failed.

The poor picador convict was now desperate, indeed. His last chance for pardon and freedom was lost. After a short rest, he appeared before the bull again, with sword and red flag, perfectly reckless as to his fate, for as now the equally enraged animal made a dash at him, or the red flag, he threw sword and flag aside and in an instant sprang between the bull's horns, clasping his arms over the horns and around the animal's neck or ears. In this position he remained for a minute as though screwed in a vise, the bull plunging and bellowing while the spectators were yelling with delight at [this] audacious act.

Exhausted, he finally dropped, when the animal ran over him. He was as before immediately carried out and restoratives administered, though most of us thought he was dead. Mexican whiskey must have miraculous power, or the Mexican, like the cat, has many lives, for soon our hero made his appearance again with sword and flag.

I think his last bold act had its effect on the Governor, for the "poor cuss" looked cheerful and confident of victory this time. It was not long before his old enemy caught sight of the exciting red flag and offered battle again.

As the animal passed under his right arm, the point of the glistening blade was seen to enter the shoulder on the inner side of the scapula, passing down and through the heart, causing almost instant death. In a moment the poor criminal was transformed into a hero. The ladies waved their white handkerchiefs, while hundreds of male voices filled the air with, "Bravo!! Bravo!! Bravo!!" This was the last I saw of the conquering hero.

Lord only knows what will become of him. In this country it may be the first step toward promotion to the office of a Major General in [the] Mexican Army.[2]

A yoke of half-starved oxen was driven in and the remains of the tortured, but game, brute dragged from the ring, and will soon be stewed or "jerked" to feed the prison and chain gang.

This afternoon seven bulls were tortured and killed for the amusement of *church members,* who no doubt took what they call the "Holy Communion" and call themselves Christians!!

This shows what education will do. No doubt, like the poor ignorant Hindu mother who takes the life of her child, they think there is no harm in it. To them tis a pleasure to torture poor dumb brutes, and mangle and maim human convicts on Sunday to entertain society, and all done by order of the Governor of the State after he has attended church and had his dinner. Oh, think of it.

If Darwin is correct, it must be the instinct of the cat torturing the feeble mouse that has been handed down from their feline forefathers.[3]

OCTOBER 7, [MONDAY] Our voyage so far has been quite monotonous. A fairly formidable breeze most of the time. Consequently, sea not uncomfortably rough, although I can feel the swells, especially in my stomach. We have a motley crowd on board. Our American boys are, of course, much more genteel than the rest, but I confess, quite lively. Have been away from home so long, and now that their faces are turned in that direction, feel keyed-up to a high pitch. New England and N. York boys take the lead when there is any mischief on hand. Our "butternut Missourians" make good *second* Yankees.

Some of our passengers have been so unfortunate as not to own a second pair of pants, or possibly [they are] waiting to purchase other clothing after arriving in the States, where they could suddenly shake off all signs of semi-barbarism through which they have passed. This class was frequently in some secluded spot, quietly but earnestly examining the seams of their old pants and woollen shirts in search of parasites.

When such a friend was reported, the hoses were soon turned in on the unfortunate soul. I doubt not, from present indications, our ship will be alive before we reach Panama, for I understand these "Kritters" like bedbugs become grandmothers in 24 hours.

110

Most of our passengers kill time playing cards and reading.

OCTOBER 10, [THURSDAY]

The ocean unusually rough for the last few days, with rather [strong] headwinds. Consequently, we are making poor time.

Today we witnessed a rare sight for landlubbers. One of our passengers, an old Belfast Captain of a whaler, reported a whale in sight. All on board were soon on deck, with eyes wide open, awaiting the monster's appearance.

We had not long to wait. As soon as the monster's head reached the surface, water was thrown to considerable height, after which the head gradually disappeared and the back appeared and finally the upper portion of the tail and all was gone.

When his lordship first blew, he was about 300 yards distant. The sight was a short one, but the old whalers assured us he would soon show, giving us another chance to examine his gigantic proportions and see him blow.

Soon enough, inside of ten minutes, his huge head made its appearance, within 200 yards of our ship, and the water flew as before. All now was excitement, from the "Old Whaler" to the "land lubber." To our utter astonishment, while the jack-tars were spinning their whale yarns, the brute made his appearance again. Closer still, say 100 yards.

The conversation at this moment began to assume a more serious tone. Our Missourian with the "butter-nut" britches asked the question in all seriousness, "What is he coming so close for? Suppose he should come up directly under us, or slap us with his tail?" The serious consideration of this question will last us several days. I doubt not we will see him no more forever.

OCTOBER 14, [MONDAY]

We have been making poor headway for [the] last few days. At times hardly breeze enough to flap a sail, while the sun is intensely hot, especially at noon, making it necessary to put up an awning over our heads. The pitch fairly stews out of the cracks on deck.

Today the boys—N. Y. and Boston—enjoyed themselves jumping off the rigging into the ocean, swimming around a few minutes, and then climbing up the rope ladders to the deck and repeat. I have no desire to jump into such deep water, even if they tell the truth when they say tis impossible to sink in this salt water. I have a mortal dread of the old shark that follows our ship. I want to carry my bones home, now that I have started.

When we kill a sheep or hog and throw the intestines overboard, it is but a few minutes before Mr. Shark makes his appearance, turns over on his back, and tries to catch them, but he always succeeds sooner or later. Never gives it up.

When the boys come out of the water, I invariably notice Shark coming from under the ship, as though looking for a lunch.

Some say a shark will not attack you while you are in motion. I don't care to risk him. My notion is when a shark is hungry and food is within his reach, he will partake thereof, and I don't propose to take any chances to satisfy his appetite with my flesh and blood. Consequently, I remain on deck.

I am getting mighty tired of this monotonous life. We don't seem to be getting anywhere, while our water and rations are getting short.

OCTOBER 15, [TUESDAY] Last night, while I was stretched out at full length on the aft cabin looking at the stars and coaxing my stomach to behave itself, the Captain and first mate appeared nearby and commenced conversation in a low tone regarding the prospects of a storm. A small cloud "not bigger than a man's hand" was seen in the S. W., and we heading for it with only a square sail. Slight breeze from N. E. I could catch a word now and then, which led me to believe we were threatened with a squall.

The weather being intensely warm in this latitude, passengers were lying round on top of fore and aft cabins, where they could be most comfortable, and even sound asleep. About midnight I heard the Captain say, "Call the boys," and take down the square sail, or words to that effect. The mate hastened to give the order, at which time for a few minutes there was a dead calm. The sail hung limp and still as death. Not a quiver could be seen on its broad surface.

The dark cloud in front could be seen coming with rapidity of a racer, and before the sleepy sailors could reach their posts, the squall struck us square in front, tearing our sail into ribbons and leaving our craft at the mercy of the seas, with not a sail of the smallest kind to steady us and hold us to the breeze. The passengers who were sleeping on the upper forward cabin deck under the square sail rolled off in every direction, and confusion reigned supreme. As usual on such occasions, the Captain, mate, and sailors did some extra cussing, all in Spanish, which did not seem to soften it any.

For a time, we seemed to be at the mercy of the sea, but a jib was soon put in place and the vessel brought somewhat under control, although the seas continued to rise higher and higher.

The sharks came near having a good lunch today. A little Spanish sailor was ordered out on the jib-boom to rig some sails, slipped, and fell into the water. As good luck would have it, he hooked the bends of both forearms round one of the ropes and held on like a good fellow, plowing headfirst through every sea. We all ran to the side of the vessel to offer aid, but could do nothing as he dare not let go to catch a line. The sailors managed to get hold of the line he was holding, and drew him up out of the water, when he was lassoed and drawn on deck, pretty well jaded. He did not object to an internal application of whiskey.

OCTOBER 16, [WEDNESDAY] We have been having a fearful time all day. From some oversight our centerboard was let down too deep in the water during the day, straining the joints and causing a leak. We have all been using our muscles today at the pumps, while the carpenter is trying to caulk the opening. This is what you call paying and working your passage at the same time.

Few persons refuse to work on such occasions but lap into it with a good will.

My stomach has been quite rebellious all day. This evening I feel like a "stuffed toad."

System all bound up, but tis work or sink, and I prefer to be industrious.

OCTOBER 20, [SUNDAY]

Storm all over and repairs made. The sea is as smooth as a floor. During the storm all we could do was to steady our vessel and float with the sea. When our Captain took reckoning today, we were near the Sandwich Islands.[4]

There is great fault found with our Captain. There is no doubt of his incompetence. The "old whalers" talked seriously of putting him in *irons* in case he behaved as badly in another storm. Captain has agreed to make the port of Realejo, Nicaragua, if possible in place of Panama.

NOVEMBER 1, [FRIDAY]

For the last ten days we have suffered terribly from heat, poor food and water. Lord only knows when we shall reach the coast of Nicaragua at our present rate of speed. At least half of the time we have had a dead calm, not breeze enough to flap a sail. Our water has been short and we are allowanced to a pint a day for several days, and it at times is quite ropy.

If it would only rain we could catch some water on our awnings. Tis so hot down here the pitch stews out of the cracks on deck where the sun gets at it. Consequently, we keep an awning all the time, night and day.

It seems too bad. So much water all round, and underneath, and yet not a drop that is palatable or will allay thirst. I often think of the lovely springs in the Rocky Mountains and the beautiful banks of snow at the South Pass when I made ice cream and we all enjoyed it so much, but such is life on the ocean wave.

NOVEMBER 3, [SUNDAY]

Same old story, but we are gradually gaining—not in flesh—on the space between us and terra firma. There is a great deal of discontent on board, but most of us are living on hope. Not good bread and water.

NOVEMBER 5, [TUESDAY]

In the dim distance we can see land, but what land the Lord only knows. We are sure the Captain does not.

NOVEMBER 6, [WEDNESDAY]

Have been running along the coast all day, trying to make the harbor of Realejo.[5] The Captain is trying to figure it out as best he can, for he is anxious to get rid of us, and I am sure we will "take to the bush" the first good chance we get and make the best of it.

NOVEMBER 7, [THURSDAY]

Thank the Lord we have cast anchor once more. This time at the mouth of a small stream which they say leads up to our long looked-for Realejo. The coast here is very flat.

The natives come out to us in small row boats, and we have engaged them to row us up to the city, which appears to be behind the timber.[6]

Tis now noon, and our baggage is on the small craft. Eight of us are saying goodbye to the old centerboard schooner forever.

Through Nicaragua and Then Home

November 8, 1850–January 1, 1851

☛ *Slipping up a small stream to Realejo, Parke and his fellow passengers arranged for transportation to Granada. Along the route he visited Chichigalpa, León (the capital), Managua, Masaya, and other towns and saw exotic flora and fauna and smoldering volcanoes. After reaching Granada, Parke sailed Lake Nicaragua in a bungo to San Carlos and from this tiny village drifted down the San Juan River to the Caribbean port of San Juan, where he lingered for several days and soaked up the local culture. He then sailed for home.* ☛ *Parke's views on Nicaragua were very mixed. Monkeys, parrots, alligators, columnar cacti, and volcanic mountains were only a few of the country's features that intrigued him. The people were generally hospitable, eager to please, and kind. On the other hand, cruelty to animals, inefficiency, stolid ignorance, corroding church-state relationships, chronic political violence, the intrusion of the military into civil affairs, and super-power machinations disgusted him. Much of what he saw flew in the face of education, reform, and progress. His disgust was heightened by delays and discomfort and an eagerness to be home. When he pulled out of the harbor of San Juan, he had had his fill of world travel—at least for a few years.*

NOVEMBER 8, 1850–JANUARY 1, 1851

NOVEMBER 8, [FRIDAY]

We are now in the City of Realejo, where we expect to remain over night.

This is an old Spanish city of 4,000 inhabitants. Over one hundred years ago this was the home or headquarters of the pirate Morgan.[1] The ruins of a fine church destroyed by him is still to be seen, the walls of which are covered with vines and moss.[2] When we left the ship, our course was up a little narrow stream, in many places nearly covered by boughs and vines. The current in places rather swift and course crooked, making it difficult for our oarsmen to steer it. This is truly a land of creeping things, not only vegetable but animal. Green lizards of all sizes climb up the small trees and shrubbery on either side as we approach, while long slender snakes are seen sunning themselves on the boughs above, or darting from place to place.

This city is regularly laid out in squares or blocks, but looks like a "God-forsaken" place, although most of the people spend many hours each day in prayer and praise. A certain amount of prayer and thankfulness is all right, but I think it would be better if these people would pray less and work more so as to have more to be thankful for.

Some of the squares are surrounded by cactus. I do not know the variety, but the stalks are about six inches in diameter and cut off about 4 feet high.[3] They stand touching side by side like one's fingers and make a very substantial fence.

The people here are very kind to us and are glad to sell us the best of all they have.

NOVEMBER 9, [SATURDAY]

We have engaged ox teams and drivers to take us overland to Granada on Lake Nicaragua, a distance of forty-eight leagues or 144 miles, for which we pay the sum of $10.00 each.[4] Our next city is Chinandega, three leagues distant, which place we expect to reach this evening.

117

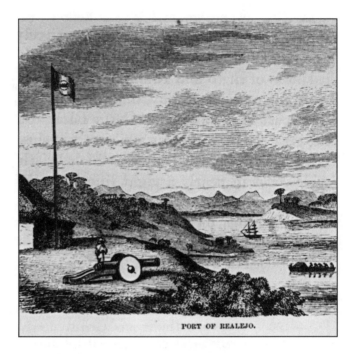

PORT OF REALEJO.

7. Port of Realejo. From E. G. Squire, *Nicaragua: Its People, Scenery, Monuments, and the Proposed Interoceanic Canal.* (New York, 1852).

It would make even our southern Negro laugh to see our outfit. In the first place, our oxen are walking scrub skeletons. They may be able to get us to our place of destination on time, but I doubt it. We understand the English mail steamer leaves San Juan every two weeks—first and middle of each month—and we hope these "poor dumb brutes" will be able to reach Granada in time. The rest of the trip will be by water down the lake and river in a Bungo, which may be as slow as Nicaraguan steers.

The oxen here are fastened together with a stick in front of the horns and bound fast to them with straps of

118

rawhide. The animals don't pull; he pushes the yoke in front of him, in which he works to great disadvantage compared to our ox yoke, where the bearing is against the top of neck and shoulders. The cart is crudeness personified. The axle is a round pole of hard variety of timber fastened to [the] bed with raw hide straps. The wheels are 6 inches wide, sawed from the end of a log 3 to 3½ feet in diameter, a hole bored through the center for the axletree.

The wheels are held on by a wooden pin through the ends of the axle. An axle only lasts a few days, as they are perfect strangers to tallow, as you might expect from an inspection of their beef cattle. The axle is kept lubricated by the driver pushing in pieces of bark from the green trees and shrubs from the road side. A great deal of this bark is very succulent, like that of the elm tree, and answers the purpose well for this lazy, indolent people. When the lazy cuss fails to feed his axle freely, the screeching is fearful and can be heard ½ a mile away. When an axle wears off, we stop by the wayside, cut down a small sapling, and make a new one. Hour after hour here we go, all of us walking, the oxen pushing the yoke against their foreheads, while the driver part of his time feeds the wheels, and the balance of the time probes the oxen with a sharp gad. With this gad he punched holes on each side of the tail. All the oxen have great sores at this point and frequently full of *maggots*. The driver keeps the hole covered with mud, which is some protection. Today I saw an ox so badly flyblown the skin could be seen moving six inches below the opening.[5]

These Spanish-Indian-Negro mongrels have some funny ways. Today we met a man coming down the road on horseback leading a cow. He had a long lasso or lariat tied round the cow's horns, while the other end was tied to his horse's tail. It seemed to me the poor old horse's tail had the worst of it. The road was not very wide where we passed, and as our carts approached the old cow made a sudden lurch toward the brush, when she brought the old horse up standing with his rear end toward her side of the road, but when the large Spanish spurs stuck into his sides

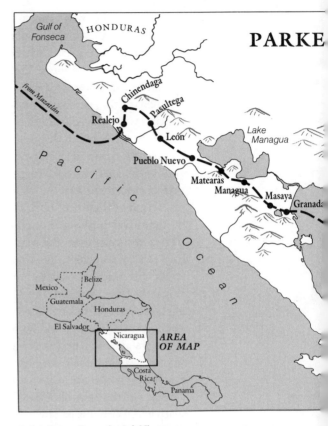

Parke's Return Route through Nicaragua

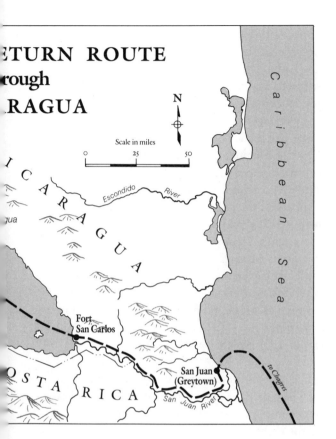

RETURN ROUTE
through
NICARAGUA

N

Scale in miles

0   25   50

Caribbean Sea

NICARAGUA

Escondido River

Nicaragua

Fort
San Carlos

San Juan
(Greytown)

San Juan River

to Chagres

COSTA RICA

his tail seemed to be inspired with power from "On high," as our good Methodist camp meeting people say, and the unruly cow had to come to time. I do not know how far this horse has to lead the cow, but I should think, if very far, in this fly country he would lose the use of a very necessary appendage.

Our outfit left Realejo early this morning, arriving in Chinandega this evening, a distance of 9 miles.

This is a beautiful old-fashioned Spanish city of 1,200 inhabitants.[6] It contains 5 fine churches. In fact, the churches are about the only fine buildings in the cities of this country, which would lead one to believe the inhabitants of this country are a very devoted set of Christians. And at this point we might with propriety ask the question, is a lack of chastity consistent with so much devoted Christianity? Too much "church and state" mixture is bad for both church and state, no matter what denomination runs the machine.

The city is regularly laid out.

NOVEMBER 10, [SUNDAY] We started on our journey at an early hour this morning, arriving at Chichigalpa at 10:00 a.m., a distance of 6 miles, and in the evening at Pasultega, 12 miles further, where we will spend the night.

Chichigalpa and Pasultega are both small towns of about 400 inhabitants.[7] The latter town has a very large church of rather odd architecture.

NOVEMBER 11, [MONDAY] Left Pasultega early this morning, arriving at Kesalguaca, a distance of 6 miles or 2 leagues, by 10:00 a.m. This is a small village of 150 inhabitants. We are now on our way to the famous city of León, 6 miles distant.

On our way to this city we passed through some fine forests of valuable timber, mahogany, and rubber trees. Before reaching Lake León [Lake Managua], I strayed ¼ of a mile ahead of the company, with rifle in hand, thinking I would have a better opportunity to see the many beautiful birds of this country.

While sitting behind a very large mahogany tree, I

heard a tremendous chattering that rather startled me. The sound was an uncommon one. Presently, I saw a regular drove of monkeys approaching, jumping from tree to tree, screeching as they jumped. I hardly knew what to make of it, although alone I concluded to stand my ground.

The squad consisted of 18 monkeys, large brown fellows with white faces, about twice as large as a full-grown Tom Cat. They were strung out in single file. A reverent-looking old fellow led off, while the sons and daughters in Israel followed, some with little young monkeys holding fast to them. The old Captain kept about 40 feet from the ground, and the same distance to the left of me.

As soon as he passed me, he stopped and faced about, keeping his eye steadily on me until the last monkey passed, when he followed, chattering as he jumped. It was a funny sight, and one long to be remembered.

When the teams came up, I told the boys my story, when one of them presented me with a little scrubby baby monkey he had picked up by the roadside. I soon gave it a wide berth as it was loaded with creepers.

Before reaching the lake we discovered a large monkey up about 20 feet amongst some vines. Two of us determined to capture the animal dead or alive. To shoot was the only way to get him. I shot 5 and my companions 3 balls before it fell. It proved to be a large brown female. I will never forget my feelings after examining the "old gal." She looked so much like an old African negro I felt as though we had committed murder.[8]

We placed her in the stern of a canoe in Lake Leon to see her no more forever.

Leon is the capital of Nicaragua and the largest city in Central America, having a population of about 40,000.[9] Tis a beautiful city. It is noted for its large churches and once-famous castle, a portion of which is still standing and used as a church. Originally, it covered a whole square, built of stone and cemented. The roof is a series of stone arches, very heavy and thoroughly cemented on top. There is a strong wall or parapet about 3 feet high all

8. Street View in León—Calle de San Juan. From E. G. Squire, *Nicaragua: Its People, Scenery, Monuments, and the Proposed Interoceanic Canal.*

around the roof of the portion now standing. Behind this parapet are several old cannons commanding different portions of the city. This castle was partially destroyed during one of their many revolutions. The wooden window blinds of the building opposite the castle were thoroughly riddled with bullets during a late revolution. Standing on the top of the castle today, I could see 5 different burning volcanoes, all in active operation and in the same direction.[10] There was a shaft of smoke spreading at the top, resembling a large umbrella. There are 5 large churches in this city.

Passing down on the west side of Lake León and before reaching the city of León, we crossed over a large lava bed,

124

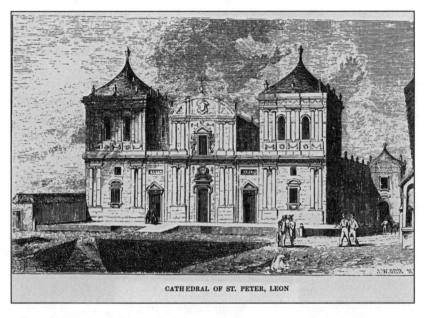

CATHEDRAL OF ST. PETER, LEON

9. Cathedral of St. Peter, León. From E. G. Squire, *Nicaragua: Its People, Scenery, Monuments, and the Proposed Interoceanic Canal.* (New York: 1852).

which extends down to the lake. During an earthquake the ground had cracked open to the extent of three feet. This was covered with a large flag stone, over which our wagons passed. The sides of this fissure seem to be like soapstone. About ⅓ of one of the towns sank about 20 feet, leaving the walls standing. The people are still living in their houses.

The "lower country" is too near the surface for me to tarry here long. In my opinion tis only a question of time when this strip of land connecting North and South America will sink out of sight, and the two oceans will run together. Then when the two waters find their level, what a mighty change there will be.

125

NOVEMBER 12, [TUESDAY] Left the City of Leon early this morning and arrived in Pueblo Nuevo this evening, a distance of 8 leagues or 24 miles. This is a small village of 1200 people and one church.[11]

Twelve miles farther brought us to the small town of Nagarote, 800 inhabitants, where we arrived at noon. This afternoon we traveled 12 miles, reaching Matearas at night.[12] Matearas is quite a small place near the lake. Said to have 300 inhabitants.

NOVEMBER 13, [WEDNESDAY] We left Matearas at an early hour this morning and reached the beautiful city Managua on Lake Leon [Lake Managua] this evening, a distance of 6 leagues or 18 miles. The location of this city is all that could be desired. There is a sameness in all the cities.[13]

NOVEMBER 14, [THURSDAY] Today we made a forced march, reaching the little town of Nindiri after dark, a distance of 8 leagues or 24 miles.[14] As I had charge of [the] company today, I determined to make the next town, a distance of one league more, and there spend the night. Nindiri has a population of 800, while Masaya has 14,000 and is a beautiful city. We reached this latter city at 10:00 p.m.[15]

One of the principal citizens came out to meet us and escort us to his house, where a bountiful supper was ordered for us consisting of tortillas, biscuits, and huevos with the most delicious chocolate I ever tasted. I don't think any of this kind of chocolate is ever shipped to this country (U.S.A.). Tortillas are corn cakes and huevos are eggs.

The American stars and stripes floated over the home of our host and hostess, who are pure Castillians, no mixed blood. He has a printing press in his house, and his beautiful daughter of 18 summers sets up type. One of our company, a young Baltimorian, I think is captivated by her charms. She has invited him to assist her in translating a public notice into English. Of course, he accepted.[16]

We shall remain here until tomorrow, when we will resume our line of march toward the city of Granada, a distance of 12 miles.

NOVEMBER 15, [FRIDAY]   Left Masaya at an early hour this morning, and arrived in this city, Granada at noon. As I anticipated, our young Baltimorian became infatuated with [the] orange-tinted senorita and refused to accompany us further. Granada is a beautiful Spanish city of 12,000 inhabitants, situated on the western shore of Lake Nicaragua. The homes are all constructed on the old Spanish plan. Very thick stone walls, tile roof, streets cross at right angles.[17]

Our trip down through the state of Nicaragua from Realejo to this city, a distance of 144 miles, has been to me a very interesting one. This people have treated us very kindly from the start. Not one disagreeable incident from the time we left Realejo.[18]

This is an interesting country. We passed through beautiful forests and orange groves loaded down with the most delicious fruit, ripe on the trees and free to us. Also, banana and pineapple plantations. The towering coconut tree is also to be seen. The trunk of this tree runs up from 20 to 40 feet without a limb, after which it branches out into a moderate top, where the coconut is grown.

Tis said the monkeys will climb to the top and throw the nuts down. The pineapple grows close to the ground in the center of long, thick leaves like the aloe plant.

The banana stock grows about 10–12 feet high, with large leaves on the top about 8 feet long. The huge bunches of fruit hang from the top when the leaves branch. The stock is about 6 inches in diameter and must be very strong to support such heavy weight. They grow in rows so many feet apart.

The ripe orange plucked from amongst the green leaves in this climate is simply delicious. Each one contains almost half a tea cup of juice. A person from the North has no idea of the difference in flavor of a large sweet orange ripe on the tree, and one pulled green to ship. Same with the pineapples and bananas.

Nankeen or yellow cotton is raised in this country, but as this is not its season I have not seen it growing. The plantain and sweet-potato grow almost spontaneously and is the principal food of most of the poor. The plantains are cut in slices and fried.

"Tortillas" as corn batter cake is the common bread. They are nothing more than coarse corn meal with water and a little salt, made into a mush and baked or rather dried on an earthen dish over the fire. In the larger cities we have been able to procure rolls or biscuits made of wheaten flour. The latter comes mostly from Chile. For the benefit of those with delicate stomachs, I will record a visit I made to a washing spring in suburbs of one of the towns we passed through. The spring was a beautiful place under magnificent shade trees. The sheet of water was about 20 feet in diameter and about 2 feet deep, with several flat rocks 2 x 2 sticking up six inches above the water.

Long before we reached the spring, we could see quite a number of females actively engaged. Our approach did not in the least interfere with their labors.

Most of them were engaged in washing, one on each rock, slashing away at a great rate like threshing wheat with a flail. Then they would rinse and wring like our own people. The most interesting sight was two of the olive-colored ladies washing corn. The corn is placed in a large stone jar or mortar 18 inches high and same in diameter. A small quantity of water is added. Then one of the fair damsels with dress about to the knees steps into it with her bare feet and tramps and tramps until the husk is softened and rubbed off the grain. Tis then rinsed and placed on a large flat stone or slab and rolled like we roll pie dough, until tis fine enough for tortillas. Corn cake made from this meal is sweeter than ours. In fact, there is more sugar in the corn and other fruit in this country than in northern countries. This is a "tred mill" sure enough. I saw the feet when they came out, and I know they were *clean*. Every time after when I ate a tortilla, I imagined I could see those beautiful clean feet.

There is nothing in Granada to attract particular attention. In fact, when you see one Nicaraguan city, you see all, excepting of course the location and surroundings. A city of this size in the States located on such a beautiful lake would most certainly have a wharf and at least one or more vessels. There is nothing of the kind here. A sandy beach and a few "bungoes" with bows pulled out of the water constitute the "merchant fleet."

A bungo is a boat shaped like a canoe or dugout, only built of plank.[19] Tis about 20 feet long by 6 feet wide and 3 feet deep, controlled by a rudder at stern, same as a canal boat. Three or four planks are spiked across the top for seats and to stay the vessel. Through the middle of the central plank is a hole for the mast. The seats being so high, the craft is rather top heavy, especially if there is much of a gale. If there was much heavy freight in the hold, the craft would be better balanced, but there appears to be none to carry.

Our principal enjoyment while here has been bathing. The beach is perfect, made up mostly of pumice stone, extending out into the lake gradually for at least 100 yards before tis 3 feet deep.

Dozens of people, male and female, old and young, are almost constantly to be seen bathing in the clean, soft water.

Tis only necessary to add, *extreme* modesty is a scarce article in this country. There are two very great drawbacks to this refreshing enjoyment. There is a little insect living in the sand called a "jigger."[20] The little cuss has a hankering after our toes, and burrows under the nails, depositing her eggs there. I have seen quite a number of people afflicted with elephantiasis and wonder if these little fellows don't have something to do in producing it.[21] I had the misfortune to get one under my big toenail the first time I went into the lake. I was made aware of its presence and had one of my companions dig him out with his pen knife, which by the way was not an agreeable operation.

This morning the seas were rolling in toward shore beautifully, running about 3 feet high. I concluded to join the crowd and share in the agreeable sport. It took quite an effort to get out 50 yards on account of the heavy waves, but glorious sport in riding in on them, or stooping down and allowing them to roll over your head.

While thus enjoying ourselves this morning, the natives gave a few unearthly shrieks—"lagarto, lagarto, lagarto"—and made for the shore in great haste. I knew there was something wrong and followed as fast as possible. It seemed to me I was an hour in getting where the water was shallow enough to permit me to run. I soon found "lagarto" meant alligator. In fact, I saw him floating on the waves like an old moss-covered log. I do not object to the Spanish girls and boys as bathing companions, but I do protest against associating in the water with alligators. This was my last swim in Lake Nicaragua.[22]

NOVEMBER 16, [SATURDAY] Left Granada at noon today for San Juan or Greytown, where we expect to meet the regular English mail steamer for Chagres. The distance down the lake to Fort San Carlos from Granada is said to be 100 miles, and from the former down the San Juan River to Greytown about 90 more.

NOVEMBER 22, [FRIDAY] Arrived safely in Greytown this morning, making the trip by bungo in 6 days.

We experienced several squalls before reaching Fort San Carlos, in one of which we fractured our mast and had to cut it away. Having no ballast but our light trunks, we were top heavy. Many amusing things happened on our way across or down the lake. It was well there were no females aboard. I will simply record the fact there was plenty of water, but a scarcity of *closets*. When our old round-bottomed craft was running with quarter to the seas, we were all compelled to "roost" on the upper side of the craft to keep her trim. This climate being warm, we did not mind the spray, which sometimes almost drenched us. Some of us were quite seasick. Our poor old "butternut Missourian" was in a dilemma. I shall never forget his countenance and his contortions. Poor old "land lubber," he was not only seasick, but had a severe diarrhoea at the same time. It matters not who may read this when I am dead and gone, but his spiral position was simply ludicrous, as both ends of the old fellow had to be over the side of the bungo at the same time, necessitating the aid of a second party to aid in accomplishing his double act and save him from a watery grave. Bungoes have no deck or canopy overhead, no bunks or places to sleep. The hard side of the cross-planks or seats, the only places to stretch out and rest. Our training in hardships for the last year makes the soft side of a plank quite endurable, if it will only bear us homeward.

Fort San Carlos is a small military post on the bank of the lake at or near the outlet into what is called San Juan River.[23]

We were halted here and our papers examined by the proper officer, after which we were allowed to proceed on our course down the river.

Alligators are quite numerous around Fort San Carlos. Tis astonishing how easily these monsters can rise, sink and move through the water without making a ripple. I have no use for them!

An old rusty cannon or two frowned down upon us from the fort. The officer in charge was quite friendly.

The river San Juan is rather a pretty stream about 200 yards wide, with a current of about 2½ knots an hour, except at the rapids, where I should guess tis 10 knots.[24]

There are two or three rapids between San Carlos and Greytown.[25] One very bad one, where the channel crosses the river, a distance of 200 yards, running very rapidly. We fairly flew, as we swung round this curve, every one holding his breath as we passed the rocks and landed in the eddy below. Here we found a small steamer, the *Orio*. She was unable to stem the current. There are quite a number of islands in this river. The banks of this river in most places are covered with trees and underbrush densely interwoven with green vines, "morning glories, etc."

How the natives *tow* their bungoes up this stream is a mystery to me, but they do it. Monkeys and parrots abound, while snakes, lizards, and all sorts of creeping things are actively playing their part in the drama of nature.

I do not know how long-lived these birds, animals, and reptiles are, but I am satisfied a white man would soon

sicken and die in this malarious region. Animal and vegetable life in this climate is being rapidly reproduced the
year through, while general decay is no less active, loading
the atmosphere with noxious gases.

If civilized man ever thinks of connecting the two
oceans via this river, the first thing to do would be to have
the natives deaden all the trees and vines for ¼ of a mile
back from the river on both sides and burn them. This
would let in the air and sun and dry the upper soil, thereby
greatly improving the healthfulness of the locality.

Greytown or San Juan is the poorest kind of a town, on
a flat beach.[26] The harbor is poor. Vessels cannot approach within ¼ mile of shore. This place seems to be
governed by a set of Negro officers under the protection
of a British Man of War, which is now anchored outside.[27] With all our haste and push, we arrived too late to
catch the English mail steamer to Chagres, consequently
will be compelled to remain here until the 3rd of December for the next steamer.

NOVEMBER 24,
[SUNDAY]

Eight of us have rented a room and will try and make ourselves comfortable until the steamer arrives. The houses
are built of plank and bamboo.

Inhabitants [are] mostly a mixture of Negro and Indian, with a slight dip of Spanish, the woolly head pre-
dominating.

There is very little work done here. Vegetables grow so
luxuriantly, the natives are natural vegetarians. It takes
work to produce animal food. These people prefer less
meat and more rest.

Young Negroes, huge mastiff dogs, and turkey-
buzzards seem to take possession of the streets. The buzzards are the principal scavengers. Lord only knows how
many different smells there would be in town if it were not
for the buzzards. They gather the filth from the streets,
and in order to be near their work in the morning, roost
on the housetops over night. There is a heavy fine against
anyone who kills a vulture, and I think tis correct as he is
the only truly industrious inhabitant of the city.

The only amusement here is the "fandango." Some of our boys attend every night. The room or hall is about 60 feet in diameter, with seats all around the outer circle. The dance is nothing more than a waltz round and round the circle until tired. Then you seat your "dulcina" and play the agreeable until rested, when you engage in another waltz.

The city or town Marshal is a big, burly Negro wearing "brass buttons." I understand he is appointed by the English government in its representation.[28] I believe England pretends to protect this place and people. I know not why.

As in all civilized, *Christianized*, and highly-cultivated countries, there is plenty of whiskey here, and is freely used at all important gatherings, especially the "fandango."

Our American boys, especially Boston and N. York boys, can easily be persuaded to take a drink with the dusky senoritas when away from home. In fact, would be too polite to refuse her. This being a fact, almost every night the dance would break up in a row, leaving the Americans and the dusky females in possession of the hall.[29]

Complaint was made to the commander of the English Man of War in the harbor as to the rowdy conduct of the foreigners. The boys always managed to keep on the soft side of the Marshal by feeding and watering him well. When questioned by the commander as to why he did not arrest and punish the disorderly persons, the only answer given was "do you tink dem Americans damn fools?" No arrests were made.

This, like all "nigger" towns is infested with dogs. Great mastiff dogs. The ingenious American has utilized the Greytown mastiff to help kill time while waiting for the steamer and also for a little amusement. Last night we coaxed one of these big dogs into our quarters, having previously prepared a sardine box with a few bullets in it. The box was securely fastened to his "nether end," the door opened, and with a rap over the back he was sent into the street. In a minute the whole town was in a commotion. The poor dog shot up the street like a meteor, howling at every jump with the whole canine population at his heels. The d——l was to pay. Our room was all dark and we in bed. Tis hard to tell what became of the dog, and we did not inquire. No doubt the Marshal thinks the dogs are becoming Americanized.

The English here must eat a great many sardines, for the back yards here are literally covered with empty tin boxes.

We have a beautiful orange tree in our yard. Tis about 20 feet high and well-loaded with lovely fruit. With a long pole we are readily select[ing] the ripe ones out from amongst the green leaves, cool and fresh. Of course we enjoy them.

DECEMBER 3, [TUESDAY]

The English mail steamer *Tay* arrived yesterday.[30] We all have engaged passage to Chagres, for which port we will sail today. We shed no tears on leaving this God-forsaken country of niggers, monkeys, baboons, and lizards, to say nothing about the poisonous reptiles.[31] The "fandango" is the only enjoyable thing here, and one would soon tire of it.

3:00 p.m. All aboard and ready to move.

DECEMBER 4, [WEDNESDAY]

Arrived off Chagres this afternoon at 3:00 o'clock after a very pleasant voyage. No passengers here when we arrived. This is another buzzard town. No attractions whatever.[32] Consequently, we anxiously await the arrival of the American ship *Philadelphia* now due. Of one thing I am certain, and that is the English Captain of the *Tay* will be glad to get rid of his Californian passengers. The *Tay* was a marvel of cleanliness, and the Captain a gentleman in every particular.

No one is allowed to spit on the deck of the *Tay*. Consequently, you can imagine how busily the tars were kept, mopping and sweeping after most of our American Californians. They are as filthy as geese, the only difference being one uses tobacco, the other grass.

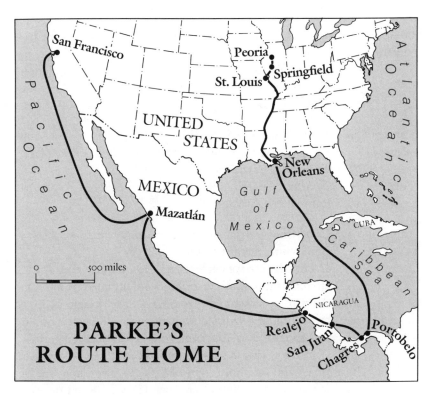

Parke's Homeward Route from California to Illinois

DECEMBER 6,
[FRIDAY]

Two sailing vessels left today with passengers for New Orleans and Appalachicola.

DECEMBER 10,
[TUESDAY]

Left Chagres today on the American steamship *Philadelphia* for N. Orleans via Kingston, Jamaica.

DECEMBER 11,
[WEDNESDAY]

We have been having heavy headwinds since we left Chagres. So much so, the Captain this evening decided to change his course and run to the nearest coaling station for fear we might run short of fuel. Porto Bello is the nearest station.[33]

DECEMBER 14,
[SATURDAY]

Arrived at Porto Bello this evening. Took on coal and water during the night, so did not see much of the place. Tis small. The coal-heavers were all blacks.

After taking on our supply, we sailed direct to N. Orleans with 332 passengers.

DECEMBER 21,
[SATURDAY]

Good thing we did not touch at Kingston, as the cholera is prevailing there at present.

First day out we made 170 miles; 2nd, 195; 3rd, 228; 4th, 250; 5th 305; 6th, 165, when we were detained by fog. On the 7th day out we made 125 miles, which brought us up to the city of New Orleans. During the last three days of our trip, the Gulf was quite calm and the evenings delightful.

There is always some bitter accompanying the sweet. When almost within sight of his Missouri home, one of our passengers died of cholera. He was sewed up in a blanket, a large piece of coal tied to his feet, and he [was] let down over the stern of the vessel to be seen no more forever. We had an Episcopal rector on board, who was a chaplain in the Navy. He read the Episcopal service before burial.

Whole distance from Chagres to N. Orleans: 1438 miles.

The island of Cuba could be seen in the dim distance as we passed.

DECEMBER 22,
[SUNDAY]

Took passage on board the steamboat *Columbia* for St. Louis.

Arrived in St. Louis early this morning. Nothing of importance transpired on our way up the river. Had serenades every night by the Negro crew.

Coming so recently from the monkey country, I can notice the strong resemblance in the actions of the two animals. I don't believe a word of the old, old story that the Negro and the white man sprang from the same original parent. The same argument would prove the beautiful humming bird, bird of paradise, and the vulture all sprang from one original bird, which would be nonsense. The truth *must be* the Creator of this universe created a *variety* of men, the same as other animals and vegetables. There is no sense in any other conclusion.

Expense Account from San Francisco

San Francisco to Realejo	$50.00
Realejo to Granada by ox team	10.00
Provisions on the way	15.00
Passage from Granada to San Juan	15.00
Provisions	4.85
Incidental expenses	3.00
San Juan house rent, 10 days	2.50
Passage on British steamer to Chagres	15.00
Board at Chagres—per day, $2.00	2.00
Passage on steamship *Philadelphia* to N. Orleans	65.00
Passage from N. Orleans to St. Louis	15.00
Passage from St. Louis to Springfield	5.00
Passage from Springfield to Peoria	5.00
	$207.85

This flower grew on the Salmon Trout River, California.[34]

Editor's Afterword

Dr. Charles Ross Parke's journey home was nearly over.[1] He pushed on to Peoria, Illinois, where he was reunited with his half-brothers—George, John, and Samuel—and resumed his practice of medicine. For reasons that are not clear, in August 1852 he moved to Bloomington, Illinois, then a town of about 2,500. He later wrote, "Bloomington was a village in the mud when I located here. A few planks laid lengthwise along the public square were the only sidewalks."[2] Conditions there must have reminded him of the California mining towns, and when he recalled Nindiri and other towns in Nicaragua, they must have seemed highly developed by way of comparison. He opened an office on the northwest corner of Center and Washington streets and became very active in the local medical scene.[3]

In order to advance his knowledge of surgery and possibly in response to a lingering desire for adventure, in 1855 he headed for the Crimean War. On August 1, 1855, he secured a commission as a surgeon in the Russian army, which was then locked in battle with British and other forces on the Crimean Peninsula. He was aided in his efforts to secure a commission by such powerful Democrats as Stephen A. Douglas, former President Martin Van Buren, and James Buchanan, the latter a close friend of his father.[4] His world travels began anew.

Upon receiving word that his commission was granted, he immediately sailed from New York to Bremen, Germany. He crossed the German states to Russia, stopping briefly in Berlin to pick up his Russian travel papers. Going on to Warsaw, he picked up his uniform and headed toward the Crimea. The broad expanses of the rolling steppes in the Ukraine made a lasting impression, possibly bringing to mind his travels along the Platte River. Upon arriving at Simferopol, northeast of the seat of fighting at Sevastopol, he provided care for the wounded in a poorly ventilated and overcrowded hospital complex.[5]

He was treated well while serving in the Crimea, and when the gentry learned that he was an American physician who was tending Russian wounded, he was treated to every kindness. In early 1856 he suffered an attack of typhus, the effects never really leaving him for the rest of his life. He was helped back to health by a Mr. and Mrs. Groton at their country home near Simferopol. In addition to being befriended by the Grotons, he made lasting friendships with the Rodivitch, Durasoff, and Toberoski families. Some twenty-four American physicians served the czar in the Crimea, ten of whom died of illnesses there.

After an armistice was concluded on February 26, 1856, Parke visited battered Sevastopol, where he was entertained graciously by British officers. He took in the grand review of allied troops before he left the peninsula. He was ordered to Kiev in May 1856 to help care for wounded who were still convalescing in hospitals. While in Kiev, the ancient center of Christianity in the Ukraine, he toured the catacombs. When his duties in Kiev had been completed, he resigned his commission, declining an offer to serve as a surgeon in the regular army on a footing fully equal to that enjoyed by Russian surgeons. He had hoped to return to the United States by means of a venturesome trip across Siberia, but he gave up this idea and returned through northern Europe. It is possible that the lingering effects of typhus forced him to reconsider his plans.

After passing through Warsaw, he pushed on to Posen, Stettin, Berlin, Copenhagen, and Stockholm, then returned to Berlin, where he spent two months with Professor August Müller, a highly respected lecturer on anatomy. While visiting central and northern Europe, Parke spent much time in museums, palaces, and other cultural attractions. Leaving Berlin, he headed west to Cologne and Brussels, pausing to visit the battlefield at Waterloo, and then continued to Paris, where he visited museums, hospitals, and other institutions of interest. While on the continent he made the acquaintance of Richard Oglesby of Illinois, and despite obvious political differences, the two men became close friends for life.[6] Parke then crossed to Britain, seeing the sites in London, and finally left Southhampton for New York on the U.S. steamer *Washington*. He arrived in New York on November 21, 1856, and made his way to Parkesburg by way of Philadelphia.

After spending the winter with his aged parents in Parkesburg, he returned to Bloomington, where he formed a medical partnership with Dr. John Sweeney, who was treasurer of the Soldiers' Orphans Home at adjacent Normal, Illinois. This partnership had a positive influence on Parke's career. Their office was opposite the courthouse on Jefferson Street on the second floor.

In spite of his lifelong adherence to the Democratic party, Parke was energetic in his support of the Union cause in the Civil War. He traveled with Federal forces into Kentucky, and after the horror of the Battle of Shiloh in April of 1862 he was dispatched to the battlefield by Governor Richard Yates to aid the wounded and prepare them for the dangerous trip home. Richard Oglesby served as a brigadier general at the Battle of Corinth in October 1862, an action in which he was severely wounded. He was brought back to his home in Decatur, and Parke went there to treat his wounds.

On October 3, 1865, Dr. Parke married Mrs. Lucy Didlake Keith of Bloomington, the second daughter of Edmund H. Didlake, formerly of Winchester, Kentucky. Their only child, a son, was born in late 1867 but died shortly after birth. Parke's wife suffered loss of health, so the couple moved to Kentucky for more than two years. By 1870 they had returned to Bloomington, Parke resuming his taxing but lucrative medical career.

Parke's reputation in the Bloomington vicinity continued to grow during the 1870s. In 1879 the Rev. Father Schreiber of St. Mary's Church in Bloomington helped launch an effort to establish a hospital. He encouraged the Rev. Mother Frances of St. Francis Hospital in Peoria to undertake the effort. Dr. Parke and Dr. Sweeney were consulted about the project, and both gave the undertaking their wholehearted support, Sweeney joining the sisters and their friends in a door-to-door campaign to raise funds. They were successful. St. Joseph's Hospital opened in late March 1880 in an old brick mansion in southwestern Bloomington.

Four sisters were empowered to run the facility. They asked Dr. Parke to put together a hospital staff. This he did, selecting six physicians, including his associate, Dr. Sweeney. Parke served the hospital well as a surgeon and for more than twenty years was its chief of staff. He was noted for keeping abreast of the latest developments in medicine and for incorporating them into his practice, and it was through his efforts that St. Joseph's Hospital earned a reputation of being one of the best-equipped hospitals in the region. His professional reputation continued to grow, resting on his precise knowledge of anatomy, his superb diagnostic skills, and his steady hand. He had always tinkered with mechanical contraptions as part of an ongoing effort to improve the care he provided his patients. One of the products of his interest in things mechanical was a "metallic adjustable fracture splint," which enabled a limb of any size to be accommodated, the device keeping constant the extension of the limb for examination and treatment. For these reasons and others, he was the acknowledged leader in the Bloomington medical world, a position he held until late in life.

Parke was highly active in medical activities and also took deep interest in civic affairs. For example, he served as first president of the George Rogers Clark Chapter of the Sons of the American Revolution. On several occasions he filled the position of president of the Library Association of

10. St. Joseph's Hospital in Bloomington, 1890s. From *Illustrated Bloomington and Normal Illinois* (Bloomington, 1896).

Bloomington. Now and then, as far back as early 1854, he contributed articles to the newspapers. Having been a free-trade Democrat and having imbibed the beliefs of Stephen A. Douglas, Parke in his later years became an ardent Bryan Democrat. He also dabbled in taxidermy and pursued other hobbies. In his civic life as well as his professional life, he did much to promote the total welfare of his community. In all of his many undertakings he was fully supported by his wife.

In his personal relations with others in Bloomington, he was known as a kindly, genial, and considerate person who went the extra mile. His overland diary and some of his Crimean War diary show him to be crusty at times and quick to see faults in others. It is possible that his kinder disposition surfaced later in life. This assumption is bolstered by some observations of Parke by his longtime friend Dwight Frink: "In his *later years*

11. Charles Ross Parke, M.D. From John Robinson, *The Biographical Record of McLean County, Ill.* (Chicago, 1899).

[emphasis added] there was a general quietness and modesty about the man that comported well with his ripening career and large achievements. . . . His high regard for personal and professional honor and his strict life of praiseworthy integrity and his companionable, brotherly disposition won all who came in contact with him."[7] Regardless of whether his mellowing took place in his later years, Parke was known for his bright disposition and modest nature, generally shunning attention for his accomplishments.

Advancing age finally convinced Dr. Parke to retire at the end of December 1902. On the first day of that month he ended his medical partnership with Dr. F. H. Godfrey, a partnership started in 1896, and by the end of the month he had stepped down as chief of staff at St. Joseph's Hospital. Although he and his wife had no surviving children, they had adopted Mana Lackey, a niece of Mrs. Parke. Mana married Virgil D. Smith, a prominent businessman from Louisville, Kentucky, and it was to their home in Louisville that Parke and his wife moved after his retirement.

He continued to take a keen interest in medical, civic, and political affairs. On April 7, 1904, for example, the McLean County Medical Society held its golden anniversary banquet and Parke attended as one of the honored guests. In response to the request of the medical society, Parke agreed to write a brief history of it, which he finished in November 1904.

Charles Parke outlived all of his brothers, half-brothers, and half-sisters, he outlived all charter members of the McLean County Medical Society, he was probably the last survivor of the band of American physicians who served the Russian wounded in the Crimea, and it appears that he was the last survivor of the University of Pennsylvania medical school's class of 1847. He also survived his wife, who died in 1906. On Friday, November 6, 1908, Charles Ross Parke—lively, interesting, venturesome, at times feisty and not likable—died of apoplexy at the home of his adopted daughter in Louisville.

Notes

Introduction

1. The reaction to American successes, the roles of volunteers in the war, and the relationships between American victories and republicanism are analyzed very ably in Robert W. Johannsen, *To the Halls of the Montezumas,* especially 279–312.

2. Newspapers in the winter and spring of 1849 brimmed with accounts of the formation of overland emigrant companies. They also informed the reader of gold-mining techniques, mileage between various points on the trail, costs emigrants could expect to incur, the advantages of various jumping-off places along the Missouri River, and the progress of cholera in the nation. There were snippets of history of California, advice from mountain guides and other experts, letters allegedly written from California, and advertisements for all kinds of equipment associated with travel and mining.

3. Henry Page to his wife, Mary, May 2, 1849, in Elizabeth Page, ed., *Wagons West,* 107.

4. Charles A. Kirkpatrick, Diary, 1849–50, June 23.

5. Bolivar Krepps, Letters, 1849, December 15.

6. This expression had been in use for some fifteen years but gained widespread popularity only in 1849 and during the rush westward. The origin and development of the expression are discussed in Peter Tamony, "To See the Elephant," 23–29, and J. S. Holliday, *The World Rushed In,* 116.

7. In Russell E. Bidlack, ed., *Letters Home,* 34.

8. Confronting new conditions and possible danger as they moved onto the trail, members of emigrant communities drew upon their personal and collective values for guidance. For the most part, these values and the institutions that embodied them were essentially agrarian, republican, and conservative. The result was a strong desire among overlanders for order and a willingness either to defer to properly constituted authority or leave the train. For more on the basic conservatism of the overland experience, see John M. Faragher, *Women and Men on the Overland Trail,* especially chapters 1, 2, and 7; John Phillip Reid, *Law for the Elephant,* which stresses the need of emigrants to take with them laws that they had known and their willingness to do so; Thomas D. Clark's introduction to Charles Glass Gray, *Off at Sunrise,* xi–xii; John Unruh, Jr., *The Plains Across.*

9. Alonzo Delano, *Life on the Plains and Among the Diggings,* June 3. Other overlanders observed the need to engage in non-traditional work. See, for example, Vincent Geiger and Wakeman Bryarly, *Trail to California,* June 2.

10. James F. Wilkins, *An Artist on the California Trail,* May 14.

11. J. Goldsborough Bruff, *The Journals, Drawings, and Other Papers of J. Goldsborough Bruff,* May 23.

12. The disintegration of overland companies is discussed very well in David M. Potter's introduction to Geiger and Bryarly, 37–40. The disruptive forces that caused the companies to dissolve were numerous and varied, and almost all trains that summer experienced stresses and strains, the vast majority of the trains at least partly breaking up. There are countless examples of wagon trains dividing into parts along the way. See, for example, Sheldon Young, Log, 1849, May 20; William E. Chamberlain, Diary, 1849, who kept joining and leaving emigrant companies; Delano, *Life on the Plains,* June 13; Augustus Rip-

ley Burbank, Diary, 1849–51, June 6; James Haines, Life and Experiences in California, June 15 and 27; Lindsey Tipton, Diary, 1849, May 5. John F. Lewis, Diary, 1849, June 5, and Amos Steck, Diary, 1849, May 28, recorded divisions of companies over disagreements about the speed at which the trains should travel. Trains continued to break up once they arrived in California; see Amos Batchelder, Journal, 1849–50, October 18. Peaceful secession and even total disintegration of entire companies had some positive features. They demonstrate that overlanders did not get locked into conditions and mind-sets from which there was no exit. They demonstrate the qualities of flexibility and practicality, as well as those embodied in voluntary association and republicanism. These qualities were very evident on the overland trail in 1849 and did much to shape the nature of migration and settlement. Perhaps undergirding the willingness of companies to split into several parts was the profound understanding that overland companies were, after all, merely the means by which large numbers of diverse people could get to the gold fields fairly quickly, nothing more.

13. For more on constitutions, see Potter's introduction to Geiger and Bryarly, 9–18, and Reid, *Law for the Elephant.* In drafting fundamental law and electing officers, at least one company took into consideration the diverse occupational and geographic backgrounds of the members, making some effort to overcome potential sources of division. See Ansel J. McCall, *The Great California Trail in 1849,* May 12.

14. For the most part, parties that were too small realized this before they pushed onto the plains, and many took the opportunity of a brief stay in the jumping-off points to coalesce into larger units, fear of the Pawnees prompting many small parties to do so. See Jasper Morris Hixson, Diary, 1849, May 19, for example, for a party of six men who teamed up with others to form a much larger organization. After falling "in with some teams with whom we

intend to make arrangements for a company," Joseph Warren Wood observed that it became necessary to formalize the arrangements by means of a constitution, by-laws, and elections. See Wood, Diary, 1849–53, May 14. Sometimes companies were too large, it becoming necessary for them to break up in order to function well. For example, Lindsey Tipton's train broke up in what is now eastern Nebraska near Salt Creek because it became "inconvenient and inexpedient to travel in a large train." See Tipton, May 5. Potter's introduction to Geiger and Bryarly, 39, focuses on the problem of overland companies that were so large that they had to break into smaller communities.

15. Some people were not pleased with the operations of companies that were established for mining. "By all means avoid companies which are got up at home for mining," one emigrant warned. "They work badly; they cramp your energies; they entangle all your operations. In the mines, it will always be necessary for you to associate yourself with one or two, and sometimes with twenty or even fifty mining companions. These associations are formed and terminate with the necessity of the occasion." See Daniel B. Woods, *Sixteen Months at the Gold Diggings,* 181.

16. Many emigrants commented on the variety of weapons carried by people making the trek. One of the most popular weapons during the gold rush was the "pepper box," a firearm produced by Allen & Thurber of Worcester, Massachusetts. It had five barrels, which rotated and cocked as each round was fired. Although this weapon was not very accurate, it was fast firing, inexpensive, and responsible for the death of countless rattlesnakes. To get ready for expected trouble, forty-niners practiced target shooting along the way, taking potshots at practically anything that flew, crawled, or hopped.

17. Unruh, *The Plains Across,* 185. The scale of Indian-white conflict has probably been overestimated. One source, for

example, suggests that between 1789 and 1898, "Indians killed 7,000 soldiers and civilians. It is improbable that more than 4,000 Indians were killed during the same period." See Don Russell, "How Many Indians were Killed?" 62. These figures may understate the scale of the conflict, but almost certainly the numbers were not enormous.

18. Bernard J. Reid, for example, was convinced of the need to buy in St. Louis a four-pound cast-iron mold for casting gold ingots, an item he discarded along the Sweetwater River. See Mary McDougall Gordon's prologue to Reid's *Overland to California with the Pioneer Line,* 26. Newspapers hawked every conceivable good and service, including bogus cures for cholera.

19. Each wagon's team usually consisted of three or four yoke of oxen. Compared to mules, the only other draft animal available, oxen had a number of distinct advantages: few farmers in the Midwest had mules, but most had oxen; they were relatively easy to handle; if they strayed at night, they were easy to round up in the morning; their stamina was renowned; they were less easily stolen at night by Indians and most Indians did not like the taste of oxen; they could live quite well off native grasses; the purchase price per animal was lower than for mules; those that survived the trek were used for clearing the land, hauling logs, and other useful chores; and, finally, some oxen ended their days as much-appreciated roasts. See Ezra Meeker, *Ox-Team Days on The Oregon Trail,* 23, for some of the advantages of oxen over mules. Late in his trek to California, Joseph Wood sang the praises of oxen: "The oxen stand it the best & have exceeded the expectations of their owners while mules and horses have fallen short." See Wood, August 13. Writing on May 11 from St. Joseph, Bolivar Krepps referred to the superiority of oxen over mules, and more than five months later he wrote from California, "I never knew the amount of hardships and suffering an ox was capable of enduring until I came on this trip." See Krepps, May 11 and October 13.

20. It is clear that the party had knowledge of the recently published guide by Joseph E. Ware, *The Emigrants' Guide to California,* a work that was both highly regarded and sometimes dangerously misleading. See Parke's entry for July 8. At least one overlander thought that no guide was necessary: "As for a guide, you need one much more to go to Chicago. Indeed, you cannot go amiss, for every road that turns out comes back again into the main track." See Israel Shipman Pelton Lord, Diary, 1849–51, July 8, 1849.

21. Some people considered cholera a punishment for immoral living and excesses, so some respectable families managed to have the cause of death listed as "unknown." See Patrick E. McLear, "The St. Louis Cholera Epidemic of 1849," 179. Wrote overlander Henry Mann: "Nearly all the sickness on the road can be traced back to intemperance in eating or drinking." See Mann, Diary, 1849, July 28. For the supposed causes of cholera and attempted cures, see James T. Barrett, "Cholera in Missouri," and Georgia Willis Read, "Diseases, Drugs, and Doctors on the Oregon-California Trail in the Gold Rush Years."

22. Cholera brought death through dehydration. Cholera patients who were plied with various liquids stood a reasonably good chance of surviving.

23. David Carnes, another diarist in the Como Pioneer Company, kept a more precise account of daily activities than Parke.

24. There may have been a psychological need to know daily mileage, one forty-niner noting, "It is unpleasant to travel without knowing something of distances. We are at present obliged to guess at it and it affords rather unsatisfactory results." He also reported, "I have conceived the construction of a roadometer, which I intend to put into operation as soon as possible." See Wood, May 13; see also John H. Benson, Diary, 1849, June 7, and Dr. T, Diary, 1849, June 18. After he arrived in California, Amos Batch-

elder wrote of his own company: "Many of the teams had instruments attached to their wheels by which the distance was measured." See Batchelder, October 20, 1849.

25. One emigrant wrote that summer, "Every night it was the business of two of us to forage for chips. I have seen fine looking ladies gathering chips in their aprons." They needed to collect the chips, he added, because "these plains were almost destitute of timber, even on the streams, and emigrants would have been utterly destitute of means wherewith to cook their meals and make the indispensable coffee, but for the droppings of the vast herds of buffalo." Quoted in George H. Woodruff, *Will County on the Pacific Slopes*, 21.

26. Awesome displays of nature sometimes overwhelmed discouraged people. After experiencing much suffering and hearing of even more, a traveler near the Little Sandy River asked, "Oh what is man in the hand of his maker [?] Here he appears almost less than nothing." See Chamberlain, June 30.

27. Parke's traveling companions did not include the type of person who infested the company to which Amos Steck belonged and of whom Steck wrote, "His mouth is full of every expression of low vulgarity. At meal time he struggles for every effort to insult his neighbors and messmates." See Steck, June 12. The presence of this type of person was bound to breed trouble. Violence erupted in the company in which Peter Kessler of Augusta, Iowa was traveling. He got into a fight with two men who tried to rob him. The two were shot by Kessler, then both were expelled from the company. See the *Burlington Hawk-Eye*, July 19, 1849. After noting that two men in his company got into a fight, one emigrant wrote that members of the company "are by turns, or altogether, cross, peevish, sullen, boisterous, giddy, profane, dirty, vulgar, ragged, mustachioed, be-whiskered, idle, petulent, quarrelsome, unfaithful, disobedient, refactory, careless, contrary, stub-

born . . . and without the fear of God and hardly of man before their eyes." See Lord, August 13. He later blamed much of the difficulty on card playing. See Lord, September 11. Examples of violence are present in most overland accounts, but the solution to tension and disagreement found by one company was quite rare. Greenberry Miller wrote, "Our company today disagreeing did not encampt together." See Miller, Diary, 1849–50, June 16.

28. The high cost of transportation boosted prices enormously. The increase in prices as goods traveled from Sacramento to the mining camps was noted by some miners. See George W. Applegate, Letters, 1849–50, August 27, 1850, for example.

29. The uncommonly sound decisions made by the company and the solid medical service offered by Dr. Parke certainly played an important role in the success of the Como Pioneer Company.

30. At least a few diarists felt the need to apologize for traveling on Sunday, or at least to explain why they felt it was necessary to travel then. E. A. Spooner, for example, wrote, "Travelled some 15 miles today although it was the Sabbath. The object of this was to overtake a train with which we wished to connect ourselves for travelling." See Spooner, Diary and Letters, 1849, May 12.

31. See Parke's entry for May 19.

32. *Missouri Republican,* December 24, 1849.

33. Information for the biographical sketch of Charles Parke was found in several basic sources: John Robinson, *The Biographical Record of McLean County, Illinois;* Dwight E. Frink, "Charles Ross Parke, M.D.";ateway Frank Sylvester Parks, *Genealogy of Arthur Parke of Pennsylvania and Some of his Descendants;* Jacob Louis Hasbrouck, *History of McLean County; Biographical History of the McLean County Medical*

Society, 1854–1954; United States Biographical Dictionary and Portrait Gallery of Self-Made Men, Illinois Volume.

34. Children of this marriage were Letitia, Caroline, John, Joseph, Samuel, and George Washington. Letitia died young. See Parks, *Genealogy of Arthur Parke,* 9.

35. Children of this marriage were Winfield Scott, Charles Ross, and Thomas G. Parke. See Parks, *Genealogy of Arthur Parke,* 9.

36. *Catalogue of Medical Graduates of the University of Pennsylvania, 1847,* 5.

37. It is significant that Parke and other emigrants did not lump all Indians and Indian tribes into fixed categories. It is true that he and other people on the trail were prone to see certain tribes in certain ways—and perhaps the Digger Indians of the Humboldt River came in for the most severe and chronic verbal abuse from the emigrants—but Parke and many other people making the trek that summer tended to treat Indians as individuals, forming positive opinions about some and negative opinions about others. The tendency for frontier women to reexamine their previously formed ideas about Indians after meeting Indians is found in Glenda Riley, *Women and Indians on the Frontier, 1825–1915.*

38. Holliday, *The World Rushed In,* 529.

Chapter 1

1. Carnes lists an organization that differs from Parke's. He has the first team consisting of Sampson, Brooks, and Carnes; the second team, Parke, Pollack, and Kelsey; the third team, L. Strope, Wm. Cushing, and F. Stiman. In both instances, Strope, Cushing, and Stiman—the

three individuals about whom very little is known—are grouped together.

2. The Indian prophet White Cloud had a village on this site. It was destroyed by Illinois volunteers on May 10, 1832, at the outbreak of the Black Hawk War.

3. Carnes notes that they stayed at Nates (?) in Geneseo.

4. Carnes does not refer to this chill.

5. Carnes writes nothing about this illness or the treatment. The scourge of cholera was treated with a wide variety of remedies, some positively zany. Patients were rubbed with brandy, plied with hot cloths, doused with vinegar, purged, swilled with liquors, bathed, starved, stuffed with foods, made to eat chicken broth, and sent to bed to get plenty of rest. The use of calomel and small amounts of opium was very common, and some physicians used quinine as well. Those patients who were encouraged to drink a lot of liquids stood a reasonably good chance of surviving, since dehydration was a leading cause of death for those who contracted cholera. Liquids containing saline and glucose were particularly helpful. For those for whom the treatments did not work, death was usually swift, the incubation period varying from a few hours to a few days. Bacteria caused the dreaded disease, but this was not known until 1883. See Raymond N. Doetsch, *Journey to the Green and Golden Lands,* 77–79, and Charles E. Rosenberg, *The Cholera Years,* 115, 135. Estimates of the number who perished from cholera vary greatly. One recent source suggests that "cholera killed at least 1,500 on the trails east of Fort Laramie" in 1849; see Holliday, *The World Rushed In,* 115. Older sources indicate that up to five thousand died; see Geiger and Bryarly, 55, n. 137. Regardless of the actual number, the fear generated by the disease was very great. All sources agree that the threat tapered off sharply after Fort Laramie. Although cholera's cause and the methods of its transmission were not understood, it was associated in the public's mind with filth, crowded

conditions, dampness, loose living, and general weakness. As a result, it is entirely likely that its frequency was underreported, since there was a stigma associated with it. See Doetsch, *Journey to the Green and Golden Lands,* 75–79; Holliday, *The World Rushed In,* 475–76; *Missouri Republican,* January 1, 3, 16, 21, 23, 1849.

6. Carnes writes that the ferry at Burlington was overcrowded, so they decided to go to Rock Island. The next day, however, Parke reports that they had decided to cross at New Boston. In the end, they manage to cross at Burlington.

7. Capsicum is made from the dried ripe fruit of the herbs and shrubs of the nightshade family. It is used as a stimulant in intestinal disorders.

8. Prairie fires, often dangerous to man and animal, were especially common in autumn, after the grasses had been parched dry and after the summer rains began to lessen. These fires, sometimes twenty miles in width, raced across the prairie and were especially awesome at night, when they caused low-lying banks of clouds to shimmer fiery orange. Small saplings and young trees were consumed in these fires, and the treeline was prevented from advancing into prairie land. With the arrival of settlers, this changed. The prairie was plowed, reducing the range of grass fires, and trees were planted. As a result, areas that were practically treeless in 1800 had a fairly large variety by 1850. Deer, wolves, and other animals took advantage of this change in the ecology and moved into the tree-planted areas in relatively large numbers, so large, in fact, that by the 1840s and as late as the 1850s it became necessary to conduct organized wolf hunts.

9. Carnes writes that the camp was on the Edwards River. It was probably just to the south of Millersburg.

10. Carnes writes that Brooks and Pollock were sent ahead to scout. They returned with the finding that it was impossible to cross at New Boston.

11. This little village was home to the *Oquawka Spectator,* a newspaper that gave much coverage to the gold rush. Unfortunately, it did not report on Parke's train.

12. A resident of Greene County, Illinois, in the early 1830s, Jeremiah Smith was elected captain of a company of the Second Regiment of the Brigade of Mounted Volunteers of the Illinois Militia in April 1832. He and his unit were mustered out of service at the mouth of the Fox River. In late fall 1833, he arrived with a load of merchandise a mile and a half west of Burlington, a place he had chosen for a farm. He was an entrepreneur and did much to promote town development. See *History of Des Moines County, Iowa,* 475; *Record of the Services of Illinois Soldiers in the Black Hawk War, 1831–32, and in the Mexican War, 1846–48,* 92; J. B. Newhall, *A Glimpse of Iowa in 1846,* 71. A good claim can be made that Smith was the first white to engage in trade in what is now Burlington; see Newhall, 71.

13. On April 18 and later, the *Frontier Guardian* and the *Burlington Hawk-Eye* referred to heavy rains, massive flooding, and loss of life. Neither, however, carried a story about the two boys. The dam was associated with the mill complex built by Levi Moffet and others, construction occurring possibly as early as 1834. It housed both a saw-mill and a gristmill, two of the first milling operations in southern Iowa. Moffet is regarded as the founder of Augusta. See *History of Des Moines County, Iowa,* 376–77, 592–96.

14. Carnes writes that West Point was "a considerable inland town."

15. Carnes observed that the Des Moines River was "a navigable river 100 miles above this [point] in high water." He also noted that Keosauqua had a population of some eight hundred people. David Carnes's cousin, William Birdsall Lorton, passed through Keosauqua on his way to the gold fields of California. On April 17, 1849, he wrote that the

village consisted of a few meager houses of little note, a square courthouse, with a cupola, on a high hill, and a tavern east of the courthouse. See Lorton, Diary, 1848–50, April 17, 1849.

16. The meaning of this term is not clear.

17. B. F. Pearson is listed as a brick mason in Keosauqua, one of two in town. See Newhall, *A Glimpse of Iowa in 1846*, 86.

18. Carnes notes that they camped Saturday night at the widow Thornton's place on the prairie. During the night, he notes, it rained and the roads were bad on Sunday. See David Carnes, Diary, 1849, April 21 and 22.

19. The fine condition of the cattle was confirmed by Carnes, who writes: "Cattle all in good condition. Cows give about five quarts each."

20. Carnes spells the name of this river the same way. All recent maps refer to it as the Chariton. Its headwaters are in south-central Iowa, south of Des Moines. The river is named for an early French trader, but it is not known exactly which trader deserves the honor. See Robert L. Ramsay, *Our Storehouse of Missouri Place Names*, 43–48.

21. The two-story log jail was constructed in 1847 and burned in 1853. See *History of Adair, Sullivan, Putnam and Schuyler Counties, Missouri*, 662. Several murder cases in Schuyler County before 1849 and afterward are discussed in this work, but there is no record of a murder case in 1849 or of the execution of a murderer. Similarly, no evidence of this murder exists in J. W. Gregory, *History of Schuyler County, Missouri*.

22. Carnes writes that this feeding was done by mistake.

23. Carnes writes that the company arrived in Winchester after two miles of travel. After he looked around the town,

he sniffed, "This is one of the best specimens of a back woods town; it consists of some ten or twelve buildings constructed wholly of logs. Scarcely a nail used in the construction." The first courthouse had been in Putnamville, and only in February 1849 was it moved to the new county seat of Winchester. In 1854 the county seat was moved again, this time to Harmony, and in 1855 the town of Harmony changed its name to Unionville. See *History of Adair, Sullivan, Putnam and Schuyler Counties, Missouri,* 464–69.

24. This claim of well-being is contradicted by Carnes, who writes on the same evening that he "could get no corn. Grass poor." Compounding their problems, he notes the next day, was the fact that on the morning of April 27 they had to search until nine o'clock for strayed cattle.

25. Carnes lends credence to the claim of feasting with a laconic "supped on Turkey." He then notes that they are traveling through Dodge County, something Parke notes the next day. Dodge County was established in 1846 and was absorbed in 1853 by Putnam County. See Ramsay, *Our Storehouse of Missouri Place Names,* 6.

26. The next day, Carnes mentions that they had camped on the Mudd River.

27. Carnes does not indicate that he felt chilly or that he took some quinine. He does confirm the price of corn, however.

28. Carnes does not mention the treatment or how he feels. He does indicate annoyance over having to look for strayed livestock until 9 A.M., and he indicates that they had to ford the East Branch at Princeton.

29. Carnes records that some goods were ferried across the river in a small dugout. He writes that a box floated out of one of the wagons and that the fording operation was not

easy, but he fails to mention that a wagon capsized. The difficult ford cost the train four hours. Carnes adds that in the evening they camped on Rock Creek.

30. Named Dallas when it was surveyed for the county seat, the town was renamed Bethany by voters in November 1845. See George W. Wanamaker, *History of Harrison County, Missouri,* 153 and 164.

31. According to Carnes, Gray's Mills was at Gentryville, near their evening camp. Carnes adds that Parke left the company to travel to St. Joseph to try to find Captain Sampson. It is entirely possible that Sampson's instructions dispatching Parke to St. Joseph to ascertain the facts concerning health conditions there were almost a month old, for on April 7 Carnes wrote that Sampson was going to St. Louis to obtain supplies. It is possible that Sampson went to St. Louis for supplies, then traveled to St. Joseph, which would help explain the absence of any reference to Sampson from early April to May by Parke or Carnes. In any case, Carnes's comments on May 2 contain no reference to cholera, which in fact was raging in St. Joseph. Two days later, May 4, Carnes reports that Parke rejoined the company just after it had encamped for the evening, adding that Parke had managed to find Sampson in St. Joseph. Probably in an effort to avoid the sicknesses in St. Joseph, the company swung north of the town and traveled up the east side of the Missouri River.

32. While Parke was on his errand, the company was, in fact, detained by wandering stock. Carnes notes that six oxen strayed, which delayed the day's trek until 3 P.M.

33. The Platte River and the Hundred and Two River flow almost straight south from Nodaway County, the Hundred and Two River flowing several miles to the west of the Platte. They join just southeast of St. Joseph. One overlander wrote, "Came to the river called 102. This is truly beautiful in the extreme." See Lorton, May 7.

34. Almost certainly this is Isaac Merrill and members of his family. He settled in 1837 south of the Rock River, just across from Sterling. In 1840 he sold out to L. H. Woodworth, whom Parke mentions on August 21. See Charles Bent, ed., *History of Whiteside County, Illinois,* 131. Both lived in Coloma Township. George W. Woodburn and his wife, Mary, were natives of Pennsylvania and had settled in Whiteside County in 1837. She died in 1846. He farmed in Sterling until 1849, "when he made an overland trip to California," a trip which lengthened into a number of years. He eventually returned to Whiteside County, where he died in June 1872. See *Atlas of Whiteside County and the State of Illinois,* xxxv, and Bent, *History of Whiteside County,* 402.

35. The place does not contain the remains of St. Joseph. The town was the product of Joseph Robidoux, an energetic member of a large family of fur traders and entrepreneurs. It was laid out in 1843 and named after Robidoux's patron saint. The town grew almost immediately, and during the spring and summer of 1849 it became a bustling, sprawling, and chaotic place teeming with overlanders, traders, animals of various types, and much commerce. Its great advantage over Independence as a jumping-off place lay in the fact that it was both north and west of Independence, which meant it was three or four days closer to the all-important Platte River. In common parlance, the town was usually just St. Joe.

36. Very possibly this is James M. Whipple, whom Parke notes on September 20, 1849. He was born in Massachusetts in November 1822, and settled just west of Sterling with his father, Colonel Jacob Whipple, in 1838. He did not marry until 1872. See Bent, *History of Whiteside County,* 391, 401.

37. Two days earlier, May 4, William Stackpole wrote of the dangers lurking in the towns that served as staging points for the overland migration. After citing some thefts of

livestock, he added, "There can be no doubt but there are many desperate characters about the frontier towns of Mo. attracted by the great body of emigrants and the many opportunities for plunder and the small risk of being brought to justice." See William Stackpole, Diary, 1849, May 4. Two days before, May 2, he had recorded a robbery and a stabbing.

38. Carnes confirms Strope's encounter with mud. In addition, he notes that the goods shipped from Burlington consisted of supplies of meat.

39. According to Carnes, a wagon needed repair. Others took damaged wagons to Savannah for repair. See Bruff, May 17. A ferry across the Missouri River operated at nearby Savannah Landing, funneling a great deal of overland traffic through Savannah. Near Savannah on May 7, William B. Lorton wrote, "We hear numerous stories from travelers about measles, cholera, small pox, & the numbers of teams." The next day, he commented that Savannah was the most flourishing place he had seen for three weeks. It boasted a brick courthouse with stone columns and stairs on the outside. It stood in the middle of the square. He also wrote, "Came along a man inquiring for Lorton, & who in the world should it be but David Carnes." He added, "He may join our company." See Lorton, May 8. If the repairs that Parke and Carnes noted involved metalwork, it is likely that the work was performed by two brothers who were blacksmiths, Jacob and Andrew Moodi. See *History of Andrew and DeKalb Counties, Missouri*, 150.

40. Less than two weeks later, another overlander described Newark: "At 11 A.M. passed through the Village of 'Newark'—the last collection of houses. This place is only a row of some 15 or 20 log houses on either side of the street—or rather road. A wheel-right's and Blacksmith's establishments here are very important in such a district, where the roads are suffered to take care of themselves." See Bruff, 447, n. 51.

41. Although a ferry across the river was in operation by mid-May and possibly earlier, Carnes records that the train forded the stream. Perhaps this was done to save money. Within days, however, other forty-niners used the ferry: "Crossed Polly's Ferry, 12 miles beyond Savannah, in a scow, drawn over by a line across the Nodaway River, which is here a pretty stream, and quite broad. We drove up a tolerable steep hill to the right of Hollister's mill, a stone building, and where good flour could be bought cheap." See Bruff, May 22. One week after the Como company passed the mill, another emigrant wrote: "Yesterday we crossed the ferry at Nodaway River. Here is a flour mill where we can get good flour much cheaper than in St. Louis." See Wilkins, May 16. The mill, three stories tall and including a dam for power, was completed in the spring of 1847 and was owned by A. G. Hollister. It was destroyed by fire before the Civil War but was rebuilt and played an important role in the county's history. See Walter Williams, ed., *A History of Northwest Missouri*, I, 532–38, and *History of Holt and Atchison Counties, Missouri*, 440.

42. Carnes, writing on May 10, claims the Merrills arrived "this afternoon." Perhaps Parke was correct in the sense that possibly Isaac Merrill's wagon arrived before he and his family did.

43. Almost certainly this mission was not the Presbyterian mission near present-day Highland, Kansas. The Como company was too far to the northeast to consider turning so far to the southwest.

44. Carnes notes merely that he was "sick myself." The next day he adds, "Rather better today."

45. After observing that Linden is a "small town. Two or three stores," Carnes writes that because it was Sunday they could get no one in town to perform the repair work, so Strope did it. The delay cost the party three hours. That

evening, Carnes says, they camped in the Nishnabotna River bottom. The seat of Atchison County is now Rock Port.

46. Carnes writes that they started the day's travel before breakfast, ferried across the Nishnabotna River, and camped within five miles of the Fort Kearny ferry. He does not refer to his illness. Bruff, May 29, commented on the ferry operation: "Spent half an hour at supper, mules in harness, and at 7 P.M. crossed the Nishnabotna Ferry in a scow, cordelled across, for which we paid 50¢ per wagon, and 25¢ per private animal. Banks steep and soft. Public house kept by the Ferryman." Compared to what members of the Como company and others were to pay on the Platte and Green rivers, these prices were very low.

47. Fort Kearny (known as Old Fort Kearny) was across the Missouri at the mouth of Table Creek. Carnes notes that they camped at the ferry and that about twenty teams were in front of them.

48. This is not the company from the town of Virginia, Illinois, nor is it the Charlestown Company, of which Geiger and Bryarly were members, from Charlestown, Virginia. It is probably another company from the state of Virginia, a company that Carnes pronounces to be "a jolly set of fellows."

49. Carnes writes that Merrill, Woodburn, and Whipple are still behind, and "we will wait here till they come up." The next day, May 17, Carnes reports that the three arrived at noon and picked up their tents. As was true of all ferries, there was a bottleneck at this one and some jostling for position. Simon Doyle, Diary, 1849, saw some two hundred teams waiting to cross on May 12–13. Somewhat later the river rose, complicating fording activities. See Bruff, May 31–June 4. Both Carnes and Bruff say they traveled three miles after leaving the ferry, Bruff (June 4) noting, "moved the train up upon the prairie, N.N.W. three miles,

to a water hole, and camped." Doyle, May 14, referred to trekking three miles "back of Fort Kearny to a small stream on the left of the road."

50. Very possibly this is the Knoxville, Illinois, company, which took the Mormon Trail north of the Platte and crossed the Missouri River on May 23–24. Evidence to support this lies in Carnes's reference to "the bluffs" (Omaha–Council Bluffs), the place of departure for emigrants using the Mormon Trail: "Sent Brooks back to the ferry to find out if the Knox Co. teams were come up yet. Returned and reported they had taken the road to the bluffs, so we struck tents and moved on hoping to fall in with . . . more teams to make up the company." See Carnes, May 18.

51. One visitor thought: the fort "is beautifully situated on a fine slope of prairie, as beautiful as ever laid out of doors, ½ mile from the river. Soil fine & timber plenty. It is only a small blockhouse with soldiers quartered." See Doyle, May 14. Less flattering were the views of Joseph P. Hamelin, Jr., Diary, 1849–50, April 19–20. The fort was erected in May 1846 by Colonel Stephen Watts Kearny and his force of dragoons. Table Creek recommended itself for the site because it was the site closest to the point where the Independence–St. Joseph Road intersected the Platte River. It was the farthest west that army supplies could be brought by steamboat. Despite these advantages, St. Joseph and Independence became the major outfitting points in 1849, only a comparative trickle of emigrants being attracted to Old Fort Kearny: perhaps only 10 percent of the total overland traffic in 1849. The post was abandoned by May 1849, a caretaker staying behind. See Merrill J. Mattes, *The Great Platte River Road*, 118; George R. Stewart, *The California Trail*, 225; J. H. Sweet, "Old Fort Kearny," 233–43.

52. Dr. Wilmer Worthington and his wife, Elizabeth, lived in West Chester, Pennsylvania in 1850. William, twenty-two,

was their son. See *U.S. Bureau of the Census, Population Schedule, 7th Census, 1850, Chester County, Pennsylvania, Part 1*, 326. Dr. Worthington, one of Pennsylvania's leading physicians, did much to prepare Parke for medical school. See *United States Biographical Dictionary*, 564; Frink, "Charles Ross Parke, M.D.," 4; *Biographical History of the McLean County Medical Society, 1854–1954*, 57.

53. According to Carnes, all was not well with the teams. He writes that the party saw a couple of Indians, which meant that close watch must be kept over the cattle. The next day, May 18, he reports: "One of the teams found an ox missing. Diligent search was made, but we [were] obliged to come off without it."

Chapter 2

1. On May 18, Carnes writes, there was not a stick or shrub to be seen. The next day he adds: "Not a tree in sight." He notes that rosinweed was gathered for fuel.

2. Salt Creek was crossed before Cottonwood Creek. Carnes says Salt Creek was too salty for drinking. Bruff, June 7, said the gases from the stream smelled "entirely like putrid carcasses, and we had to hold our noses." The stream, he claimed, was full of small rattlesnakes. Another traveler agreed that the creek was very salty, noting that it was some thirty feet wide, but then he wrote that fish were caught in the creek where a small tributary of fresh water enters it. Doyle, May 17. See also Wilkins, May 26.

3. Some overlanders found it difficult to get used to using buffalo chips for fuel, but the role chips played in saving countless emigrant lives is significant. On the Great Platte River Road and beyond, wood and other forms of fuel were scarce—often extremely scarce—and only buffalo chips (the *bois de vache* of French trappers) were available.

Buffalo chips enabled those heading west to cook and boil water for coffee, tea, soup, and various drinks. The boiling of water undoubtedly helped to restrict the spread of cholera and other diseases and enable the weak and the sick to live.

The zeal with which chips were gathered impressed Wellman Packard: people would "jump from the wagon, gunny-bag in hand, and make a grand rush for the largest and driest chips; the contest was spirited, but short and always fun provoking." The contest, he wrote, was heightened when two people raced for the same chip, and he concluded that "the most expert chip gatherer was a treasure." Packard, *Early Emigration to California, 1849–1850,* 5–6. For a good account of an earth oven, the use of buffalo chips, and overcoming aversion to the chips, see Reuben Cole Shaw, *Across the Plains in Forty-nine,* 36–37. See also Steck, June 4; David Cosad, Diary, 1849, May 20; Batchelder, June 23; Lord, June 12. When chips were too fresh or were wet after a rain, gold seekers complained, one grumbling after a heavy rain that "buffaloe chips wouldn't burn." Chamberlain, June 10. Another traveler simply stated, "No wood and buffalo chips wet." Young, May 31.

Emigrants used chips for a purpose that may have protected health. Joseph P. Hamelin, Jr., wrote from Green River that he and his companions "made a patent mosquito bar by getting in the smoke of burning ox chips." Hamelin, July 19. Another said his party used buffalo-chip fires "all around the corrall to drive the mosquitoes away." Charles Gould, Diary, 1849, July 1.

Editor Edward Everett Dale writes: "Had it not been for buffalo chips and cow chips the plainsman would have had much difficulty in providing himself with fuel. Buffalo chips long afforded ready means for cooking his food and warming his camp." See *The Journal of James Akin, Jr.,* 11 n. 22. Nearly all overlanders complained about the absence of wood for fuel. Had it not been for chips, one wonders whether tens of thousands of emigrants could have survived the trek to the coast—or even attempted it.

Perhaps it is not too much to claim that chips made the overland surge possible.

4. Carnes notes that Elk Creek was a good stream with cottonwoods and the terrain was "covered with loose boulders" in places. He also reports that the company was carrying fuel continually for emergencies, a fairly common practice among emigrant companies, but one that generally faded with time.

5. The only man named Fields who is recorded as leaving Adams County in 1849 via the overland route is Golder Fields of the Mill Creek area. He left with a party of twenty-six on or about April 10. *History of Adams County, Illinois,* 307. Intestinal disorders went by various names, including *inflammation of the bowels, diarrhoea, dysentery,* and *colik.* Diarrhea and similar disorders were feared because they were seen as precursors of cholera, and indeed they were present when cholera ran its course. One man wrote from the South Platte ford: "There is a good deal of diarrhoea in the camp. It is said to be the forerunner of cholera, and it naturally creates no little apprehension. We passed one tent with a man sick of diarrhoea who is expected to die." See Benson, June 5. Impure water, unusual diet, irregular hours, and the novelty of the trek contributed to diarrhea in virtually every overland train. Two days later, on May 24, Parke confirms that Fields has cholera. He also suspects that a man by the name of Miller has it. This was probably O. F. Miller of Adams County, Illinois, who left Quincy in early April for St. Joseph. His company numbered well over fifty. *History of Adams County, Illinois,* 307.

6. Doyle, May 21, was impressed by both the river bottom and the adjacent upland prairie: "Upland today rather finer than for several days previous; being the finest prairie for agricultural purposes, lacking only timber. The bottom in which we travelled 12 miles is a fine rich alluvial-covered [land] with rich grass." Carnes exclaims, "Here is the most beautiful bottom prairie I ever beheld."

7. The devastating fierceness of this storm was noted by others, Carnes writing that the "storm beat under the tent and completely saturated the blankets." McCall, May 24, wrote, "After dark the rain came down furiously, as though the windows of heaven were opened. Such thunder and vivid lightning I never witnessed before." He added that tents were of little protection. Gray, May 25, reported that the previous "night was bitter cold & the wind blew violently & the rain came down in torrents, by which everything was completely drench'd through." Geiger, May 24, commented on "the most crashing thunder and vivid lightning." Wilkins, May 25: "The wind blew with a fury known only on these immense prairies. The tents were all blown down one by one." Writing on May 24–25, Delano, *Life on the Plains*, devoted much space to the awesome storm. As far east as the Missouri River, Bruff (May 24) felt the fury of the wind and rain. The storm moved Hamelin, May 24, to poetry, and it was probably the same storm that inspired Gustavas C. Pearson, writing sometime in late May, to exclaim, "Language cannot convey the least idea of the force of the wind and of the gloom and utter darkness when not lighted by the glare of sulphurous discharges so continuous and deafening as to deaden thought. United with these, torrents of water poured from the whistling clouds that drag along the earth. The lightning followed the ox chains, the tires of the wheels and gun-barrels hanging to the wagon-bows, and everything metallic seemed in flames. Imagine the feelings of one lying in the wagon upon a hundred and fifty pounds of powder with the roaring of the storm without and the incessant playing of the lightning about us! Add to these the bellowing of the terrified cattle, which had been chained to the wagons to prevent their stampeding, and one has a faint idea of our sensations." The next day, Pearson noted that the only loss of life had been three yoke of oxen, apparent victims of lightning. Pearson, *Overland in 1849*, 22.

8. The warlike reputation of the Pawnees caused overlanders to expect much trouble, so they entered Pawnee country

warily and bristling with weapons. Joseph Sedgley, *Overland to California in 1849,* June 8, was worried: "We are now in Pawnee country; watchfullness and care are necessary." David Dewolf, "Diary of the Overland Trail," June 2, claimed: "The Pawnees are a thieving set of Indians, consequently we have to keep a close watch on our stock." See also Delano, May 27; Niles Searls, *The Diary of a Pioneer and Other Papers,* May 29; Bernard J. Reid, May 26; Gray, May 20. Expecting much trouble, emigrants were delighted when they encountered very little; the fact was, there were few Pawnees to be found. Searls, May 29, for example: "Not a single Indian has made his appearance since we entered the Pawnee Country." See also Benson, June 5; Lucius Fairchild, *California Letters of Lucius Fairchild,* June 5; David T. McCollum in Bidlack, June 27; and "Pawnee" in *Missouri Republican,* June 4. Several factors account for the absence and weakness of the Pawnee Indians in the spring of 1849; their archenemies, the Sioux, had been pummeling them for some time, and they were spending much of their time and energy trying to keep away from the Sioux; diseases—and news of diseases—had spread among the Pawnees and they associated these misfortunes with the arrival of thousands of whites, many of whom they knew were dying of cholera; the emigrants streamed across Pawnee country in numbers that dwarfed all other migration across the plains to that date, and the emigrants carried with them weapons of every description; it appears that the game on which the Pawnees depended was either fleeing the surging columns of emigrants or was being killed off by heavily armed, quick-to-shoot emigrants. In any case, some forty-niners knew of the plight of the Pawnees. Bruff, June 10, wrote of the diminished condition of the Pawnees: "The great warriors, Arabs and terror of the plains, turned out to be a badly reduced, starving, contemptable race!" Hamelin, May 20, referred to them as "a miserable looking crowd" and said two thousand Sioux were on the prowl for them. At least one overlander gave hearty thanks to the Sioux for "keeping off the Pawnees, Cheyennes, and Arapahoes, otherwise no white could get through." Isaac Jones Wistar, *Autobiography of Isaac Jones Wistar, 1827–1905*, June 7, 1849.

9. The village of the Grand Pawnee on the Platte is on the south side of the river about thirty miles upstream from the place where the Loup fork enters the Platte, or about seventy-five miles downstream from Fort Kearny. Looting of abandoned Indian property and desecration of Indian burial sites were fairly rare occurrences, but on June 17, Benson mentioned that emigrants had torn a body from its burial tree "and scattered the bones for rods around, the rotten flesh still clinging to them." Wrote Benson: "I rather take my chance with that heathen Indian than with the ghouls that scattered his bones." Probably much more typical of the treatment accorded Indian sites was that described by Searls, June 19, and Bernard J. Reid, June 19. Parke's description of the village conforms closely to Bruff's lengthy description of June 12. Wilkins and his comrades visited the village and found, much to their surprise, "an old Indian, stone blind, alone and apparently left there to perish. He was frightened at first, but was soon pacifyed. He excited so much the sympathy of the company, that bread and bacon poured upon him." Wilkins said the old Indian was grateful, and "he signified his wish to accompany us, and altho' it was contrary to our laws to allow any Indians in the camp, his was such a hard case that the rule was dispensed with, and he was allowed to accompany us." Wilkins, May 31. The sustained Sioux campaign against the Pawnees probably forced them to abandon the village. Doyle visited the place on May 23 and concluded that the village "is deserted on account of the number of Palefaces which travel the road." See also John A. Markle, Diary, 1849, May 18; Isaac Foster, Diary, 1849–50, May 24; Tipton, May 17; and Waldo R. Wedel, *An Introduction to Pawnee Archaeology.*

10. A Mr. Woods left Quincy before April 10 with O. F. Miller in the same large company, which departed about the same time as Golder Fields's company, suggesting that the

two groups either were traveling together or were traveling near each other. See *History of Adams County, Illinois,* 307–308. Carnes notes that Woods's antelope was the first shot by members of the train; he also laments the scarcity of fuel.

11. Fort Jessup, abandoned in 1846, was in Louisiana midway between the Red and Sabine rivers. Clearly, Parke is in error here. The junction to which he refers is that of the road from Old Fort Kearny, coming down from the northeast, and the Independence–St. Joe Road, coming up from the southeast from a bend in the Little Blue River. The junction was perhaps twelve to fifteen miles east of Fort Kearny. See Doyle, May 27–28; Wilkins, June 4 n. 15. Almost certainly Parke is in error when he maintains that he camped near the junction of the two roads. Two pieces of evidence argue against his claim. First, Carnes notes that they passed the junction at 10 A.M., much too early to have camped. Second, on May 30 both Parke and Carnes indicate that after breaking camp in the morning they traveled only three miles before reaching Fort Kearny and that they then traveled another fourteen miles before camping for the night.

12. Mystery shrouds the identity and fate of David Harris. He was almost certainly axed to death for making advances to the wife of another emigrant, but uncertainties persist. Writing on May 27 from Fort Kearny, G. C. Hard stated simply, "The grave of Dr. David Harris is close to our camp this night. There is nothing left to tell where he is from." *Rockford Forum,* July 4, 1849. "Pawnee" wrote from Fort Kearny, "A serious difficulty occurred a day or two since between two emigrants in this vicinity, in which one of them by the name of Harris lost his life. It appears that this man had been making advances towards the wife of a man by the name of Shields which coming to his (Shields') ears, induced him to lay open his (Harris') head with an ax. He died instantly." See *Missouri Republican,* June 9, 1849. On July 25, the *Oquawka Spectator* ran the

following: "A man named Harris from this place was literally cut to pieces for attempting improper liberties with the wife of one of the emigrants. A year earlier he was tried for rape before Judge Williams." About two weeks later in the same newspaper, "W" recounted that Shields was from Mercer County, Illinois, and Harris was from Burlington, Iowa. On the trail they shared a mess, argued much, and Harris persisted in his advances, causing Shields to strike Harris twice in the head with an ax. Sentiment, "W" added, was in favor of Shields. *Oquawka Spectator,* August 8, 1849. See also *Burlington Hawk-Eye,* July 19, and *Iowa State Gazette,* July 19. P. C. Tiffany, Diary, 1849–51, May 20, 1849, wrote substantially the same thing but added a new twist. Harris, he claimed, was not a physician but "a man of no character" who had worked as a blacksmith in Burlington. After the killing, he wrote, the officers at the fort conducted an inquest, "but the matter was dropped and the parties permitted to pass on." It is possible, however unlikely, that *two* men—perhaps even two men named Harris—were killed in two incidents, but the weight of evidence suggests otherwise.

13.   Although many emigrants had encountered swarms of humanity at St. Joseph, Independence, and other outfitting points, the heavy concentration of teams along the route surprised many overlanders, some of whom expected to be members of solitary trains. H. Egan wrote on May 31 from a point just east of Fort Kearny: "Today we have passed where the St. Joseph and Independence road intersects this road; there is one continual string of wagons as far as the eye can extend, both before and behind us." *Frontier Guardian,* July 11, 1849. Another traveler wrote, "The number of teams on the road is immense." See Wood, May 14. Still another commented from South Pass in mid-July: "The road looks like a great thoroughfare in the midst of a thickly populated country . . . like a mighty stream they pour along unceasingly." Thomas Eastin, Diary, 1849, July 17. Additional accounts of crowded routes are plentiful: Gurdon Backus, Diary,

1849, July 2; Delano, July 1; *Richmond Palladium,* August 15; Lord, June 29; Spooner, June 14; Mann, June 27; Benson, July 4; Steck, June 2; John A. Johnson, Note Book, June 17. From one end of the route to the other, the crush of humanity and livestock was truly impressive, resulting in bottlenecks at ferries, jostling for fuel and water, and shortages of nourishment for emigrant and cattle.

14. Carnes says they learned of the seriousness of cholera along the route after joining emigrants from St. Joseph at the junction of the roads. Many overlanders that summer kept tallies of grave sightings, and some, like Bernard J. Reid (James M. Hutchings, *Seeking the Elephant, 1849*), kept very accurate lists of people who died.

15. In May 1846, Congress directed the construction of a fort to protect people going to Oregon and to keep peace between the Sioux and the Pawnees. The site was selected by Lieutenant Daniel Woodbury in the early autumn of 1847, but the Mexican War and other factors delayed construction until the spring of 1848, when Colonel L. E. Powell began work, naming the post after Colonel Thomas Childs. On October 31, 1848, General Stephen Watts Kearny died, and the fort was renamed after him two months later. (Both Childs and Kearny were Mexican War heroes.) The fort often was called New Fort Kearny to distinguish it from the fort at present-day Nebraska City some 180 miles to the east. Lieutenant Colonel Benjamin L. E. Bonneville arrived in late May 1849 to take command. In appearance the fort was not impressive to most people—some overlanders ridiculed it—but it did provide comfort and services to emigrants, and perhaps the Indians found it imposing. For emigrants coming up from western Missouri, Fort Kearny marked the end of the first tenth of the journey to the gold fields. As such, it was a place where people took stock of their situation; some found everything fine and resolved to push on; others, perhaps feuding with messmates or unhappy with

the state of affairs, coalesced into new overland companies; others—many others—found that they had packed too many things, and they began to pitch; still others, plagued by doubts about the whole enterprise, returned home. The fort's physical presence and symbolic presence were both important. Troops were withdrawn from the fort in May 1871. Francis Paul Prucha, *A Guide to the Military Posts of the United States, 1789–1895,* 82; Lyle E. Mantor, "Fort Kearny and the Westward Movement," 175–207; Mattes, *The Great Platte River Road,* chap. 6; Stewart, *The California Trail,* 227–42; Irene D. Paden, *The Wake of the Prairie Schooner,* 83–84.

16. Benson, Farnham, and McCall, all in the immediate vicinity on May 30, wrote that they, too, were delayed by heavy rain.

17. A full account of these soldiers and their journey to Oregon is found in Raymond W. Settle, ed., *The March of the Mounted Riflemen.*

18. Those who gave up and returned home—"gobacks," "turn-arounds," or "turn-backers"—tended to be rumor-mongers who exaggerated hardships. Some did tell the truth, however, and some carried mail for those who wanted to write to relatives back east. See Unruh, *The Plains Across,* 122–31. One emigrant wrote that he had heard "the most frightfull stories" of what lay ahead, which were "told by Californians who have backed out and wish some excuse to give." Fairchild, June 5, 1849. Some of those who returned bitterly resented having to do so. Elijah Bryan Farnham, "From Ohio to California in 1849," May 29.

19. Very likely members of the Merrill family, but by June 4 the Merrills are with Parke again, so it is unlikely that all of the Merrills were two days behind on May 31.

20. Virtually every wagon that went overland in 1849 was overloaded, so great was the desire of emigrants to take

every conceivable article. Although some people began pitching belongings long before they reached Fort Kearny, the area around the fort became a favorite dumping ground. Benson, May 28; Markle, May 24; Steck, May 28; and Spooner, May 26. Evidently, there was a scale at the fort for one overlander mentioned that he and his company weighed their wagons, then "sold some flour and bacon" to lighten the load. Burrell Whalen Evans, Narrative, 1849, May 23. One individual displayed rare insight when he reported from St. Joseph: "All load[s] too heavy." Lord, May 13. Material possessions were not the only items thrown away; not far from the fort, Lord discovered T. R. Waring from Andrew, Iowa, who had been pitched because he had cholera. On the same day, Lord wrote that emigrants were taking too many boxes and trunks, so he urged people to put things into bags of various sizes that could be shoved into corners and odd places. Lord, June 2. Some people put to good use things that others threw away. Isaac Jones Wistar, for example, used discarded bacon to build a brisk fire. Wistar, May 30.

21. Carnes, June 1: "I have omitted to mention that we are organized under the title of the Illinois California-Bound Invincibles. The [company] is composed of 13 teams, 36 men, 4 women, & 4 children, have 116 head of cattle and horses." The Como company had metamorphosed into a new organization with a constitution and bylaws. As individuals and groups of people joined existing companies, they had to agree to abide by the constitution and laws of the company. See Bruff, May 12; Delano, *Life on the Plains,* June 17; Owen Cochran Coy, *The Great Trek,* 98–103; McCall, May 12; Wilkins, May 23 and June 4; Wistar, May 21; Geiger and Bryarly, 213–22; Cosad, June 21; Dean J. Locke, Diary, 1849, July 29; David Brainard, Journal, 1849, April 2; O. J. Hall, Diary, 1849, June 18 and July 3; Joshua D. Breyfogle, Diary, 1849, August 13; Farnham, July 25; Wood, May 14; and Leslie L. D. Shaffer, "The Management of Organized Wagon Trains on the Overland Trail," 355–65. As a general rule, companies that were

organized as joint-stock enterprises were more likely to have detailed constitutions and elaborate laws than were companies that appeared to coalesce spontaneously. Moreover, it appears that companies from New England and from areas in the North where New Englanders settled were more likely to have highly structured companies.

22. Dr. T. A. Livermore was a surgeon-dentist from Galena. He had lived there since 1834 and had been an active Mason since 1846. See *Weekly North-Western Gazette,* July 10, 1846, and *History of Jo Daviess County, Illinois,* 521.

23. Carnes: "The roads are covered with teams as far as the eye can see either way." From virtually the same place on the same day, another emigrant reported "hundreds of teams continually in sight." Steck, June 2, and Doyle, June 3.

24. Wistar noted on June 2 that the town was several miles long and the animals' excavations made it difficult to navigate the wagons. P. F. Castleman, Diary, 1849–51, June 6, and D. Jagger, Diary, 1849–50, June 9, repeat the story that prairie dogs and rattlesnakes lived together. See also Lord, June 6; Shaw, 38–39; John F. Lewis, Diary, 1849, June 4. McCall, June 3, wrote a very lengthy and at times amusing account of the prairie-dog town. Carnes refers to the dogs' "spirited barking."

25. Carnes notes the departure: "Two of the companies teams became dissatisfied and left the train. Merrill & family and Whipple are the persons." On June 3, Parke wrote: "Will lay over tomorrow and have some washing done," implying that someone else was going to do the washing, not Parke. The first entry of June 4 indicates that poor Mrs. Merrill was the person, and it is not unreasonable to think she resented it. She was not very typical if she growled about having to do the wash, however, for most women in wagon trains accepted their traditional chores without a murmur. For accounts of women doing the wash on the

trail and accepting the underlying assumption that they should do the wash, see Faragher, *Women and Men on the Overland Trail,* 78–79.

26.　On their way to Ash Hollow and the North Platte, emigrants could cross the South Platte practically anywhere along the forty-five-mile stretch separating the Lower Ford (the new ford) from the Upper Ford. Most chose the Upper Ford, which was several miles west of present-day Brule, Nebraska, but the lower crossing, near present-day Hershey, was almost as popular. Parke and his comrades chose it. Using the crossing the same day, Doyle wrote that the water was "2½ feet deep, 1000 yards wide"; Carnes finds it knee deep and a mile wide. Benson's entry for June 5 stressed that the ford was new. McCall's company had quite an ordeal in crossing: "We entered upon the toilsome and difficult task of fording this fickle and uncertain stream. It is near a half a mile wide, its bottom a bed of quicksand. All hands were compelled to take hold and steady the wagons down the steep bank. When the wheels struck the quicksand, the swift water washed it from under, so that the wheels are constantly running uphill, making a constant buzzing like an engine letting off steam. The moment the wagon or team halts, they are going down—down, and would be soon entirely buried." McCall, June 5. For more on the effects of quicksand, see Delano, *Life on the Plains,* June 2; Hutchings, July 9; Gould, June 25; Carnes, June 5; Farnham, June 5. See also Dale L. Morgan, "The Ferries of the Forty-Niners"; Mattes, *The Great Platte River Road,* 264–67; Unruh, *The Plains Across,* 256–60, 477–79.

27.　Indian-emigrant hunts were not terribly common, but they did occur. The hunt and the presence of Sioux caught the attention of a number of diarists. One overlander wrote: "As we were re-arranging our teams after crossing the river, two buffalo were seen on the gallop a short distance away. The Indians put out on horseback, and the next I saw was a white woman who had traveled near us today on horseback. She led off at full speed. Several of our men joined in the chase on foot. Some who had not seen the woman start thought her horse was running away with her." He added that the woman got in the first shot at the buffalo, helped kill it, and "the woman passed us in about an hour with a lot of meat hung to her saddle. I saw her husband when she was in the chase, and he appeared to be very proud." This was truly an extraordinary event, one rarely seen elsewhere. The chase resulted in the killing of two buffalo. For more, see Granville, Ohio, Company, diarist, Diary, 1849, June 5. Hunting was almost solely a male activity, one in which men enjoyed themselves, demonstrated aggressiveness, and acted out fantasies. For more on the subject, see Faragher, *Women and Men on the Overland Trail*, 85–87, 99–102, 135–36. On the day of this unusual hunt, June 5, McCall was on the scene and described it: "These Sioux were here on their annual hunt and were entirely friendly. They were fine, stately-looking fellows, plump and well-fed, with prominent features." Others were equally impressed; see Joseph H. Johnson, Diary, 1849, May 20; Dr. T, May 25; Tipton, May 19; and Steck, June 5–6. Steck observed that the Indians were outstanding horsemen, "were very shrewd and equal to the white man in bargaining" but had a weakness for whiskey. Farnham, June 5, referred to the Sioux as "a proud noble race of good proportion, tall strong athletic and good horsemen."

28. An emigrant somewhat to the west noted that hail "about the size of pigeons' eggs covered the ground white in a few minutes." Gray, June 6. For more on the storm, see Geiger and Bryarly, June 6; Benson, June 6; McCall, June 6; and Doyle, June 6, who reported being "deluged with rain."

29. Perhaps the game had been killed off or chased away by the great throng of emigrants, for during the day's travels Carnes observed that "the road in front and rear for two miles each way was filled with wagons, etc."

30. After crossing the Lower Ford on June 5 and pitching camp a short distance from the ford, Benson commented on the Indian village two miles away and the fact that during the evening a "good many Indians" visited the camp to trade moccasins and animal skins. The next day, June 6, he noted that it had showered during the night and "we started out quite late. In two miles we came to the Indian village. I think there are about 200 huts, made mostly of buffalo skins. These are made round and large at the bottom, with poles from 20 to 25 feet long, coming together at the top. I should think they have a thousand horses. They seem to be possessed of the necessities of life, and to be contented and happy, and I could not help wondering what they really thought of us bull wackers, with our assumption of superiority trudging along (going somewhere) at the rate of a few miles a day. We would not trade places with them for anything in the world and they would not trade [places] with us. Some of the emigrants were trading with the Indians for buffalo robes, a good robe for a pair of breeches or a peck of beans. It was unfortunate for us that we had thrown away all our beans before we got here. It was thought that a diet of beans was bad in cholera time, and we cast them away." Doyle, encamped just north of the crossing, also was visited on the evening of June 5: "3 Sioux Indians visited our camp this evening, among whom was the Chief, Bulls Tail, & his daughter of 18." The next day, after noting that the women have "beautiful features," he wrote that the chief displayed a number of certificates given by whites that testified to the good character and honesty of his tribe. The chief asked the captain of Doyle's train for a certificate, and the captain gave him one saying the tribe had treated the whites with civility but warning other overlanders "to be on their guard for they are the most complete thieves he ever saw." He then recounted two instances of theft; Doyle, June 5–6. Another overlander complained that some miscreant had plied the Sioux with "Old Rye," which "had made them crazy," and since he was encamped about a mile from the Sioux, he could hear

"their yells all night." McCall, June 5. These somewhat negative views of the Sioux were the exception, however, and much more typical were those held by Steck, June 5–6; Krepps, June 14; Wistar, June 7; and Farnham, June 6.

31.   Castle Rock is seven miles west of Ash Hollow, but relatively few diarists mention it.

32.   Ash Hollow is mentioned by the vast majority of diarists. Its vegetation, clear water, high cliffs, and general grandeur contrasted sharply with the comparatively featureless plains over which emigrants had traveled before reaching Ash Hollow. Parke was somewhat disappointed, but Carnes and other forty-niners were not. See Doyle's and Wistar's entries for June 9. Others were equally impressed; see Hale, June 7; McCall, June 8; and Benson, June 8. Compared with other emigrants' experiences, that of Parke and his companions at Ash Hollow was easy. By crossing the South Platte at the Lower Ford and following the south side of the North Platte to Ash Hollow, they avoided the awesomely steep declivity at the south entrance.

33.   Stackpole, June 5: "The appearance of these Indians and their mode of living was far above what we had expected to see and altogether superior to those near St. Joseph. Their lodges are constructed of dressed Buffalo skins stretched over poles much in the shape of a round tent. They are large and commodious and seem to have been constructed with great care." Benson, June 8, was impressed by the fact that the Indians had "white wolves trained for dogs." Israel F. Hale, writing on June 7, was surprised by what he saw: "These Indians appeared much more comfortably fixed than I expected to see them. They looked clean and were well dressed and had several good horses. I presume they were some of the better class." Hale, "Diary of a Trip to California in 1849"; see also McCall, June 8; Abram Minges, Diary, 1849, June 2; Delano, *Life on the Plains*, June 4; and Gray, June 4, who

wrote: "Passed an encampment of the Sioux Indians; there were about 20 of them, male & female. They were Frenchmen with Sioux wives & some of the children were as fair as our home productions." Referring to the mixture of blood, he added: "These Indians didn't look very Indian like I thought."

34. Carnes: "A crowd of wagons as usual. The bottom was literally alive with cattle." After referring to "a compact line of canvas covered wagons" that stretched back for nearly a mile, McCall, June 8, added: "It was a magnificent sight. I estimated the number at not less than five hundred, the greatest number that I had ever seen massed together."

35. Writing on June 8 from Ash Hollow, the Granville Company diarist reported: "Saw a young man that had shot himself by a pistol going through his thei. The ball went through his thei and then a foot in the ground. He was from Missouri. We carried him in our wagon until we came up with his train at Ash Hollow." Perhaps this is the same man Farnham mentioned on June 9: "A man belonging to one of the trains ahead . . . had shot himself with a pistle while loading it. The ball went through the calf of his leg." In any case, accidents were very common on the overland trail because the emigrants were armed to the teeth, had relatively little experience in handling weapons, were jumpy and nervous much of the time, and were often tired and irritable. In short, conditions were right for a rash of accidents. Delano sized up the situation correctly when he wrote, "When we first crossed into the Indian territory above St. Josephs, every man displayed his arms in the most approved desperado style, and rarely thought of stirring from the train without his trusty rifle." It was perhaps inevitable that such a concentration of firepower would lead to numerous accidents. Charles A. Tuttle, Letters, 1849, May 16; Vincent Hoover, Diary, 1849, May 29; McCall, June 11; Delano, *Life on the Plains*, May 27, June 4, June 28; Reuben Miller, Diary, 1849,

August 29; Markle, June 28; Charles Tinker, "Charles Tinker's Journal," April 11; Locke, June 27; Young, May 22; Andrew M. Orvis, Diary, 1849–50, June 28; Gould, June 29; Eastin, June 27. After encountering very few real threats, Delano wrote: "By degrees the arms were laid aside, and by the time we reached Fort Laramie all were abandoned except a knife, and sometimes a pistol, which might be seen peeping from a pocket." Delano, *Life on the Plains*, July 22. Weapons laid aside, emigrants were far less prone to fire at the slightest provocation. As a result, only one-tenth of the fatalities caused by accidental shootings occurred west of South Pass through 1850. See Unruh, *The Plains Across*, 412–13.

36. Rain during the night and early morning, Carnes notes, caused the train to delay its start until 8 A.M. Spring Creek was "a stream of clear, but rather warm water." Geiger and Bryarly, June 8.

37. Parke's view of Castle Bluffs was shared by Geiger and Bryarly, who wrote on June 8 that the bluffs were "only bleak sandy hills, but little resembling castles or houses of any description." Delano, *Life on the Plains*, June 5, was a little more enthusiastic, noting that the bluffs "were looked upon with curiosity and interest." Bernard J. Reid, June 20, was highly pleased by the rock formations, seeing in them features that resembled "turrets, castles and embattled fortresses, crowned by a few stunted cedars." See also Hale, June 8; Holliday, *The World Rushed In*, 161; and Doyle, June 9.

38. Carnes confirms both the deep sand and the poor grass.

39. At this point, John H. Benson, who had been traveling abreast with Parke for some time, began to fall a bit behind. On June 10, after commenting that "there is sickness to a considerable extent in nearly every train," Benson wrote that he had met a mail carrier and three wagons from Salt Lake City. Almost certainly this is the individual

who was carrying Parke's letter. McCall, also a bit behind Parke, wrote on June 10 that he had encountered a small party of Mormons heading east. Both men indicated that the Mormons had given them useful information about conditions to the west.

40. This storm made a deep impression on more than one emigrant. Geiger and Bryarly, June 10: "The thunder burst forth in deafening peals & the lightening played & flashed in the heavens, assuming shapes & colors never before witnessed—with a strong S.W. wind, and then poured down the hail in torrents. The ground was covered like snow. The tents beaten through and the wagon covers almost riddled." William W. Chapman, Diary, 1849, June 9, reported a "dreadful storm" near Chimney Rock in which six oxen were killed by lightning. Spooner, June 10, attributed at least one aspect of the storm to divine displeasure: Just beyond Chimney Rock, "a thunderbolt descended & struck two of Col. Avery's oxen dead. I could not but think it was an exhibition of the displeasure of the Almighty for the violation of his holy day." Writing on June 9, Spooner exclaimed, "The heavens seemed to be in a continuous blaze of the most vivid lightning for an hour or two, and the successive peals of thunder were of the most startling character." See also Stackpole, June 9; McCall, June 10; Farnham, June 9.

41. Simon Doyle camped quite close to Parke's company on the night of June 10. He wrote on June 11: "Wilson's train from Missouri stampeded just after night. Broke out of the corral, breaking 2 wagons and scattering over the plains." Wilkins, June 11; Benson, June 11; Hale, June 11; George Gibbs, "The Diary of George Gibbs," June 11. Carnes says it "required all hands to keep our tent down."

42. Francis Parkman had warned that for those who wanted to sleep on the plains "the pertinacious humming of unnumbered mosquitoes will banish sleep from his eyelids." See *The Oregon Trail*, 32. The mosquito was more dreaded

and caused more commotion than either the ubiquitous rattlesnake or the wolf. Markle, July 16, had a tough time trying to sleep. As early as May 22, Gray was much annoyed by mosquitoes. Not far from Parke on June 10, the Granville diarist complained about mosquitoes, adding the next day: "Our blood was about all sucked out by the mosquito." Amos Steck, very close to Parke's location on June 11, wrote, "Musquetos most horribly pesterous. The cattle becoming almost crazy and hard to guard." Hoover, June 6: "Last night the musquitoes almost ate the cattle." See also Chamberlain, June 11; Octavius Thorndike Howe, *Argonauts of '49,* 153; Bernard J. Reid, June 20–21; Holliday, *The World Rushed In,* 162–63; Wilkins, June 19.

43. Alonzo Delano passed this spot on June 6 and identified the man from Michigan as George W. Tindal, "a young man from Tecumseh, Michigan, who had died of consumption." Delano had run across him on his passage from St. Louis to St. Joseph and was much impressed by him. Hale, June 8, "passed the grave of a man by the name of Tindall. He died about four days since." He then claimed, erroneously, that Tindall hailed from Wisconsin. Markle, June 5, wrote, "During the day we passed 2 graves. One was Tindell from Michigan, who was buried on the 4th. The other was William Stephens from Boone County, Missouri, who they were just about to bury. They wraped him in his clothes, and put him in a sand hole." Markle said there was fear that wolves would unearth Stevens. The fear of wolves was justified, for on June 7, Joseph Wood, coming upon Tindall's grave, wrote, "We have passed the grave of a young man from Tecumseh, Mich., who died three days ago. The wolves had tracked over it and commenced digging." The grave had not been disturbed as of June 6, at least according to William Stackpole. On that date he noted: "We passed the grave of a young man from Michigan 23 years of age. He died June 4th 1849." Evidently, the graves of Tindall and Stevens were some miles apart, for Stackpole cited Tindall's grave on June 6 and Stevens's on June 7. Hale supports this

conclusion by citing Tindall's grave on June 8 and Stevens's the next day, writing, "After a drive of about five miles we passed a grave. It was a Mr. Stevens of Boone County, Missouri. He died on the sixth of consumption. He was traveling for his health." James M. Hutchings wrote that William P. Stevens died on June 6, was twenty-four years old, and was from Boone County, Missouri. Hutchings, *Seeking the Elephant, 1849,* 189. See also Stackpole, June 7, and Steck, June 11.

44. No person by the name of Boil appears elsewhere in Parke's diary or in Carnes's. On September 20, Parke joined Isaac Boyle and John Boyle in a mining operation in California; both men were from Iowa. It is likely that Parke is referring to Isaac or John, either or both of whom may have joined the Como train by June 12. Almost certainly Corrington is in fact Joseph A. Farrington of Lyndon Township, Whiteside County. He was born in January 1829 in New York, and his parents brought him to Whiteside County in 1836. Bent, *History of Whiteside County,* 282.

45. Solitary Tower was also known as Solitary Rock, Solitary Castle, Lonely Tower, and Lone Tower. In reality, it consisted of Courthouse Rock and Jail Rock. When seen from the east, however, the two landforms appear to be one. They were also known as the Church and Prairie Church and the Castle (not to be confused with Castle Bluffs west of Ash Hollow). There were many variations of these names, and many different spellings were associated with the variations. For a detailed sorting out, consult Mattes, *The Great Platte River Road,* 346–47.

46. Consisting of volcanic ash and Brule clay, this landform was mentioned by practically every diarist. For a thorough and rigorous discussion of Chimney Rock, "Eighth Wonder of the World," see Mattes, *The Great Platte River Road,* chap. 12. Carnes writes of Chimney Rock: "This is called a rock, but it is in reality a clay, so cemented as to

resemble rock and will crumble at the slightest touch." He adds, "It can be seen 30 miles distant, at which distance it resembles a hay stack, with a pole running far above the top." He thinks the "pole" is 100 feet high and 8–10 feet in diameter. Emigrants knew of Chimney Rock from a variety of sources and were on the lookout for it as they approached from the east. This posed a problem, for distances were very deceiving, as some overlanders learned. Carnes writes on June 10: "The atmosphere is so pure that a person is often deceived in the distance, supposing from appearances it to be much nearer than it really is. I think the naked eye can desern objects at double the distance than it can in Illinois." Others arrived at similar conclusions. Delano, June 7, wrote of how Courthouse Rock "appeared to recede." See also Wistar, June 12. The phenomenon of magnification is discussed in detail in Mattes, *The Great Platte River Road*, 389–92. See also Merrill Mattes, "Chimney Rock on the Oregon Trail."

47. Parke is essentially correct, except that sandstone is found in Courthouse Rock, Scott's Bluff, and other landforms in the vicinity, all of which are higher in elevation.

48. Horse Creek flows into the North Platte from a south-westerly direction in present-day Scotts Bluff County.

49. Of all the major landmarks along the North Platte valley, Chimney Rock is mentioned by 97 percent of the journals, diaries, and guidebooks. Scott's Bluff comes in second, being mentioned in 77 percent of these sources. Mattes, *The Great Platte River Road*, 380. There are many variations of a story of how a trapper by the name of Hiram Scott became sick in the late 1820s, was abandoned by his companions, and, crawling a considerable distance, finally died at the base of the bluffs. In any case, the looming bulk of the landform is impressive, as it was to overlanders in 1849. Carnes writes: "The road . . . passes in [the] rear of Scotts Bluffs and in 8 miles we arrive at the highest point

in the gorge. Here we had some of the richest scenery yet presented to our views [and] we get a fine view of the Rocky mountains, for the first time." Unlike Parke, Carnes refers to the trading post operated by the energetic Robidoux family, with Joseph Robidoux, Sr., probably heading the operation. See Mattes, *The Great Platte River Road*, 449–53. Carnes writes about a Frenchman who "resided at these bluffs and kept a small shop to trade with emigrants. Also a blacksmith shop. Sold whisky, &c., &c."

50.   Fleming Dunn of Indian Town (now Tiskilwa), Illinois, left Peoria on April 4 as a member of a large emigrant company. Charles W. Haskins, *The Argonauts of California*, 413. Charles G. Hinman also was a member of the company and wrote about the cholera attack that killed Dunn about 10 P.M. on June 13: "We buried him at 8 oclock the next morning with as much decency as if he had been in the States, put a sand stone up with his name, age, &c., cut on it, and left him. He was a young man and left a wife and one child in Indian Town, Ill. His name was Dunn." Hinman, *"A Pretty Fair View of the Elephant,"* June 17. On July 7, Bruff noted that Dunn was twenty-six, the same age recorded by Hutchings. Hutchings, *Seeking the Elephant, 1849*, 189. Fleming's brother, Ellis, also went west and died in California shortly after his arrival. *Biographical Record of Bureau, Marshall, and Putnam Counties*, 595. See also John Edwin Banks, Diary, 1849, June 14; Mattes, *The Great Platte River Road*, 445; *Missouri Republican*, August 29, 1849.

51.   At many places along the route, informal "post offices" were established. These varied in size and other ways, but essentially they were places where emigrants left messages, directions, and warnings to individuals and groups of people they thought were behind them on the trail. Notes were sometimes attached to trees, sometimes to stakes and posts driven into the ground.

52.   Carnes says they were one mile above Fort Laramie. Situated on the west side of the Laramie River about a mile

south-southwest of the Laramie's confluence with the North Platte River, the fort was about one-third of the way from St. Joseph to Sacramento. In 1834, William Sublette and Robert Campbell constructed Fort William (after William Sublette). Soon afterward it was purchased by the American Fur Company, which changed its name to Fort John (after one of the company's officers). In 1841 the company built a new fort and also called it Fort John, but Fort John on the Laramie soon became Fort Laramie to trappers and traders. (It is possible that the two forts coexisted briefly in 1841, one being maintained until the other was finished.) The Mexican War delayed construction on the site of a military post for overlanders using the Oregon Trail, but on June 16, 1849, soldiers under the command of Major Winslow F. Sanderson arrived; they were Company E of the Mounted Riflemen. Ten days later, Fort Laramie became a military post when, for four thousand dollars, title to it was transferred to Major Sanderson by the Rocky Mountain Fur Company. The fort was near the boundary line of two natural environmental regions: the western edge of the High Plains and the eastern edge of the region of the uphill trek toward the Rockies. In 1849 the fort became the place where emigrants had to make one of three decisions: reduce loads, repair worn equipment, rest animals, and push on in wagons; abandon wagons and virtually all nonessential possessions and pack on foot and with horses; return to the States. Some overland companies spent two or three days at the fort, resting, catching up on work, and making decisions. The fort also marked the region where cholera tapered off sharply and scurvy and dysentery became more common. Troops were stationed at Fort Laramie until March 1890. See Mattes, *The Great Platte River Road,* 480–505; Aubrey L. Haines, *Historic Sites Along the Oregon Trail,* 135; a remarkable statement in a letter written by Merrill Mattes to Gregory W. Franzwa on February 13, 1982, in Franzwa's *Maps of the Oregon Trail,* 106; Prucha, *A Guide to the Military Posts of the United States, 1789–1895,* 84; Paden, *The Wake of the Prairie Schooner,* 152–56; LeRoy

R. Hafen and Francis Marion Young, *Fort Laramie and the Pageant of the West*. Nearly every diarist mentioned the fort. For some particularly useful descriptions, see Lord, June 27; Benson, June 18; Farnham, June 16–17; Gray, June 11; Geiger and Bryarly, June 14; Gibbs, June 22–23; Osborne Cross, "The Journal of Major Osborne Cross," June 22; Dewolf, July 7; Bruff, July 11; and McCall, June 27.

53. Carnes does not mention this misfortune.

Chapter 3

1. Carnes writes that the wagon beds were shortened to about ten feet, the projections being removed. Others truncated their wagons, too. See Geiger and Bryarly, June 16. At Fort Kearny and all along the trail between Fort Kearny and Fort Laramie people pitched surplus possessions, but it was at Fort Laramie that the most serious efforts to "lighten up" were made. Virtually every writer on the scene in 1849 mentioned both Fort Laramie and the vast amount of abandoned wagons, furniture, weapons, clothing, tools, and other items, including food and even people. Foster, visiting the fort on June 16, wrote, "Here we found plenty of provisions without money and without price; as you pass along you see piles of bacon and hard bread thrown by the side of the road; about 50 wagons [were] left here, and many burned and the irons left; trunks, clothes, boots and shoes, lead by the hundred, spades, picks, guns and all other fixings for a California trip." Hutchings, July 21, found at Fort Laramie not only abandoned goods but three wounded men who had been left behind by their companions. Another individual recorded that after he and some friends forded the Laramie River and got soaking wet, the rest of the company "drove off and left us in distress." Chapman, June 13. Some people complained that when goods had to be abandoned the

owners often destroyed the goods or burned them. Benson, June 18, grumbled about emigrants who "seem to burn their wagons for pure cussedness. Because they cannot sell them, they seem to be determined that they shall be of no use to anyone else." Searls, June 27, also noted burned wagons. The discarding and destruction at Fort Laramie were noted by many others, including Castleman, June 28–29; Evans, June 17; Searls, June 27–29; Greenberry Miller, June 13; Shaw, *Across the Plains in Forty-nine*, 53–56; Henry J. Shombre, Diary, 1849, June 17; Dr. T, June 3; Wood, June 14; John Prichet, Diary, 1849–51, June 17, 1849; Spooner, June 13; Benson, June 18–19; David T. McCollum to J. H. Lund, June 27, 1849, in Bidlack, *Letters Home*. The area around the fort served the emigrants as a dump; the fort itself provided services to people, animals, and equipment. See Stackpole, June 13; Hutchings, July 21; Bruff, July 10. Refitted, refreshed, and relieved of unnecessary belongings, the forty-niners pushed west from Fort Laramie and continued to pitch goods along the trail.

2. On July 18 the temperature of Warm Spring was 71 degrees. Howard Stansbury, *Exploration and Survey of the Valley of the Great Salt Lake of Utah*, July 18.

3. Carnes claims two miles, but he agrees that it is "the finest stream of cold water yet seen" and adds that the spring from which the stream flowed was twenty by forty feet and ice cold. Most diarists referred to Bitter Creek as Bitter Cottonwood Creek, one of many small North Platte tributaries that flow northeasterly between Warm Spring and Deer Creek.

4. Stansbury, July 21: "A beautiful stream of running water, clear, soft, and very cool." See Delano, *Life on the Plains*, June 15; Bernard J. Reid, June 30; Farnham, June 20.

5. Carnes confirms the antelope kill. Emigrants welcomed a chance to deviate from their diet of salt pork.

6. A very accurate estimate.

7. The massive mountain, some 10,300 feet high, was topped
    with snow into the summer. Delano and Gray both saw
    snow on June 12. Dewolf, July 4, referred to its top as
    "being covered with snow." On July 7 he wrote to his wife
    and again noted snow on Laramie Peak. However, Bruff
    mentioned the peak on July 7, 11, and 12, and at no time
    did he mention snow. Nor did Hutchings on July 20. The
    accounts of Bernard J. Reid, June 30 and July 1, and Searls,
    who viewed the peak through a telescope on July 1 and
    declared it to be "entirely barren," compound the confu-
    sion: neither mentions snow. It is likely that by late June
    and early July snow was (or was not) seen, depending on
    the time of day, the angle of sighting, and other factors.
    The flint rocks, which resembled snow, caused difficulties.
    Carnes, June 20, reports for the second time that sand and
    flint fragments are hurting the oxen's feet. This probably
    resulted in the additional discarding of belongings along
    this stretch. The manner in which some people pitched
    goods angered McCall. Writing near La Bonte Creek on
    June 21, he heaped scorn on someone who "had an over
    supply of sugar and coffee, instead of placing them where
    they might do somebody good, scattered these desirable
    articles, as he went, in the dust. Such a wretch richly
    deserves starvation." For more on the destruction of
    goods, see Benson, June 19; Stansbury, July 21; Farnham,
    June 19; McCall, June 19–21.

8. Carnes: two miles west of La Bonte Creek. F. D. Everts,
    Diary, 1849, June 21, noted that the creek was twelve feet
    wide and a foot deep.

9. The next day, perhaps twelve or fifteen miles to the east,
    Amos Steck wrote, "Passed some military who had ar-
    rested one young man for stealing a horse and yoke of
    oxen. Was bringing him back to Fort Laramie." Steck
    went on to claim, however, that the theft had occurred
    more than a hundred miles west of Fort Laramie. Even so,

it seems likely that Steck and Parke are referring to the same person.

10. Wistar was on La Bonte Creek on June 20 and wrote of "buffalo in countless masses," remarking that "it is hard to tell how these immense herds live on the thin and scattered grass."

11. Carnes names the same three trees and refers to La Prele Creek as swift and pure. Everts, June 22, noted that it was a rod wide and eighteen inches deep.

12. Carnes confirms the color, noting that the countryside turns red west of La Bonte Creek. When passing this spot the next day, Benson wrote: "Some of the hills in the distance have the appearance of blazing fires. We traveled in one continuous cloud of red smoky dust." McCall, June 21, commented on "a fine, red impalpable dust, very disagreeable to pass through." See Edward J. Willis, Diary, 1849, June 20; Bernard J. Reid, July 2; Farnham, June 21.

13. Carnes notes that the stream is twenty feet wide and clear. Everts, June 23, recorded twenty feet wide and eighteen inches deep. Foster, June 21, thought it to be thirty feet wide and two feet deep. The stream is now called Boxelder Creek.

14. Deer Creek, the largest tributary of the North Platte between the Laramie and Sweetwater rivers, was attractive, and many emigrants camped there. McCall, June 23, liked it because it was "a most lovely stream of clear crystal water, bordered by oak aspen groves. The woods were filled with camps and provided a brisk and lively appearance." See also Carnes and Everts, June 23. Benson, June 23, did not comment on the river but did say, "The country seems to be covered with camps, but little for the cattle to eat."

15. The North Platte River was ferried at the mouth of Deer Creek and at various points from there thirty miles up-stream on the North Platte. It was a very congested and dangerous place. Foster arrived here on June 22: "Found a ferry at the mouth of Deer Creek and hundreds of teams gathered around the creek; in the space of several miles were several ferries; stream rapid and difficult to ferry; several men drowned at one place by the upsetting of [their] raft in the current and five more in attempting to ride and drive over a lot of horses and mules." Benson, June 23, also cited the congestion and a drowning. A near drowning is recorded by Bernard J. Reid, July 2. See also Wood, June 21; McCall, June 25; Geiger and Bryarly, June 20 and 22; Jessie Gould Hannon, *The Boston-Newton Company Venture,* July 15. On July 25, Stansbury wrote of a drowning the day before: "They told us that this man made the twenty-eighth victim drowned in crossing the Platte this year; but I am inclined to believe this must be an exaggeration." As a matter of fact, this figure seems entirely reasonable, if not low.

16. The blacksmith operations were observed by McCall on June 23: "An extemporized smith shop was running, shoe-ing oxen and horses; wagons were being repaired." Al-most certainly this smithy was fueled with coal from nearby deposits. See Mann, June 23; Searls, July 3; Wistar, June 24; Hutchings, July 30; and Stansbury, July 25, who found a stratum of coal some three or four feet thick on the left bank of Deer Creek where the road crossed it. Spooner, June 20, also observed portable smithies using coal at the mouth of Deer Creek.

17. Carnes notes that the layover was for shoeing some of the oxen and doing related work.

18. McCall penned the following on June 23 at this site: "Some were washing and some mending; in fact almost everything was going on."

193

19. A great many ferry operations were flourishing by the latter half of June between Deer Creek and Mormon (Upper) Ferry, some thirty miles upstream. Some of these were run by people who were on the scene for some time, others by emigrants who dallied a few days and earned a little money by running ferries. Rather large numbers of overlanders purchased boats, rafts, and other vessels from emigrants just ahead, ferried themselves across, then sold the craft to those just behind. Some intrepid souls tried to ford the swollen North Platte, often with disastrous results. Unruh, *The Plains Across,* 258–59. The primary ferry services were those at the mouth of Deer Creek and those thirty miles upstream at Mormon Ferry, but there were many makeshift services all along the thirty-mile stretch.

20. Since Parke's outfit traveled only eighteen miles from Deer Creek before arriving at this ferry, almost certainly this is not Mormon Ferry. The many opportunities to cross almost anywhere in the thirty-mile stretch are illustrated by numerous diarists. For example, Searls wrote on July 3 from Deer Creek, "Emigrants are crossing from a short distance below us to a point thirty miles above, at every place practicable. The usual method is to prepare some two or three 'Dug Outs,' pin them together by means of cross timbers, thus forming a kind of scow capable of carrying a wagon. The builders, after crossing, sell out to some other company, who do the same to a succeeding one. Our company has purchased two of these rude machines, one near us and one two miles below." Along the thirty-mile stretch, he said, some two thousand wagons were trying to cross. For a similar account, see Benson, June 25. Somewhere between Deer Creek and Mormon Ferry, McCall (June 25) saw "a temporary ferry established by an emigrant" consisting of "three canoes rudely dug out from cotton-wood logs, and fastened together by hewed planks." When the craft was loaded, it was drawn across the river by oxen pulling ropes. On the return trip, the empty vessel was pulled across by hand. McCall's company bought the contrivance for seven dol-

lars and sold it to the next emigrant group for five. For more on ferry operations, including the threat of drowning, see Delano, *Life on the Plains*, June 18; Gray, June 18; Hutchings, July 31; Searls, July 5; Bruff, July 17–19; Bernard J. Reid, July 3–4; Dr. T, June 10 and 13; the Granville diarist, June 24–25; Joseph Hackney, Diary, 1849, June 21; William G. Johnston, *Overland to California*, June 4. So many people were funneled into this section of the river to ferry across it that Benson wrote on June 26: "The river bank has the appearance of a town with the encampments."

21.   Carnes: "A mule company was unfortunate. They drowned one of their mules in swimming them over. Accidents of this kind are by no means uncommon." Emigrant drownings also continued. J. B. Colton, writing on July 17, reported fifty drownings within a fifteen-mile stretch of the fording area, all within a week. *Oquawka Spectator*, October 3, 1849. He may have exaggerated the number of drownings, but others noted a number of people who drowned. Zirkle D. Robinson, *The Robinson-Rosenberger Journey*, June 14; Young, June 22; Chamberlain, June 20; Geiger and Bryarly, June 20.

22.   In the days immediately after the ferrying of the North Platte, complaints about cattle getting sick from alkali water were numerous. The region was comparatively inhospitable. On June 26 within a very short distance of Parke's company, McCall observed, "We are now in the Alkali region and the roadside is strewed with dead cattle, poisoned by drinking the water. We watch ours closely to prevent them from getting a draught of the dangerous element." Carnes mentions the problem, as did Benson on June 28–29. See also Johnston, June 5; Geiger and Bryarly, June 23; the Granville diarist, June 28; Bernard J. Reid, July 9; Dewolf, July 22.

23.   Carnes: "Unfortunately the lightning struck a whole team of 8 oxen dead, which had just been unleased of avoid the

storm. It descended upon the yoak of [the] hind cattle and followed the chains forward, killing all instantly. A man who was at the wagon off about 20 feet received a slight shock. No other damage done." Passing the site on June 27, McCall wrote: "A thunder storm came up and an emigrant, driving four yoke of cattle, wheeled them around out of the road so as to have the storm on their backs, when an electric spark struck them dead on the instant, and there the bloated carcasses lay side by side. The fluid [lightning] probably struck the chain to which they were attached. The driver was uninjured. Such are some of the calamities that befall men which no foresight or care could avoid." See also Benson, June 29, and the Granville diarist, June 28. In all likelihood, these were the carcasses Stansbury saw when he arrived July 27.

24. Maybe so, but at least one person found ground-up beetles quite tasty. One morning after he and his companions were tormented for hours by swarms of beetles, it was Niles Searls's turn to make coffee. He discovered that the coffee mill was full of dead beetles. Try as he could, he could not remove the beetles, so he poured the coffee beans into the mill and ground up both the beetles and the beans. He served the resulting beetle-flavored coffee to a friend, who liked the concoction so much that he suggested Searls always make the coffee. Searls, June 4.

25. McCall, June 26, described how the alkaline deposits formed "in broad and perfectly white sheets, from one to two inches thick, very much resembling snow." Two days later, Carnes saw some deposits and reported them to be several inches deep in places.

26. McCall, visiting Willow Springs on the evening of June 27: "There is here a small spring of fine, pure cold water which comes from the hills; it was far better than any we had tasted in some time, and the poor animals were allowed to drink their fill." Two days earlier, Wistar visited Willow Springs, sniffing at the "dwarf willow scrub,

NOTES TO PAGE 43

among which there was some scarce and bad water." Perhaps the storm on June 26 replenished the supply of pure water in the spring.

27. Carnes reports that the train did not start for Independence Rock until 1 P.M. The rock was a natural focal point for emigrants. The day before, for example, Mann wrote that some three hundred wagons had just camped there. Mann, June 27. The landmark, some nineteen hundred feet long, caught the attention of most diarists, many joining Benson (July 1) and Parke in noting its tortoise-like shape. Virtually every diarist who mentions Independence Rock refers to the thousands of names that were painted, tarred, carved, or chiseled onto or into the surface, causing the rock to be dubbed the Great Register of the Desert. Carnes writes: "Thousands of names are recorded by travelers, and this season has added more than all the previous ones." Since the rock is igneous and does not resemble other rocks in the vicinity, Chapman may have been closer to the truth than he suspected when he wrote on June 27, "It seems to have been ushered from the bowels of the earth." Independence Rock may have received its name from Tom Fitzpatrick, who cached furs there on July 4, 1824. Gregory Franzwa, *The Oregon Trail Revisited*, 258. Load lightening continued at the rock, goods being abandoned all around it.

28. Carnes notes that the river is forty feet wide, consists of good water, and is fordable. At the southwest end of a stretch of alkali flats and wretched water, the cold and sparkling waters of the Sweetwater were welcome relief.

29. These measurements grossly understate its size. In fact, the north end is more than 190 feet above the valley floor. Franzwa, *The Oregon Trail Revisited*, 257.

30. Unlike so many of the names that overlanders wrote on Independence Rock, this one survived for a while, at least until William Birdsall Lorton arrived on the scene on

197

July 13 and made a drawing of the rock that included "Como Company, Ill" on it.

31. Carnes writes: "It is about ¼ of a mile long, 40 yards wide, and now has verticle walls 400 feet high. The water is obstructed in the passage by broken fragments of rock, and in one place has a perpendicular fall of 10 feet." John F. Lewis, on the scene the same day Carnes and Parke were there, was much taken by Devil's Gate: "My curiousity led me to stroll up into it and found a greater curiousity than I have seen since I left home." Even more captivated was Stansbury, who wrote on July 31, "Through this romantic pass the river brawls and frets over broken masses of rock that obstruct its passage, affording one of the most lovely, cool, and refreshing retreats from the eternal sunshine." Devil's Gate lies some six miles west of Independence Rock and was an oft-mentioned landform on the Oregon Trail.

32. The relatively good mileage over difficult terrain, Carnes notes, was the product of a 5 A.M. departure.

33. Benson, July 2 and 3, noted that the grass was actually quite good. There was no need to haul oats. Carnes claims he found "luxurious grass."

34. Forty-niners continued to abandon surplus belongings as fatigue, disease, and other difficulties continued to take their toll of oxen and mules. The stench of dead animals impressed many emigrants. Carnes, July 2, saw twenty dead oxen, and on the same day Benson saw eight. Delano, *Life on the Plains,* June 28, attributed the oxen deaths to weariness and foul water but also suggested another cause: "the rarification of the air."

35. Perhaps referring to the same crime, Joseph Warren Wood wrote on July 1: "A man who was reported to be drowned in the Platte is suspected to have been murdered, and two men are arrested on the suspicion. I hear they are to be

198

tried on the 4th at S[outh] Pass." About two days east of South Pass on July 5, Sheldon Young reported, "There was a man arrested for murdering a man that was packing. Took his horses and four hundred dollars and put out. He committed the act on the Platte." Henry Rice Mann's account of July 4 is the lengthiest reference to the crime, although it is somewhat at odds with Parke's: "Judge Lynch is holding a court today at the Pacific Springs [just beyond South Pass] on the case of a man by the name of Reed. It seems that Reed and another man were packing through and Reed shot him through the heart, leaving him laying in the edge of the Sweetwater 10 miles east of the Pass. When he overtook a train that he was acquainted with, he gave out that his partner was drowned in crossing the Platte and he saw him go down the last time. He had some $400.00 in money, and the subsequent finding of the body, led to his arrest and he will probably never see California." On July 10, Mann again commented on the case: "I heard today that the man who had his trial near the South Pass for murder has been aquitted. No positive proof being adduced in the trial, and he is wending his way on to California with the rest of us." See also Foster, June 30–July 1, and McCall, July 2–3. An emendation was made at this point in Parke's diary in what appears to be Parke's hand: "This man was afterward hung by Vigalence Committee in California." It is possible that this flurry of legal activity pertains to more than one crime, but there is no evidence to this effect.

36. A tributary of the Sweetwater.

37. Many diarists reflected on the rather mundane appearance of South Pass. Charles Gould, Diary, 1849, for example, wrote on July 26, "We could hardly believe that we stood upon the dividing ridge between the Atlantic and the Pacific oceans. It seemed more like a rolling prairie." Geiger and Bryarly, June 29, claimed that people "generally have a very erroneous idea of this South Pass," observing that it was not narrow with rugged, towering walls on

both sides. Stansbury, August 6, referred to the locale by noting that it "has nothing remarkable in its features." Even so, virtually everyone was much impressed by the symbolic significance of crossing the Continental Divide because they realized that a great hurdle had been overcome. The pass, 7,550 feet in elevation, allows travelers relatively easy passage through the southern end of the Wind River Range of the Rockies. It was discovered in 1812, and its name is derived from the fact that it lies south of the passes used by Lewis and Clark.

38.   A reference to Robert Pollock. This must be an emendation or a rewriting of the diary, for James Pollock served as Whig governor of Pennsylvania from 1855 to 1858.

39.   In the mid-nineteenth century, perhaps more than at any other time in our nation's history, the Fourth of July was celebrated with abandon. Americans celebrated this day with speeches, exhortations, drinking, the firing of guns, and general merriment that often continued well into the night; overlanders were no exception to this public outpouring of national sentiment. McCall, July 4, referred to a "rousing salute" at dawn with guns and pistols, followed by speeches, drinking, the singing of boisterous and patriotic songs, and similar activities on "our great national holiday." Charles G. Hinman wrote of a celebration at South Pass. Bernard J. Reid, July 4, recorded "a jollification in honor of the 4th" consisting of "volleys, cheers, songs, toasts, and carousals." Both he and McCall said everyone reverted to childhood on this day. One emigrant engaged in a sort of national communion with his fellow countrymen elsewhere by imagining celebrations "in the cities and towns of our glorious Republic." Backus, July 4. Doyle and Gray are two of the very few emigrants who fail to mention festivities. See also Mann, July 5; Searls, July 4; Benson, July 4, who referred to a "fusilade in every direction"; Bruff, July 4, whose train enjoyed apple pie and wine; Geiger and Bryarly, July 4 and July 5; Delano, *Life on the Plains*, July 4.

40. About fifteen miles west of South Pass, emigrants crossed Dry Sandy, which is usually very nearly a dry gulch. Geiger and Bryarly, June 30, found water in it but wrote that neither man nor animal should drink it. Gray, June 30, "did not dare to trust the water." On the same day another overlander found it "not inaptly named, for it was the dry bed of a creek where salt and unpleasant water could anywhere be found at a depth of six or eight inches below the sand." Delano, *Life on the Plains*, June 30. See also Searls, July 19; Bruff, August 3; and Stansbury, August 6.

41. Located about three miles beyond the divide, Pacific Spring was something of an oasis amid bleakness. Its clear, cold waters produce Pacific Creek. Emigrants were very much aware that this was the first westward-flowing stream on their journey. Geiger and Bryarly pronounced the spring to be large, fine, and clear and noted that within a "fifteen minutes walk you can drink from the flowing waters of both the Atlantic & Pacific oceans." Geiger and Bryarly, June 29. Today the spring is surrounded by a bog.

42. Others commented on the poor grass and brackish water. Perhaps these conditions led to a sharp increase in the number of livestock that died. "We saw more dead cattle the first day after crossing the Pass than at any other time until we reached the Great Desert," writes Delano on June 28.

Chapter 4

1. Little Sandy received a mixed review from overlanders, some finding adequate food and water there and others finding the stench of dead livestock and little feed. See Delano, *Life on the Plains*, June 30; Bernard J. Reid, July 20; Benson, July 10; Geiger and Bryarly, June 30. Diarists McCall and Farnham do not mention Little

Sandy. Benson, July 10, found Big Sandy to be fifty yards wide and two feet deep. See Gray, July 2 and Bruff, August 4. Cross, July 18, reported good grass and water, especially when compared with the rather thin fare they had endured on Little Sandy: "Even the sound of the waters of Big Sandy, as it ran rapidly over its pebbly bottom, seemed to have a charm in it." The real significance of Big Sandy, however, lay in the fact that it was the jumping-off place for the trek across a desolate desert. Emigrants knew this and used Big Sandy to replenish food and water, rest, refit, and discard additional surplus goods. See Delano, *Life on the Plains,* July 1; Searls, July 20–22. Unfortunately for McCall and his companions, the rest and recuperation at Big Sandy was not pleasant or relaxing. The wind blew, sand flew into the face, and the men were in something of a snit. A squally time was had by all. McCall, July 8. He said those who had joined "Walkers' Train"—those who had left their trains and were proceeding west on foot—were especially snarly.

2. Estimates of distances vary according to variations in routes taken and the perceptions of diarists, but almost certainly it was about three miles from the divide at South Pass to Pacific Spring, about eleven miles farther to Dry Sandy, probably twelve or thirteen from Dry Sandy to Little Sandy, and six (or slightly more) from Little Sandy to Big Sandy.

3. Several miles east of Little Sandy crossing, Sublette's Cutoff veers straight west from the Oregon Trail and runs almost due west across Little Sandy and Big Sandy to cross Green River just downstream from La Barge Creek. (The Oregon Trail continues down Big Sandy toward Salt Lake City and is known as the Mormon Trail as a result.) It is possible that William Sublette, for whom the cutoff is named, blazed the way in 1832, but Caleb Greenwood may have used the route somewhat earlier (the route was first known as Greenwood's Cutoff). Although Sublette's

Cutoff took emigrants across bleak wasteland, it became popular very quickly and carried the bulk of the overland traffic.

4. Joseph E. Ware's thin volume *The Emigrants' Guide to California, 1849* was highly touted and widely used. It was also in serious error here. Ware had never been on the overland route, and his work was published hastily for the emigrant market of 1849. Perhaps the printer accidentally transposed the numerals, for all diarists recorded higher mileage, ranging for the most part between 45 and 55 miles, depending on where they started on Big Sandy and where they struck Green River. For example, Delano, *Life on the Plains,* July 1, recorded 54 miles; Searls, July 23, 52 miles; Cross, July 19, 50 miles; Carnes, July 8, 52 miles; Hale, July 5, 51¾ miles; Bernard J. Reid, July 22, 51 miles. Some of the suffering emigrants were so angry about their ordeal that they said Ware should be lynched for his mistake. Little did they know that Ware, making the overland trek himself that summer, became sick east of Fort Laramie, was abandoned by his friends, suffered much, and died miserably.

5. Carnes: "Country remarkably hilly and abrupt near the Green River." Cattle died by the score along the march, especially in the last few miles.

6. Carnes says the company arrived at the Green River at noon, thoroughly fatigued after some twenty hours of travel. Others who reached the river via Sublette's Cutoff also were exhausted. Gurdon Backus wrote on July 4: "We reached Green River at 11 o'clock a.m. where we camped . . . amid sand and sage, with poor grass for our jaded animals and about 170 wagons to go over before us. Having had no sleep last night and the weather being cold this morning, we feel depressed in spirits and long to see an end of this toilsome journey."

7. Almost certainly this statement contains an element of sarcasm. Emigrants complained about the cost of the

Mormon ferry service here. Some French Canadians, however, were providing an alternative ferry service as early as June 14, charging only three dollars per wagon. Cosad, June 14. Geiger and Bryarly, June 2, found the French Canadians charging eight dollars to ferry a load of three wagons. By the time John Benson arrived on July 11, a group of men from Iowa had established another ferry, albeit a temporary one: "There are two ferries, one conducted by the Mormons, and the other by men from Iowa. They charge $2.00 a wagon. Before the Iowans had set up this opposition ferry, the Mormons had charged $5.00 a wagon. We crossed with the Iowans. They have been here six days. They expect to leave tomorrow. Their company has gone on." (Benson also noted that the river was fast flowing, two hundred yards wide, about ten feet deep, and home to fish.) Since both Parke and Carnes cited a price of six dollars per wagon on July 9 at the Mormon ferry, perhaps the salutary effect of competition from the Iowans had not yet been felt. By July 23, however, conditions had changed, for on that day Searls and Bernard J. Reid recorded a price of two dollars per wagon. By mid-July, in fact, at least four competing ferries were functioning on a three-mile stretch of the river. Unruh, *The Plains Across,* 259. For more on the crossings at Green River, see Cross, July 20; Geiger and Bryarly, July 2; Delano, *Life on the Plains,* July 3–6; Gray, July 3; Bernard J. Reid, July 23; Doyle, July 8; Unruh, *The Plains Across,* 259.

8. The next day, however, Carnes says they had to drive cattle four miles to find grass.

9. It appears that some of these were the same individuals seen by Joseph Middleton, who arrived on August 4: "Yesterday afternoon went up the Creek a little way to a tent where there were 5 French-Canadian Indians, half-breeds, and some whites living with the Snake Indians with their squaws. Ten of them (the men) were playing at a game of cards called Monte. There was from $12 to $16

down on the red blanket every deal. One of them, a trader with the Indians, of the name of Robinson, called on us today and bought a pair of red blankets for $15 and a few other trifling things." Joseph Middleton, Diary, 1849–51, August 4. The game of monte was very popular among members of the gambling set that summer and in the gold fields of California. Writing from the river on July 25, Searls lamented: "Every few days we come across a canvas lodge occupied by some Canadian Frenchmen who dignifies his establishment by the name of trading post, though the name of 'Gambling Hell' would convey a more correct idea of its uses. In general, the proprietor is a man who, destitute of character, has wandered off among the Indians; and with a squaw for a wife, lives in all respects like the natives, except that he gambles to thrive in the region." See also Bruff, August 7; Farnham, July 11; Bernard J. Reid, June 23; Cosad, June 14; and Carnes, July 9.

10. Carnes saw Captain Hawkins "of the Arazona Train" on July 8.

11. One of them may have been that of a man who drowned July 9 while trying to swim a horse across the river. Carnes, July 9.

12. The small stream was probably Fontenelle Creek, a tributary of Green River. Carnes confirms both the good water and snowdrifts at least twenty feet high.

13. It was Ham's Fork, which joins Black's Fork near the Mormon Trail, from which point the combined waters flow into the Green River. They nooned there, Carnes reporting that the river "abounds with fish." The next day, July 14, Farnham and his companions nooned in the same place, caught some fine trout, and found that Ham's Fork was about two and a half rods wide and three and a half feet deep.

14. At almost exactly the same place five days earlier, another overlander had lamented, "The musquitoes were larger &

more numerous here than any place we have yet passed. Many of our men who are not used to such plagues in life were much troubled by them, their sting proving very poisonous." Geiger and Bryarly, July 8.

15. Carnes confirms that this was the Thomas Fork and mentions a good supply of fine grass.

16. According to Carnes, it was necessary to lock the two rear wheels to slow the descent. Even so, one wagon turned over.

17. The Snake Indians were also known as Shoshones. Carnes writes: "Some Indians and traders encamped here and Mormons, butchering and selling beef to other emigrants." For more on the Indians, consult Delano, *Life on the Plains,* July 10. This trading post was established by Thomas L. ("Pegleg") Smith, a colorful mountain man. He was born in Kentucky in 1801 and spent his early years in the Southwest, trapping and stealing horses from the Spaniards. While near the headwaters of the South Platte, he was shot in the left leg just above the ankle. Using a knife and a saw, and possibly with some help from companions, he amputated his shattered limb himself and then spent time with the Ute Indians, recovering and being fitted with a wooden leg. By 1848 he established his trading post, consisting of four cabins and some Indian dwellings, near present-day Dingle, Idaho. He carried on trade with Indians and others. By all accounts he was intelligent, happy, and hospitable. He had a number of Indian wives and numerous offspring; his wife at this trading post was sixteen and a bit plump. Misfortune dogged him, and by 1860 he was living near San Francisco, dying there in October 1866 under greatly reduced circumstances. Chamberlain, July 8, found him to be quite rich, hospitable, and kindly toward the Indians, having saved a number of them from starvation the previous winter. Mann, July 13–14, wrote that Smith was "a liberal-hearted old fellow" who had an "interesting squaw." For

more on this celebrated figure, see Hixson, June 26; James A. Pritchard, *The Overland Diary of James A. Pritchard,* July 18; Farnham, July 18; Delano, *Life on the Plains,* July 12; Geiger and Bryarly, July 10; Bruff, August 15; Paden, *The Wake of the Prairie Schooner,* 272–73; Hale, June 15–17; Shaw, *Across the Plains in Forty-nine,* 99; John Steele, *In Camp and Cabin,* 276–77; Alfred Glen Humphreys, "Thomas L. (Peg-leg) Smith," 311–30; Unruh, *The Plains Across,* 248, 264, 389.

18.   It is possible that the sick man was either a person by the name of Titus or a person by the name of Bay. Both were at Smith's trading post on July 17 and both were sick. It is entirely likely that Parke saw one of them before he left the trading post. Hale, July 16–17.

19.   Almost all diarists mention the scores of springs found here, especially Soda Springs, Steamboat Spring, and Hooper Spring. Hale, July 20, says Soda (or Beer) Springs "did not boil like the others but was rather sour. It tasted like the bottled soda of St. Louis." Delano, *Life on the Plains,* July 13, was impressed: "These springs are one of the greatest luxuries on the whole route. They are highly charged with carbonic gas, and are as delicious as they are refreshing." See also Cross, August 1; Bernard J. Reid, August 2; Geiger and Bryarly, July 11, who gave a detailed account; Searls, August 5; Bruff, August 17, who claimed that only lemon syrup was needed to make a perfect soda drink; according to Geiger and Bryarly, July 11, cooks found that the water's soda content made bread rise without the need for anything else; Farnham, July 20, wrote extensively on the springs, and his description of Steamboat Spring is likewise excellent. Carnes makes many comments on the springs, noting that some of the men drank a great deal from the springs and suffered no ill effects. Although most of the springs, including Steamboat Spring, are now submerged under the impounded waters of Soda Point Reservoir, Hooper Spring still delights visitors.

20. Alexander Crater lies just over seven miles west of Soda Springs. Set in the midst of a bleak plain, the cone of cinders rises some one hundred feet above the surrounding plain and has an interior depth of perhaps sixty feet. Delano, *Life on the Plains,* July 14, saw two craters and walked to the southernmost: "Its form was conical, about eighty feet high, the crater being oval shaped, and probably two hundred feet in its greatest diameter, and about forty feet deep." See also Bernard J. Reid, August 2, and Farnham, July 20. Carnes observed that volcanic fragments made the road difficult.

21. Near the western edge of present-day Alexander and just northwest of a very sharp bend in Bear River, Hudspeth Cutoff struck a course almost straight west for some distance. (The cutoff was also known as Myers Cutoff and Emigrant Cutoff.) Benoni Morgan Hudspeth and John J. Myers audaciously led a train due west from Soda Springs on July 19, 1849, cutting some twenty-five miles off the established route, which bore northwest to Fort Hall. Hudspeth was the train's captain, Myers its guide. Myers had spent a number of years trapping in California and elsewhere in the West. The train they led was from Jackson County, Missouri, had 70 wagons and 250 people representing a motley assortment of humanity; fortunately, both Hudspeth and Myers were excellent managers of people. Although the cutoff they began to establish on July 19 was rough and challenging, most forty-niners and later overlanders used it, causing Fort Hall to suffer a loss of trade. Hudspeth's Cutoff became popular so quickly that when Farnham arrived at the junction the next day, July 20, he was simply amazed at how many people were using it. Parke and his companions, using the route the very day Hudspeth and Myers blazed it, were among the very first people across it. Although Parke was quite restrained in his reaction to the novelty of the situation, Carnes was much more impressed: "We fell in with the train of Hawkins of 64 wagons, and they have a guide who has been this route with Fremont. There was never a

wagon across it yet." This was the only major new route established by forty-niners. A few weeks later, Hudspeth and Myers led their train on a difficult and circuitous journey through northern California, for which they received much blame.

22. Almost certainly Fish Creek.

23. The large stream is the Portneuf River and the last stream is Dempsey Creek. Both Parke and Carnes claim to have crossed the Pannack River. Actually, the Bannock (also spelled *Pannock*) lies well to the west.

24. Carnes says the road was good but notes that the country was broken, steep, and dusty.

25. Carnes writes that the group ascended a hill for eight miles and then descended into a beautiful valley that had wood, grass, and water.

26. This is probably the Little Malad River, which is the first river Parke and his companions encountered, after taking the Hudspeth Cutoff, that flows south into the Great Salt Lake.

27. According to Carnes it was already dark when they arrived at the summit.

28. Carnes writes that it was a good spring, one set in a grove of aspens and willows. He also indicates that cattle were giving the company problems. Strope had lost an ox the previous evening, and on the evening of July 23 it took until 10 P.M. to get the animals corralled.

29. The company was now in the land of the Diggers, who were reviled by virtually every emigrant who saw them. Their name was derived from the fact that they used sticks to dig in the earth for roots and little animals, which they then ate, a practice emigrants found loathsome. On the same day, July 23, and just a few miles to the east, Elijah

209

Farnham came across some Diggers who made a very unfavorable impression on him: "We saw Indians today more filthy than any that we had before seen. These are the diggers, a tribe the most degraded of all. These it is said live upon ants & grasshoppers—anything that crawls. Yes, they pick lice out of their heads and eat them. We saw them do it. And we did not wish to be near them." Another practice of the Diggers enraged the emigrants even more: at night they lurked around emigrant camps and at opportune moments shot arrows into the livestock, causing the forty-niners to abandon the disabled animals. The next morning, the emigrants sometimes would travel only a few hundred feet before they saw the Diggers descend on the disabled animals to feast. See Hale, August 6, 9, 15, 16; Farnham, August 19; Wood, August 1, who said they were the ugliest and most treacherous tribe of Indians he had encountered; Dewolf, September 17; Wilkins, September 21; Delano, *Life on the Plains,* July 29, August 3, 6, 8; Bernard J. Reid, August 22, September 16; Bruff, September 3, 9; Castleman, October 4; McCall, August 14, 24; Gray, July 28; Hutchings, September 23–25.

30. Carnes corroborates Parke's comments about sage, but he also notes good feed and water. He adds that during the day they could see the Great Salt Lake from the tops of mountains.

31. Carnes claims they moved out at noon, not one o'clock. One of the reasons for the late start may have been the fact that they did not succeed in getting their animals corralled until 11 P.M. the previous evening. Carnes, July 24. Writing on the evening of July 24, Carnes, knowing they were a short distance from the Fort Hall Road, claimed they had saved forty miles by taking the Hudspeth Cutoff, certainly something of an exaggerated figure. Some who took the cutoff, such as Elijah Farnham, made no claim concerning miles saved. Joseph Wood, who took the Fort Hall route instead of Hudspeth's Cutoff, hooted a bit at

those who chose the latter. Coming down from Fort Hall, he encountered the train led by Hudspeth and Myers: "Capt. Hudspeth's train of 60 wagons under the direction of Myers as guide left the old road at the north bend of Bear River to strike west across the hills and make a cut-off, instead of going north to Fort Hall. We took the old road and our train parted from his at the point of the Cutoff. He got to his place two hours before we did, and we are now ahead of him. He undoubtedly saved two days' drive in distance, but lost it in time on account of breaking a road." Wood then conceded, "Some future trains may be benefitted by the cutoff," an observation that was already true.

32. Carnes: the group started at 5:30 A.M. and arrived at the road three miles after crossing a creek.

33. This was Cassia (also spelled *Cachia* and *Cache*) Creek, and Parke was heading west toward present-day Connor.

34. Camp was probably twelve miles or so northeast of present-day Almo. Joseph Wood, traveling the same route on July 26, wrote, "Feed in this valley has been good so far, though rather course," then added at evening camp, "We have good feed tonight." Carnes concurs, noting that feed and water were good but adding that the roads were very dusty because of the presence of light clay.

35. Carnes found a number of good springs at evening's camp, which was located in what later became known as the City of Rocks, some four or five miles southwest of present-day Almo. The City of Rocks was a truly impressive assortment of rock formations and did much to excite the imagination of overlanders. Carnes, for example, writes of "tall spires and jags of rocks" that reminded him of "the spires of village churches." He declared it to be "one of the wildest places we have yet seen." Joseph Wood, viewing the scene in the morning of July 27, wrote: "The hills here are the roughest the imagination can con-

ceive. Bare granite rocks are heaved up hundreds of feet high and stand isolated or compose large hills. They assume fantastic forms, are white and beautiful. There are ledges of mica slate, and micaceous quartz abounds also." His afternoon travel led him to more striking formations. Bernard J. Reid, August 11, wrote of "sphynxes and statues of every size, and haystacks and wigwams and castles, towers, and pyramids and cones and projecting turrets and canopies, and leaning columns, and so on throughout a thousand varieties of fantastic shapes." Bruff, August 29, has a lengthy and interesting account; See also Geiger and Bryarly, July 19; Wilkins, August 13; Lord, August 17; Hutchings, September 14. Farnham, July 30, was one of the very few diarists who passed through these weird landforms without recording his thoughts.

36. Emigrants followed Goose Creek, a tributary of the Snake, upstream and entered Nevada. The route to Goose Creek took Parke by the junction of the road to Salt Lake City, across a tributary of the Raft River, through Granite Pass, and across the rough terrain surrounding Birch Creek, a tributary of Goose Creek.

37. Carnes writes that they got an early start, enjoyed a good road, had fine grass and water, and six miles after leaving camp came to the road to Salt Lake City, the western end of the Salt Lake Cutoff. (He claimed the city was 183 miles from the junction.) The junction served to fuse that stream of emigrants which had veered off toward Salt Lake City just west of South Pass with the stream that went west from South Pass to Soda Springs and beyond. The migration traffic was once again surging westward along a single route. There was a "post office" here for overland emigrants. Delano, July 23. It consisted of a number of sticks driven into the ground to which notes and letters were attached for emigrants still behind.

38. Carnes wrote that the road was very hilly the last twelve miles. The last part, the section west of Granite Pass, was especially wretched. The Granville diarist, for example,

wrote on July 31: "If those hills was [*sic*] in the States, no body would try going down one of them with a loaded wagon." Farnham, also July 31, gives a vivid picture of the descent, as does Bernard J. Reid, August 12. See also Hutchings, September 14; Geiger and Bryarly, July 20. The river bottom was home to Goose Creek, from which Geiger and Bryarly, July 20, pulled some fine trout.

39. An obvious error. It was Sunday, not Saturday.

40. Camp was probably in or near a dry wash several miles west of the point where Goose Creek turns sharply north. Problems were very severe along this stretch of the overland trek and produced crises in a number of trains. Carnes writes of cold nights—ice forming a quarter-inch thick—and blistering-hot days, conditions aggravated by poor water, inferior grass, and a road laced with volcanic cinders and "black glass." These factors and general exhaustion resulted in death for many oxen and other animals. Grumbling was rampant, social cohesion spongy, and morale weak, causing many trains to disintegrate and not a few people to become a bit unhinged. Joseph Wood, writing on July 29 from almost exactly the same place as Parke, observed of his company, "The boys in the other team are talking about dividing their things, and I suppose they will." He then wrote that they had in fact split.

41. Carnes attributes the early start to the need to find water and feed.

42. Carnes's account is at variance with Parke's on a couple of details. Carnes says they traveled ten miles before coming to Well Spring, not thirteen. He records a noon layover until 4 P.M. to let the livestock rest. The evening camp was probably on the upper reaches of Rock Springs Creek, which constitutes the northern arm of the Thousand Springs Valley drainage basin.

43. Carnes records a 6 A.M. start and notes a good road that was level. The springs impressed him: "Here is something

worthy of note." Carnes stresses that these were hot *sulfur* springs and that they were "hot enough to boil eggs in 10 minutes." The main stream, he says, was eight feet wide and a foot deep. See also Farnham, August 3, and Wood, July 30–31.

44. "Here we took a bath," Carnes writes, adding, "We could choose such temperatures as suited, from almost ice cold to 170 degrees of Fahrenheit." He notes that the whole region had a volcanic character.

45. Two routes lead from Thousand Springs Valley to the Humboldt River. The more difficult of the two strikes southwest through Bishop Creek Canyon. The other heads in a more southerly direction toward present-day Wells before turning west. Parke and his companions took the latter route, and that evening they were rewarded for their efforts with "the greatest abundance of excellent feed." Carnes, August 2.

46. This refers to one of three or four streams that flow northwest from the northern edge of the East Humboldt Range into Bishop Creek, which is one of the major tributaries of the East Fork of the Humboldt River.

47. Joseph Wood was on the scene the same day, August 3, and wrote that "clover abounds here." Carnes: "Not a tree is to be found, but the river bottom is a mile wide" and "covered with a heavy growth of nutritious grasses, such as blue joint clover, and a wild wheat, and other seed grasses."

Chapter 5

1. The North Fork of the Humboldt.

2. Emigrants were forced to cross and recross the Humboldt River many times to find the path of least resistance.

214

Endless fording, stenchy water, offensive Diggers, and rotting carcasses combined to make the Humboldt route a path of misery and woe. Even so, had it not been for the Humboldt River, it is safe to claim, virtually no company would have been able to traverse northern and central Nevada. Clearly, the silvery (and often muddy) ribbon of water was the means of sustenance for those rushing west for gold. The river supplied feed, water, and game, enabling people and animals to forge on. Alonzo Delano passed through this place on July 30 and recorded the presence of ducks, sage hens, geese, cranes, and fish. Charles Gray was there August 4 and wrote, "Four of our shooters went out early, & at noon returned with 51 large Sage hens, about the size of full grown fowls." Three days later he wrote, "The hunters again brought in 30 fine birds." See also Wood, August 5–6.

3.   Carnes says the camp was on the east bank of the river.

4.   Probably Maggie Creek near present-day Carlin.

5.   This valley is Emigrant Canyon, which enters the Humboldt River bottom about six miles east of present-day Beowave. Camp was near Gravelly Ford. During the day, Carnes complained that "the clouds of dust [are] almost insufferable," and wrote the next day that "our camp last night was a poor one. Everything is dust." Traveling within perhaps twenty miles of Parke this day, Charles Gray was much bothered: "The dust today was excessively thick & of a different character from any I have seen before, it acted upon me like lime, burning & irritating the skin." Gray, August 7. Not far away, Delano reported on August 7: "The ashy dust was very deep, and when we turned aside to find better walking, the parched and dry alkaline crust broke under our feet like frozen snow, making it excessively fatiguing to walk." Joseph Wood was practically traveling with Parke's company on August 7 and wrote of an ox which was "nearly blind on account of the dust." Dust was only one problem confronted by

overlanders at this point. Brackish water, poor feed, increasing depredations by the wily Diggers, and general fatigue continued to take their heavy toll. Wagon trains disintegrated, individuals bailed out of companies and joined "Walkers' Train," and still others sought to remedy their unfavorable situation by ousting their leaders and pushing on with new ones. Individuals responded to the hardships of the Humboldt in different ways. Elijah Farnham, for the first time on the overland journey, rode instead of walking. Farnham, August 9. Those who served guard duty at night took to firing their weapons into the night to keep away real or imaginary wolves and Diggers. Delano, *Life on the Plains,* August 6 and 8. Other individuals became excessively contentious and fights broke out. An emigrant a few days behind Parke's company wrote, "The boys got to disputing and had a little 'knock down,' nothing serious," then added, "It is strange that there is no more fighting than there is, for the men seem to have lost all restraint." Clearly, life in the Great Basin was rough, but every overlander knew that ahead lay the Sierra Nevada.

6. Traveling through this area on August 14, Ansel McCall wrote that he and his companions had been warned about the Diggers: "It is said they use a poisoned arrow with which they wound cattle from which they are sure to die. Their dead carcasses furnish them with sumptuous feasts." From the same general area Delano reported on August 3 that "manifestations of Indian hostility began to appear. We saw an ox which had been shot during the night with arrows, which were found sticking in him in the morning. The same company lost several head of oxen the same night, and taking their trail into the mountains, found the remains of two, which the Indians had slaughtered and eaten." See also Geiger and Bryarly, August 1–3; Gray, August 11; Wood, August 8. To prevent depredations by Diggers, wagon trains increased their security at night and guards became much more prone to fire. Those who sought to punish thievish Diggers by sallying up ravines

after elusive Indians were sometimes rewarded for their efforts by being made to step lively by Diggers who rolled boulders down the hills or suddenly turned and fired at their pursuers.

7. This is Stony Point, which is several miles northeast of present-day Battle Mountain.

8. Carnes confirms distance, direction, and condition of vegetation. He also describes the surface of the land: "The soil is a whitish limey clay at this season perfectly dry for several feet in depth."

9. Israel Hale passed through this area in the middle of August, writing on the fifteenth: "It has been their custom to cripple stock in such a way that it would become useless to the owner and they would leave it, when the Indians would return and carry off the meat. But this year they pursue another course. They drive off cattle, horses, and mules and in large numbers. We have passed several wagons that had lost their stock by the Indians and were unable to pursue their journey in consequence of it." Actually, the Diggers continued to disable as well as steal. On August 11, John F. Lewis wrote from a spot quite close to Parke: "There is great complaint here of the root digger indians shooting and steeling. Passed a train of 3 waggons this morning which last night lost 10 of their cattle. 5 others were wounded. The arrows still remained in them til they were found." And then he repeated an oft-told complaint about the elusive nature of the Diggers: "We are never able to see one of the indians." For more on disabling and theft, see Kirkpatrick, August 11.

10. This person's name appears in no contemporary account, census, or history. Evidently, Parke knows the individual, but Carnes fails to mention him. Perhaps this man was the person Delano encountered on July 25–26, "a gentleman named Beckwith, from Rock Island, Illinois." Beckwith and another man were riding horses to California after

abandoning their wagons, cattle, and other belongings. In any case, the presence of individuals and small groups on foot and on horseback indicates dissolution of many wagon trains. This fact was noted by Elijah Farnham, who passed through several days later: "There are a great many packers along here now. They have a great time of it a camping in the willows or in the dust plains at night without tenting." And see Delano, *Life on the Plains,* August 11. The "low hills" that were crossed were those located several miles northeast of present-day Golconda, and camp was probably straight north of Golconda across the river.

11. Carnes says there was a "marshy flat cut up by sloughs filled by bullrushes. Here the grass is excellent and in great abundance." D. Jagger was a day or two ahead of Parke at this point and wrote on August 12, "Here we encamped and, as we expected to find no more feed for 70 miles, picketed our animals, cut the grass, and carried it for nearly a mile through water knee deep, and they fared sumptuously." Joseph Wood, arriving on the scene August 13, wrote, "We found excellent feed for our cattle, but the grass generally is dry and dead. Fires have run in places, and it makes the prospects look dark for those who are far behind." He added, "The water in the stream is becoming poor & muddy, & as it dries down it will be still worse." See also Geiger and Bryarly, August 3, and Holliday, *The World Rushed In,* 239.

12. Carnes grumbles about the difficulty of getting through the sand and says the roads were "the worst roads yet seen." See also Farnham, August 20, and Wood, August 13.

13. Carnes confirms this, adding that the cattle were much fatigued. Referring to the difficulties of traveling through sand, Joseph Wood wrote on August 13, "The oxen stand it the best & have exceeded the expectations of their owners while mules and horses have fallen short." Another person who had a high regard for the stamina of

oxen was Bolivar Krepps, who wrote home from California on October 13, "I never knew the amount of hardships
and suffering an ox was capable of enduring until I came
on this trip."

14. Three trans-Sierra routes existed by mid-August: the Carson route, the Truckee route, and Lassen Cutoff. The
cutoff noted by Parke is the Lassen, or, as it is sometimes
called, the Applegate-Lassen Cutoff. Named for Peter
Lassen, the route was used by many diarists: Farnham,
Doyle, Foster, Middleton, Hinman, Delano, the Granville diarist, Hale, Gray, Bruff, Benson, Wistar, and others. Since it skirted the northern edge of the awesome
Sierra Nevada Range, its main advantage was the absence
of a rampart barrier, such as that found at Donner Pass, an
unhappy place well known to emigrants in 1849. However, the Lassen Cutoff suffered from a number of disad-
vantages: the terrain over which it ran was rugged; the
deserts were bad, especially the Black Rock Desert of
northwestern Nevada; and the total distance for those
taking this route to the Sacramento Valley exceeded the
distances of the other two routes by 135 miles. One of the
fundamental problems with the Lassen Cutoff was that
nobody really knew what lay along the trail; it was, in its
essential features, unknown. Even so, since Hudspeth and
Myers and others were known to have taken it, by August 20 large numbers of people used it, so many in fact
that traffic heading toward the Humboldt Sink was reduced to a trickle. In 1849 at least eight thousand people
entered California via this route, at least seven thousand
used the Truckee route, and some six thousand took the
Carson route. For the most part, those who used Lassen
Cutoff in the hope of avoiding difficulties were keenly
disappointed. Delano and Bruff were only two of the
diarists who recorded difficulties. The rigors of this route
humbled even John J. Myers—the "great desert god"—
and his party. See Stewart, *The California Trail*, 215–16,
269, 272–92; Donald Dale Jackson, *Gold Dust*, 195–96,
198–99; Holliday, *The World Rushed In*, 247–51.

15. This is not Dr. William Swain, who was some five weeks behind Parke.

16. Carnes confirms the rain. On the same day, Henry Rice Mann, traveling only a few miles away, wrote, "We had a novelty this afternoon in the shape of a copious shower, the first we have seen since we struck the Sweetwater. It was delightful travelling after it, roads being good and weather cool." Parke referred to the "Sink," but this was not the Sink of the Humboldt, which was still several days' travel away.

17. Carnes claims the banks were fifty to one hundred feet high. Today they vary widely in height, from only a few feet to perhaps one hundred. In any case, Carnes says steep, high banks kept the stock from getting to the water, which accentuated their thirst and overall misery. He makes no effort to explain why the emigrants did not bring water to the cattle. Perhaps the quality of the water was poor; perhaps the emigrants were too weary.

18. Carnes refers to this place as "a high plain which is perfectly barren."

19. This was probably just southeast of present-day Lovelock. Carnes appreciates the fact that it had "plenty of grass and water." The lush abundance of grass here stood in sharp contrast to the scarcity of grass during the past several days. As a result, a number of trains stopped here and at places a day's journey or two just beyond. Some stopped for several days to cut grass, cure it, and recover from recent travel.

20. Carnes is elated by the superb grass: "The luxuriousness of this slough is unsurpassed." He describes the plain as "being clothed with a heavy coat of green virdure. This affords great relief to the already jaded animals and is a splendid place to recruit them for a journey of 60 miles [across the desert to the Truckee River] without a single spear of grass."

21. The Sink of the Humboldt was ahead. Parke and his companions arrived there on August 22, at which time Carnes wrote that the Humboldt River disappears by sinking into sand and by evaporation. He puts the dimensions of the sink at fifteen miles by five miles or ten miles.

22. Almost certainly Leonard H. Woodworth, who had settled just across the river from Sterling in Coloma Township not far from Daniel Brooks and Isaac Merrill. Originally from the Northeast, he went to California in 1849 and returned to Illinois by 1851, where he served in several low-level offices in Whiteside County. He is listed in *Holland's Sterling–Rock Falls Directory for 1875–76*, 178. The federal census of 1850 lists an Alice Woodworth, age twenty-nine, from Vermont, and three children, including Leonard, who was fourteen and born in Illinois. Dora Wilson Smith, *Whiteside County, Illinois, 1850 Census*, 17. See also Royal Brunson Way, *The Rock River Valley*, I:636, and Bent, *History of Whiteside County, Illinois*, 126–31. According to one source, Leonard Woodworth traveled west in 1849 as part of an Odd Fellow outfit: "The Odd-Fellow Wagon, from Chicago consisting of H. P. Woodworth, Wm. H. Hebbie, L. H. Woodworth, Sterling, Ill." *Frontier Guardian* of May 30, 1849.

23. Carnes: Sulphur Springs was five miles below the sink, and they arrived there at 4 P.M. McCall, August 27, called the springs "a slimy, filthy place, and the water really unfit for man or beast. It is fetid and acrid, but necessity compels its use." Geiger and Bryarly were here on August 11, and it is possible that the water was not so bad then: "The water was very like many of our sulphur springs at home. The animals drank it freely & it seemed to do them no harm."

24. Geiger and Bryarly, August 11, agreed with Parke's description of the route, noting that it was "as smooth as a table & hard as a rock." Carnes writes that in the morning

they passed through countryside consisting of loose ashes eighteen inches deep in places.

25. During the night's journey, they passed the point where the Carson River route forked off to the left. Along the same stretch on the same day, Henry R. Mann observed, "The road was strewen with dead cattle, waggons, long chains, and ox yokes. I have counted more than 200 chains in the last 16 miles." He noted the same day at Boiling Springs that some people were boiling meat and some were boiling clothes. Carnes found Boiling Springs barely adequate for cooking, but he was happy to report, "Here we had a cup of tea without the aid of fire." John Prichet, August 17, noted that the water temperature exceeded 190 degrees Fahrenheit but claimed it made men and animals sick. The springs served yet another purpose: forced at last to abandon many of their remaining possessions, some weary overlanders—perhaps out of anger or spite— dumped them into the springs. Also, whether by accident or by design, animals also wound up in the boiling water. Paden, *The Wake of the Prairie Schooner,* 432. One emigrant reported that some oxen and a little dog were killed by jumping into the boiling water. Jagger, August 19; Geiger and Bryarly, August 12, 13, and 15; and McCall, August 29, who provided a detailed description of the springs. They were much more than a curiosity; in reality, they were the only natural source of water to be found in the blistering wasteland north of the Truckee River.

26. The Truckee River, also known as the Salmon Trout, was named by John C. Frémont in 1844. *Report of the Exploring Expedition,* 316. The Truckee route was first called North Pass. Its advantage over the Carson River route lay in the fact that water was available at Boiling Springs; the major disadvantage was that the Truckee route went through Donner Pass, a notoriously difficult one. Moreover, the Truckee route twisted through narrow canyons, but the Carson did not. For those taking the Truckee, it was necessary to cross the river dozens of times; those taking

the Carson route did not have to cross that river once. The fork dividing the Truckee route from the Carson was about twenty-five miles southwest of present-day Lovelock near the junction of Interstate 80 and U.S. 95. Paden, *The Wake of the Prairie Schooner*, 459–60, and Stewart, *The California Trail*, 206, 292.

27.   Carnes confirms these points. Henry R. Mann reached the Truckee River at 1 P.M. the same day. After writing that "hundreds were compelled to leave their wagons and drive their stock to the river, water them, and go back after their loads," he said, "The river was a beautiful, bold mountain stream, lined with the cotton wood and willow." The trees were the first they had seen for weeks. For more on impressions of the Truckee, see Geiger and Bryarly, August 13; McCall, August 29.

Chapter 6

1.   Carnes confirms the seven crossings. He notes that most of the trees were one thousand to fifteen hundred feet up the mountainsides and says the "Truckee River is a fine stream of pure water," observing that it was three feet deep and had large loose stones in its bed.

2.   Geiger and Bryarly, August 16, related some amusing incidents of people and mules trying to ford the river, but some individuals were not at all amused by what they found. The rocks on the bottom were very loose and treacherous, which caused several drownings.

3.   Carnes confirms the seven river crossings and says the morning's travel was through a canyon. In the afternoon they forded twice, he says.

4.   Carnes also calls this basin "Muddy Valley" and assigns it a width of ten miles. The calm waters of the slough "are

well stored with fish, the chief kind Salmon Trout," he says. One emigrant wrote of "blue grass to the horses' knees" in the "beautiful, green, velvety valley, which, upon first coming in view, presented a most cheering appearance." Boggy conditions caused some difficulty, he said. Geiger and Bryarly, August 17.

5. Carnes says that by the end of the day they had forded the Truckee twenty-seven times since encountering it.

6. Geiger and Bryarly, August 19, referred to "large trees of pine, cypress, & lignum vitae. The banks of the river & the sides of the mountain are also covered with them."

7. The basin, Carnes writes, was about a mile from the summit. He adds that the atmosphere here reminded him of atmospheric conditions back in the States in October.

8. Probably the same valley Geiger and Bryarly wrote about on August 20: "A beautiful little valley with a very steep hill to descend to it. We went down in the valley & nooned. This valley is oval in shape & had plenty of good grass & water in it."

9. Organized by George and Jacob Donner, this party numbered nearly one hundred when it left Independence in the spring of 1846. Swelling to nearly two hundred through additions along the way, the party divided at Fort Bridger. The smaller group, numbering eighty-seven, experienced delay, extreme hardship, and social disintegration before becoming trapped in the Sierra Nevada and reverting to cannibalism. See Bernard DeVoto, *The Year of Decision: 1846;* George R. Stewart, *Ordeal by Hunger.*

10. On August 21, 1849, Wakeman Bryarly saw the same structure: "This [cabin] was still standing. It was two in one, there being a seperation of logs between. The timbers were from 8 inches to a foot in diameter, about 8 or 9 feet high & covered over with logs upon which had been

placed branches & limbs of trees, dirt, &c. The logs were fitted very nicely together, there being scarcely a crevice between. There was one door to each, entering from the north and from the road." He then mentioned finding animal bones, human bones, and fragments of clothes. Henry R. Mann, August 29, saw this cabin and the others and referred to them as "cannibal cabins." He, too, saw bones and pieces of clothing scattered all around. John Prichet, August 25, visited the site and found clothes and human bones strewn around the cabins.

11. Parke seems to have doubts that cannibalism was practiced here. Bryarly, August 21, had no doubts and found evidence to support his thinking. Near one cabin he "found many human bones. The skulls had been sawed open for the purpose, no doubt, of getting out the brains, & the bones had all been sawed open & broken to obtain the last particle of nutriment." He added, "There seems to be a sad, melancholy stillness hanging around these places, which serves to make a gloom around you, which draws you closer & closer in your sympathies with those whom hunger compelled to eat their own children, & finally to be eaten by others themselves, & their bones now kicked perhaps under any one's feet."

12. Carnes concludes that the snow must have been six feet deep since the stumps of the trees used to build the Donner cabins are at least six feet high. Mann, August 29, wrote, "The trees are chopped off about 10 feet from the ground, showing the depth of the snow." It is not unlikely that the height of the stumps varied according to the depth of the snow. For a lengthy account on the Donner tragedy by a forty-niner, see McCall, September 7. A superb account of the Donner site and the events associated with it is found in Markle, August 20.

13. Overwhelmed by the stupendous difficulties, Carnes exclaims, "This is the elephant." As was true of so many emigrants that summer, the Sierra Nevada proved to be

the last straw. Parke, Carnes, and the others had to man-handle the wagons up to the summit, the animals alone being unable to pull the loads over the tortuous trail, which existed in little more than name alone. The party finally reached the summit at 6 P.M., Carnes writes, at which time "we gave loud and long cheers for our success." They could see green valleys beyond.

14. The presence of good grass is confirmed by Carnes, who also observes, "The country is timbered the whole way with the largest trees I ever saw."

15. Missourians were known as pukes because of the way the Missouri River "pukes" into the Mississippi River just above St. Louis.

16. Wakeman Bryarly trekked along here on August 23 and was deeply impressed by the condition of the road: "The road was rougher than we have before seen it, immense large rocks. The road was also up & down hill; one in particular, about 5 miles from starting, was so rough & steep as to have to let our wagons down by ropes. In getting thus far we passed 6 lakes, some upon each side, & of considerable size, measuring several miles in length." Carnes writes simply: "The road is of the worst kind to day—one pile of rocks, peak after peak." He says they camped at the foot of the peak and reports that the American Fork of the Sacramento River headed at the base of the peak.

17. The only naval lieutenant who fits this description is Strong B. Thompson, who entered service as a midshipman on April 13, 1832, was promoted to lieutenant on July 24, 1843, and resigned on June 24, 1850. Edward W. Callahan, ed., *List of Officers of the Navy of the United States and of the Marine Corps from 1775 to 1900*, 542.

18. With good reason. Carnes notes that they had to unyoke the cattle and lower the wagons over the cliffs by rope, an arduous undertaking. At the same place about nine days

earlier, Bryarly devoted four lengthy paragraphs to describing the numerous difficulties associated with travel. So impressed was he by the day's toils that he wrote, "Everyone is liable to mistakes, & everyone has a right to call a road *very bad* until he sees a worse. My mistake was that I said I had seen 'The Elephant' when getting over the first mountain. I had only seen the tail. This evening I think I saw him in toto." Geiger and Bryarly, August 24.

19. Both Geiger and Bryarly, August 25, and Carnes agreed with the observation that the roads were indeed vile. Greenwoods Camp, as it was called, was named for a group of miners from Oregon, known as Greenwood & Co., who in 1849 discovered a bar on Jefferson Creek, a small tributary of the South Fork of Yuba River about a mile below Washington. Carnes refers to it as Greenwood's Camp. Erwin G. Gudde, *California Gold Camps*, 175.

20. Bear River (or Creek) flows westward from the Sierra Nevada into the Feather River, a tributary of the Sacramento.

21. Carnes: "This is the most difficult descent yet. It is necessary to rough lock the hind wheels and secure all fast by chains." Geiger and Bryarly, August 26, gave a vivid account of the process.

22. This is clearly not Leonard H. Woodworth from Sterling, whom Parke saw on August 21.

23. Carnes describes the soil as being like pulverized brick.

24. Carnes writes that emigrants cut down small oak trees to feed the livestock and that "poison laurel abounds and of this cattle are sickened by eating of it." Poison laurel was encountered by Bryarly on August 28.

25. The day before, Carnes wrote, "It may be said we are now in the diggings."

26. Steep Hollow Diggings, north of Dutch Flat, is on Steep Hollow Creek, a tributary of the Bear River.

27. The use of the cradle or rocker was widespread at this time, along with pans, plates, and bowls. The cradle, essentially a one-man operation, was an improvement over the pan. For an outstanding account of the use of the cradle and the pan at this place, see Geiger and Bryarly, August 29. Carnes reports that some of the miners were doing quite well.

28. Carnes says some members of the train did not succeed in getting to the top of the mountain because their animals gave out.

29. This is not to be confused with Woodworth's Bar, which was just downstream from the confluence of the Rubicon and the Middle Fork of the American River.

30. Carnes: "Here we will encamp some time to recruit our stock, &c., and make preparations to dig *gold.*" This was very close to the spot where Bryarly and his associates made a decision concerning the recruitment of animals and other matters. Geiger and Bryarly, August 30.

31. These are probably David B. Woods and Dan T. Woods, members of a train of more than thirty people that left Indiana on March 26. David B. Woods was elected captain on May 21. (In 1851 he and three companions were killed by the Pitt River Indians near the head of the Sacramento River.) Henry J. Shombre met this party on April 17, April 18, and June 8 and left somewhat garbled accounts of his encounter with "D. Wood" and other members of the train. There is strong evidence that David B. Woods was both a Presbyterian minister and the junior editor of the *Wayne County Whig.* The *Richmond Palladium* of November 7 and December 6, 1849. See also Haskins, *The Argonauts of California,* 397.

32. There is no reference to the given name of the elusive Mr. Beesely of New Jersey. Henry J. Shombre regarded him as

a friend, but even he referred to him on at least three occasions as "Mr. Beesley" of New Jersey. Shombre, May 27–29. They had tea together and went buffalo hunting together near Fort Kearny, but no given name was used. Perhaps he is the "J. Beasley" in Haskins, *The Argonauts of California,* 377.

33. Carnes claims they traveled twelve miles. He also reports that they camped near Rose's Corral. John Rose was a Scottish pioneer of 1840 who was a landowner and something of an entrepreneur. From the adobe and corral he built here by the summer of 1848, he traded with Indians. In early June 1848, gold was discovered downstream on the Yuba River a couple of miles from the place where Deer Creek enters the Yuba, and John Rose began operations there at a place that became known as Rose's Bar. Gudde, *California Gold Camps,* 296. Except for some sporadic summaries, Carnes's diary ends here.

34. Parke does not record the distance traveled on this day, but it must have been quite great, possibly fifty-five miles.

35. Parke's thoughts concerning Sacramento were shared by others. John Benson, September 24, described Sacramento: "The city, if it can be dignified by such a name, is not easy to describe as it is such a jumble. I do not know what is city and what is camp. I am informed that the first frame building was started here in January of this year. A large proportion of the people are living in tents. Most of the business houses are crude and roughly built. I would think half of them are saloons, gambling houses and sporting houses." Backus, September 5, wrote that Sacramento was a "town of cloth containing about 3,000 inhabitants." Lucius Fairchild wrote J. C. Fairchild on October 13, 1849, from Sacramento: "This town is built mostly of canvas, a collection of tents, frames covered with cloth, with a few wooden & zink houses, & every house almost has some kind of gambling going on in it." See also Joseph Wood, October 19.

36. John McWhirter was born in County Antrim, Ireland, in October 1813. After arriving in the United States in 1840, he lived for several years in Baltimore before moving to Iowa. His trek to California in 1849 was extended three or four years, but he returned to Iowa and married Catherine Gift. Six of their children survived his death in early January 1901 at Fairfield, Iowa. *Fairfield Ledger,* January 9, 1901, and *Jefferson County Records,* III:36, IX:347.

37. An emendation was made after this day's entry in what may be Parke's hand: "1892 now Marysville." It's logical that this was Marysville, which was on the east side of the Feather River at its confluence with the Yuba.

38. There is near unanimity on this matter. The absence of theft and other crimes in mining camps and towns in the early days of the gold rush is related in great detail by many emigrants. The reason for the absence of serious crime had a great deal to do with the fact that punishment was severe, public, and nearly certain and the fact that most miners felt little need to steal, since they hoped to become wealthy by mining. Furthermore, miners—even fifteen-year-old miners—took an active part in making the laws of the mining camps, and transgressors were viewed as people who voluntarily made war against society. Richard J. Oglesby, who later served three terms as governor of Illinois, was a lawyer who yielded to gold fever and trekked to California. He observed life in the mining camps and wrote, "As regards the state of society in those parts of California over which I have traveled, especially in mines and towns near them, it is as moral as could be desired, and far surpasses the expectations of every one—no murdering, no riots, and but little drunkenness—far less of this latter evil than is seen in the country towns of Illinois. A strict compliance with contracts and a universal desire to preserve order and good feeling among the citizens seems to be the ambition of every man." Richard J. Oglesby, "Richard J. Oglesby: Forty-Niner," 170. G. B. Stevens visited Sacramento on

July 18, 1849: "A million worth of goods are here of all kinds piled up under the trees. Everything is safe. No thieves." He said that when the rare crime did occur, "robbers, murderers are ferreted out, caught, whipped & hung—and now there is hardly a case of theft. Stores of all goods without doors left open all night." He went on to tell about a theft of gold dust from a hard-working miner. The miners caught the thief, tried him, and sentenced him to be hanged, but his friends interceded and he got off with just fifty lashes, the amputation of his ears, and a warning to leave the mines and never return. G. B. Stevens, Journal, 1849. One miner was so impressed by the tranquility he found in the gold camps that he wrote: "The mines are the most quiet place I ever saw. A man is as safe here as he would be locked up in a room at home. They deal very severely with a man for stealing or robbing in this country. For stealing any small article they tie him to a tree and whip him severely, and then cut off both ears and let him go." He said property was perfectly safe without locks because miners walked around heavily armed ("yet no one fears his neighbor") and punishment was speedy and condign. He concluded, "Order prevails here to an alarming extent, and lawyers have nothing to do." Peter Decker, *The Diaries of Peter Decker*, 321–22, 319. Perhaps engaging in some unintended exaggeration, an emigrant wrote about the desire for law: "There was absolutely no thievery. Although beyond the jurisdiction of the law they were still law-abiding, and in their dealings with each other they were governed by a spirit of fairness and justice that was most commendable. And all this, too, while far away from the tender, restraining influences of the home and of society." W. J. Pleasants, *Twice Across the Plains, 1849 . . . 1856*, 102. See also *The Gold Rush*, 89 and 123; Oscar T. Shuck, ed., *History of the Bench and Bar of California*, passim; the *Placer Times*, December 15, 1849. Even though the mining society was heterogeneous, a mixture of elements from all over the world, one miner thought two factors produced respect for law: the stunning American success in the Mexican War awed people into believing that Americans were superior, and "the large infusion of law and order men from" other parts of the nation. Quoted in John Phillip Reid, *Law for the Elephant,* 7–8. A brilliant analysis of the situation, in which "there was very little law, but a large amount of good order" in the early gold fields, is found in Daniel J. Boorstin, *The Americans: The National Experience,* 81–86. Of enduring value on this topic is Charles Howard Shinn, *Mining Camps,* especially chap. 12.

Chapter 7

1. Founded by John Bidwell, a close associate of John Sutter, Bidwell's Bar was on the Middle Fork of the Feather River not far from its junction with the North Fork. There was no Oregon Bar in this area, so it is possible that the reference is to nearby Oregon Gulch.

2. There is no record of this mining company or its operations. Philadelphia is in Marion County, Missouri, northwest of Hannibal. Fairfield, Iowa, is the county seat of Jefferson County. In early January 1849 a group of people indicated an interest in forming an overland company to go to California. After meeting in the courthouse, the Iowa Drug Store, and the Presbyterian church, the interested individuals succeeded in drafting a code of laws and electing officers. The organization was known as the Fairfield Company. Randall Rice served on the committee that drafted the code of laws and was elected lieutenant, J. T. Hardin serving as captain. The company consisted of thirty-three people and eleven teams and departed Fairfield on April 19. On the membership rolls were Randall Rice as lieutenant, Isaac Boyle, John Boyle, John McWhorter, ——— Thompson, A. Daniels, ——— McCutchen, James Kenyon, J.Q.A. Thompson, and a woman and three of her children. *Jefferson County Records,* III:37, 56–69. Fairfield's *Iowa Sentinel* reported on Friday, April 20, 1849: "This company embraces some of our best and most estimable citizens, and they go with the sincere

wishes of all whom they have left behind." It added that the party was well furnished and included some additional people from the county who were not formally members of the company. This increased the number of participants to more than fifty and the number of teams to nearly twenty. The paper then listed the members of the company. A Tommy Thompson is listed as a member of the company in *Jefferson County Records*, III:60–61. For more on this company, see *Fairfield Ledger*, January 9, 1901, and March 7, 1906; *Jefferson County Records*, II:54, IV:86. Virtually nothing is recorded about the men from Philadelphia.

An examination of the 1850 federal census records for a number of counties in California failed to identify any of the men in this mining company with any degree of certainty. An examination of county history records of Marion County, including marriage records and census records, revealed very little useful information. George Terrell was born in Kentucky in 1826, was brought to Marion County in 1829, and trekked to California in 1849, where he stayed five years, engaging in mining and stock raising. Upon returning to Marion County, he married and turned to farming. *History of Marion County, Missouri,* II:745. A "Mr. Terrel"—no given name—was listed as living at Deer Creek, Nevada County, in 1850. Thomas R. Stoddart, *Annals of Tuolumne County,* 32. An individual by the name of Nathaniel Dunn was born in Kentucky in 1822, came to Marion County in 1827, became a farmer, and married in 1859. *History of Marion County, Missouri,* II:732. Fragmentary evidence suggests that most of these men were young, the majority being in their early twenties, and few of them who did not return to their respective counties left many tracks that appear in histories and reports. For example, not one of the men from Jefferson County is listed as being one of the original landholders in that county. *Jefferson County Records,* VII.

3. The fluctuating water level was a problem for miners. With the onset of the rainy season in late October and

early November, there was flooding and interruptions of work. With the beginning of the dry season in April, the water level was sometimes too low to operate races. One miner wrote, "In general there are two seasons—a wet and a dry." He then went on to give some figures for rainfall in 1849 and 1850: two days of rain in October; fourteen in November; eight in December and one day of snow; seventeen days in January of 1850 and three of snow; four days in February and three of snow; nine days in March and one day of snow; one day of rain in April. Woods, *Sixteen Months at the Gold Diggings*, 15–16. Writing to his brother James on April 21, 1850, Cornelius Reardon, mining on Deer Creek, said that because of the approaching dry season he would have to abandon Deer Creek and move elsewhere. Reardon, *Letters,* 1850. By mid-December, miners had flocked to San Francisco and Sacramento. Many of these men were skilled and many were members of professions, prompting an emigrant to remark that the cities soon would be "densely populated and overrun with men of all professions." Evans, December 16. Perhaps only half the men in the gold fields actually engaged in mining at any time, the rest performing other work or remaining idle. Krepps, October 16.

4.   At least one person predicted the floods. Writing from Sacramento to his mother on August 18, 1849, Joseph S. Stidham said that within the last twenty years the site occupied by Sacramento had been under water four or five feet in March. *Richmond Palladium,* October 24, 1849. One emigrant wrote of the floods on January 9, 1850, "To day the river commenced rising and at 9 oclock eve. the City of Sacramento was covered with about 5 feet of watter; we had 3 feet on the floor of our house and was obliged to take refuge in the loft of a house unfinished." The next day, he said, the water was still rising, destroying much property, and noted that people were crowding aboard ships to avoid the floodwaters. Backus, January 9 and 10, 1850. For some people the flooding began much earlier. Writing in Sacramento on December 10, 1849, one

person noted that "the water is about 3 feet deep in our house at this time and rising" and that many people were seeking refuge aboard ships. Soon afterward he wrote: "We have moved up stairs where we spend the time in eating, sleeping, some singing, some playing cards, some checkers, some telling yarns, some few reading, not having much reading matter." The novelty of being driven upstairs by floodwaters soon wore thin, however, and by December 13 the emigrant complained: "We have been close prisoners since Wednesday evening last, 20 of us confined to the second story of a small house. Such close confinement may do for a day but when it goes beyond that it becomes irksome." Prichet, December 10 and 13. See also John Ingalls, *California Letters of the Gold Rush Period*, 160. December 1849 was exceptionally rainy, some twelve and a half inches falling that month; the December average from 1849 through 1879 was slightly more than four and a half. *History of Sacramento County, California*, 238.

5. This particular incident and skirmish are not recorded elsewhere. Friction between the emigrants and Indians was not uncommon, and on occasion it triggered violence and bloodshed. When miners felt aggrieved or threatened, they sometimes launched private punitive expeditions against those Indians whom they believed to be the offenders. On one occasion, the horses of some miners on Deer Creek were stolen and they thought they knew who had taken them. They promptly tracked a number of Indians across the countryside and eventually killed twenty-two. At the same time, some two hundred emigrants were organizing another punitive expedition. Frequently these chases were fruitless, and every now and then they led to stinging defeat when the miners blundered into ambushes. *Sacramento Transcript*, April 5, 1850.

6. Parke's familiar reference to McCabe suggests that he knew him back east. This possibility is bolstered by the fact that the 1850 federal census records for Whiteside

County include a household headed by Moriah McCabe, a woman of thirty-eight who had seven children living with her, the oldest of whom was fifteen. It is not clear whether the black to whom Parke refers was owned by McCabe or merely employed by him. Slavery in the gold fields was never strong, and the fluid conditions of the region did nothing to strengthen it. For more on slavery in the gold fields, consult Rudolph Lapp, *Blacks in Gold Rush California.*

7. Dr. Blake was possibly James Blake, who was born about 1810 in Great Britain and was living in Sacramento County in 1850. Alan P. Bowman, comp., *Index to the 1850 Census of the State of California,* 146. A James Blake, physician, was living in Sacramento in 1854. Samuel Colville, *Samuel Colville's City Directory of Sacramento, for the Year 1854–5,* 23. Dutch Charley's Flat, or Dutch Flat, was on a branch of Honcut Creek in Butte County just southwest of Forbestown. Gudde, *California Gold Camps,* 104. William Smith O'Brien, a Whig member of the Protestant aristocracy in Ireland, was a champion of Catholic emancipation and social justice. He withdrew from Parliament in 1841 and began to agitate for Irish independence, his activities culminating in a feeble 1848 revolutionary action which was squelched by the constabulary. He was arrested, convicted, and transported, as were some of his followers. He returned to Ireland in 1856 and abstained from political activity, dying in 1864.

8. This may have been the same girl reported by Charles Main in Marysville: "There are eight young ladies dealing monte. One is reported to be a very handsome miss of about seventeen years old." Quoted in Holliday, *The World Rushed In,* 355.

9. William Clingan Miller was the son of Dr. Warwick Miller and Martha Clingan Miller, who were married in 1820. J. Smith Futhey and Gilbert Cope, *History of Chester County, Pennsylvania, with Genealogical and Biographical*

Sketches, 659. Dr. Andrew Murphy, a physician, lived with his large household in Sadsbury Township, Chester County, Pennsylvania. His age is listed as forty-eight in the 1850 federal census, and he is enumerated immediately after a David Parke and his household. *Federal Census, Sadsbury Township, Chester County, Pennsylvania, for 1850,* 332.

10. Numerous sources provide lists of names of forty-niners from Illinois. No one by the name of Dixon is included.

11. Evans Bar was in Butte County on the north side of the Middle Fork of Feather River. Gudde, *California Gold Camps,* 112.

12. Lieutenant George Frederick Ruxton attended Sandhurst, fought a bit in Spain during its civil wars, then served in Her Majesty's Eighty-ninth Regiment in Canada. While serving in Canada, he became interested in Indian life and the West. He resigned his commission to live with Indians and trappers and was happy with this life. Later he explored Africa. His book *Life in the Far West* was published by Harper & Brothers in 1849. The November 28, 1849 issue of the *Rockford Forum* (Rockford, Ill.) carried a notice of his death in St. Louis.

13. Carnes's cousin was William B. Lorton. An entry in Carnes's diary is concise on this meeting: "Met Lorton at Bidwell's Bar May 8, 1850." The diary kept by Lorton records the trek he made via the southern route from Salt Lake City, but it ends before May 1850. Lorton was born in New York, attended school in New York City, and as a young man engaged in the clock business. He went to Illinois and became a member of a large train that formed in early February 1849 at the courthouse in Oquawka, a train captained by William Findley. Lorton returned to New York City in 1854. He married, had a family, and served in the Seventh New York Regiment during the Civil War. After the war he engaged in the sewing-

machine business until his death. There was no Holt County in Illinois during the 1840s.

14. John C. Calhoun, the ardent and intellectually powerful defender of Southern interests, died on March 31, 1850.

15. Evan Jones married Parke's half-sister, Caroline, and they lived in Sadsbury Township, Chester County, Pennsylvania. He was forty-one years old in 1850, was a miller, and he and his wife had eight children. *Federal Census, Sadsbury Township, Chester County, Pennsylvania, for 1850,* 303. The other men were almost certainly neighbors of Evan and Caroline Jones, but they are not recorded.

16. Defunct or otherwise, these men probably were not Methodist preachers. No mention is made of them in any contemporary source, and they are not cited in C. V. Anthony, *Fifty Years of Methodism: A History of the Methodist Episcopal Church within the Bounds of the California Annual Conference from 1847 to 1897.*

17. Perhaps this is the Dr. Jackson mentioned several times by Elisha Douglas Perkins, *Gold Rush Diary,* and Joseph Middleton. Perkins, June 14, 21, and 25, 1849, and October 6, 1849 (Dr. Jackson was in a train that kept abreast of Perkins's train). Middleton, August 7. The only Dr. Jackson listed in Boston's almanacs during this period is a Dr. Joseph Jackson, who practiced medicine at 102 Court Street well into the 1850s. *The Boston Almanac* for the years 1847 through 1854.

18. No one by the name of Dick (or Richard) Jefferies appears in any source pertaining to Chester County. The reference to "one from my Brothers from Little Detroit" is not clear.

19. Nelson Creek, a tributary of the Middle Fork of the Feather River, is in Plumas County and was the site of rich strikes in 1850. These deposits were found after a

scramble for the fabled Gold Lake, and it appears that Parke's reference to the deposits is a very early one. Gudde, *California Gold Camps,* 135, 236–37.

20. Neither bar is mentioned in Gudde, *California Gold Camps,* or other sources. It is likely that the reference to the Fairfield Bar indicates that some other miners from Fairfield, Iowa—perhaps friends of those from Fairfield who were members of the Union Bar Company—were in the immediate vicinity.

21. This is possibly a reference to some grudge between miners from Missouri and miners from Pike County, Illinois, or Pike County, Missouri.

22. Julia and Florence Sampson were first cousins to Captain Simeon Sampson's wife, Caroline. Caroline Sampson was the daughter of William and Caroline Sampson. William's brother was Henry Briggs Sampson, and Henry and his wife had a number of children, including Julia and Florence. William and Henry and their respective families arrived at Como in 1839. Julia was born on June 16, 1825, Florence on April 2, 1832, both in Massachusetts. At the time they wrote to Parke, they were still single, Julia marrying Charles Russell in December 1851 and Florence marrying Edwin Whitman in October 1855. Bent, *History of Whiteside County, Illinois,* 251–52.

23. Dr. Martin Greenman was in a large company that left Peoria, Illinois, on April 14, 1849, and included Fleming Dunn and Charles Hinman. Haskins, *The Argonauts of California,* 413. Greenman, born in 1804 in Herkimer County, New York, was self-educated and arrived in Bureau County, Illinois, in 1847, settling at Indian Town (present-day Tiskilwa). He practiced medicine in California until 1852, then returned to Illinois before making another trip to California in 1854, after which he returned home and died in 1877, leaving a wife and children. H. C. Bradsby, ed., *History of Bureau County, Illinois,* 533–34. See also Hinman, October 7.

24. If this mock funeral was intended to be merely a tacky political stunt, it certainly had an unintended macabre element to it, for President Zachary Taylor had died less than two months earlier, on July 9. Since "San Franciscans saluted the late President Taylor with an elaborate funeral procession in late August," it seems highly likely that news of Taylor's death would have reached Sacramento by September 6, the date of Parke's comments about the mock funeral. Jackson, *Gold Dust,* 290–91. News of Taylor's death circulated in the gold fields no later than September 18. Bruff, September 18.

25. The dispute that led to bloodshed was between people who claimed lands under titles issued by Captain Sutter and those who had squatted on the lands and refused to budge from them. After the courts had ruled, authorities tried to eject the squatters, and this triggered the disturbances. The trouble began to bubble on August 10, and by August 13 events were becoming ominous. Possibly several hundred men were involved in the disturbances on August 14 and 15; several on both sides lost their lives, and a number were badly wounded. Among the dead were Sheriff Joseph McKinney, City Assessor J. M. Woodland, at least one leader of the squatters, and Hardin Bigelow, mayor of Sacramento, the first to die. (One fiery leader of the squatters, Charles Robinson, later became governor of Kansas.) For more on this subject, see Jackson, *Gold Dust,* 292–94. Bigelow and McKinney had been elected to office the previous April. *Sacramento Transcript,* April 5, and the *Placer Times,* April 13. A very good account of these riotous days is found in *History of Sacramento County, California,* 50–56. A detailed first-hand account is in Jacob D. B. Stillman, *Seeking the Golden Fleece,* August 10–27. See also Backus, August 14–17; Ingalls, *California Letters,* 177; Hubert Howe Bancroft, *California Inter Pocula,* XXXV:408–10.

26. Many people commented on the forest of ship masts in the bay. George W. Applegate, writing to his brother

from San Francisco, expressed astonishment at the idle armada of vessels: "I was never more surprised in my life than I was in this place. There is between five hundred and one thousand sails now within my view lying in the harbor and 300 in Sacramento City, and the daily arrivals are about 5." Applegate, April 8, 1850.

27. The process of leveling the hills and filling in part of the bay, Hubert Howe Bancroft wrote, worsened an already defective drainage system. *History of California,* V:201.

28. Parke is correct in attributing the absence of catarrhal difficulties to the presence of salt and iodine.

29. During this week and other weeks in September and October, the *Daily Alta California* of San Francisco ran scores of advertisements and business notices for clippers, brigs, barques, and steamships but only a few for schooners. None of the items concerning schooners mentioned a Spanish captain or a destination of either Mexico or Panama. Also, in the lists of passengers for various ships clearing the harbor at San Francisco, there were no Parkes or Sampsons. Finally, the lists of arrivals at various San Francisco hotels did not include Parke or Sampson. It seems likely that they took rather ordinary lodging in which the names of guests were not printed in the newspapers. Judging from Parke's account of the subsequent voyage to Central America, it is likely that the schooner on which he sailed adhered to no schedule and was a ramshackle operation that did not seek publicity through the press.

Chapter 8

1. An overlander who visited Mazatlán on his voyage home saw "all kinds of fruit in the market, oranges, pineapples, bananas, tomatoes, coconuts, etc.," and said the food was

inexpensive, the beach pleasant, and the town remarkably clean. He did notice a few beggars, however. Prichet, January 9, 1850.

2. After the Mexican War, Americans were eager to heap scorn on Mexican leaders, including those of the Mexican army. American attitudes toward Mexican elites are discussed fully and ably in Johannsen, *To the Halls of the Montezumas*.

3. It is not known whether this is a reference to some of the very early writings of Charles Darwin or a reference to something written by his grandfather, Erasmus Darwin.

4. Since the Sandwich Islands are today's Hawaiian Islands, it seems that Parke is making fun of the Captain's navigational skill.

5. According to a census in 1846, Realejo had only one thousand people. It is likely, however, that many people (especially men) were not counted. The people feared that the census was a precursor of either a military draft or more taxation. Ephriam George Squire, *Nicaragua*, I:32.

6. Overlanders who returned home via Nicaragua reported that at the harbor local people clustered about the ship, selling bananas, oranges, pineapples, and other fruit. L. N. Weed, Journal, 1850, November 4, 1850; Stillman, *Seeking the Golden Fleece*, November 30; and Hiram D. Pierce, *A Forty-Niner Speaks*, November 18, who notes that the fruit caused some sickness.

Chapter 9

1. Parke's knowledge of Realejo is imperfect. Realejo was Nicaragua's chief port from 1550 to 1850, being superseded by Corinto at the entrance of Realejo Bay. The gold rush

did cause it to boom, but its population in 1850 was almost certainly not four thousand. The census of 1846 listed one thousand inhabitants in Realejo, a figure cited in 1854. Squire, *Nicaragua*. I:32; Carl Scherzer, *Travels in the Free States of Central America,* I:112. Ephriam Squire quoted the census figure of one thousand, but when he visited Nicaragua in September 1849 he thought the town was home to about one thousand two hundred people. Squire, *Nicaragua,* I:366. The "pirate Morgan" to whom Parke refers was probably Sir Henry Morgan, an English pirate who sacked Spanish towns and treasure all over the Caribbean during the 1660s and 1670s. There is no evidence, however, that he ever made Realejo his home or headquarters.

2. For descriptions of the ruined church and accounts of the general decline of the town, see Stillman, *Seeking the Golden Fleece,* 198–202; Pierce, November 19, 1850; and Scherzer, *Travels in the Free States of Central America,* I:111–12, who claimed that the church was Moorish in style and that on the outside of it was an inscription in English for the benefit of forty-niners requesting them to not smoke in the church or engage in "any other indecorous behaviour." Squire mentioned preparations to build the new town of "Corinth" on the harbor and predicted the decline of Realejo. Squire, *Nicaragua,* I:366–67.

3. Evidently, the cactus that impressed Parke also caught the attention of Hiram Pierce, who wrote twelve days later from Realejo: "It grows up with a fluted shaft or trunk 20 or 25 feet high where it is not cut off, & 5 or 6 inches through . . . & is a beautiful green. It has no branches & where it is cut off even it makes a beautiful fence." Pierce, November 20, 1850.

4. Parke and his companions probably paid top dollar for this form of transportation. Eleven days after Parke's group engaged the teams and drivers for ten dollars each for transportation to Granada, Hiram Pierce arranged for

similar transportation to Granada for only six, as did Jacob Stillman less than two weeks later. Pierce, November 20, 1850; Stillman, *Seeking the Golden Fleece,* 201. Perhaps the demand was much greater in early November than later.

5. For more on ox-cart transportation and the harsh treatment of the oxen, see Pierce, November 20 and 23, 1850, and Stillman, *Seeking the Golden Fleece,* 201.

6. A slip of the pen may have caused Parke to err here, for the actual number of inhabitants of Chinandega was at least eleven or twelve thousand. The census of 1846 reported some eleven thousand people, but Ephriam Squire, who cited the census figure, claimed that by September 1849 there were "some fifteen or sixteen thousand" inhabitants, who were supposed "to be the most industrious and thriving of any in the Republic." Squire, *Nicaragua,* I:32, 353. Pierce, November 20, 1850, produced a figure of twelve thousand inhabitants. When Carl Scherzer passed through four years later, he recorded eleven thousand. Scherzer, *Travels in the Free States of Central America,* I:111. Stillman did not offer a population figure, being content to observe that the town was overrun with gaunt yellow dogs who were "so weak that they often fall over in the effort to bark." Stillman, *Seeking the Golden Fleece,* 204. Squire liked the town very much, heaping praise on the broad avenues, gardens, fine houses, and energetic populace and concluding by noting, "Altogether, Chinandega has an air of thrift and enterprise which I have seen nowhere else in Central America." Squire, *Nicaragua,* I:353, 365.

7. Parke probably underestimated the size of both towns. Ephriam Squire offered the 1846 census figures, which indicated that Chichigalpa had two thousand eight hundred inhabitants, Pasultega nine hundred, but upon visiting them in September 1849 he found the former had three thousand to five thousand people and the latter only five

hundred to six hundred. He found Pasultega "an unpretending town," and Chichigalpa was "regularly laid out, and has a neat and attractive appearance." Squire, *Nicaragua*, I:32, 350–51. Pierce, on the other hand, thought Chichigalpa and Chinandega had about the same number of people, twelve thousand, while Pasultega had three thousand. Pierce, November 21, 1850. Stillman agreed that the two towns had about the same number of people but gave no figures.

8. When Hiram Pierce passed along this route just ten days later, he, too, was impressed by the flora and fauna: "It is an unbroken wilderness, inhabited by monkeys, birds, & serpents & beasts of prey. Mahogany, nigerauger logwood, satinwood, rosewood, lignum vita, &c., grow in abundance." Pierce, November 21, 1850. In the late summer of 1849, Ephriam Squire was taken by the beauty of this region but he also knew that the dark, thick forests were home to robbers. Volunteers from Chinandega and León hunted the robbers like beasts and shot them, he said. Squire, *Nicaragua*, I:346–47.

9. Travelers wrote much about León, until 1855 the capital of Nicaragua. It was founded in 1523 at the head of the western bay of Lake Managua and was relocated in 1610. Its public buildings, gardens, fine residential areas, and excellent streets were especially noteworthy. The massive and ornate cathedral, constructed between 1746 and 1774, caught the attention of visitors, Pierce noting that its length was 350 feet, its width 170 feet, and its cost $1,800,000. Pierce, November 22, 1850. Damages from civil strife also caught the attention of visitors. León was the champion of liberal and democratic causes and suffered much from the forces of the aristocracy and clerical interests with headquarters in Granada. The population of forty thousand mentioned by Parke is probably correct, but the city was stagnating because of the chronic feuds that swept the country. For more on the subject, consult Squire, *Nicaragua*, I:242–343; Pierce, November 22, 1850;

Scherzer, *Travels in the Free States of Central America,*
I:84–91; Stillman, *Seeking the Golden Fleece,* 206–10.

10. The volcanoes actually lie to the north, east, and southeast
of the city.

11. Pierce said Pueblo Nuevo had just 360 inhabitants and
Stillman dismissed it as "a small and indifferent place."
Pierce, November 23, 1850; Stillman, *Seeking the Golden
Fleece,* 210. Squire, on the other hand, wrote that he and
his companions were treated to a fine dinner and received
many courtesies. He also noted that every house in the
village was surrounded by fences of columnar cactus,
which in places rose fifteen or twenty feet and formed
palisades. His one annoyance was being saluted by large
numbers of noisy dogs when he entered the village.
Squire, *Nicaragua,* I:240–42.

12. Travelers formed strong opinions about the little town of
Nagarote. Hiram Pierce, who called it Margareta, had a
good supper there and generally liked the place. Pierce,
November 23, 1850. After referring to the village as "a little
scurvy looking place, redeemed by but one really good
looking house," Ephriam Squire wrote that he was deeply
moved by the deep piety of at least one of the village's
residents. Squire, *Nicaragua,* I:237–38. Jacob Stillman
and his fellow travelers were gouged for the services they
received: "Here we met with the shabbiest treatment we
had yet experienced." This treatment, he said, was at the
hands of an American, a rascal who owned a house and
delighted in overcharging his guests for weird food and
inferior accommodations. Stillman, *Seeking the Golden
Fleece,* 210–11. Little was written about the village of
Matearas, Pierce noting that it contained 345 souls. Pierce,
November 24, 1850.

13. The census of 1846 reported twelve thousand people in
Managua, but Hiram Pierce says there were sixteen thou-
sand. Squire, *Nicaragua,* I:32; Pierce, November 24, 1850.
Four years later, it was reported to have had only ten to

twelve thousand inhabitants despite the fact that it was obtaining the seat of government. Scherzer, *Travels in the Free States of Central America*, I:75. The warm hospitality encountered by visitors was impressive. See Pierce, November 24, 1850; Stillman, *Seeking the Golden Fleece*, 214; Scherzer, *Travels in the Free States of Central America*, I:75. Practically nothing of a derogatory nature was written by the visitors. Ephriam Squire was lionized with shouts of "Vivan los Estados Unidos!" and "Vivan los Americanos del Norte!" He heard people shouting hurrahs in the streets for General Zachary Taylor, the principal hero of the Mexican War, and for the American flag. Squire, *Nicaragua*, I:228, 230. A leading resident of the town spoke at great length and in great earnestness about his affection for the United States and his hopes that Nicaragua soon would become part of the United States and would receive an influx of settlers from the northern republic. Stillman, *Seeking the Golden Fleece*, 217–18.

14. Nindiri captivated those who saw it: "Nindiri! How shall I describe thee, beautiful Nindiri, nestling beneath thy fragrant, evergreen roof of tropical trees, entwining their branches above thy smooth avenues, and weaving green domes over the simple dwellings of thy peaceful inhabitants." These words were only part of a paean penned by Ephriam Squire in *Nicaragua*, I:216. His sentiments were shared by Jacob Stillman, who gazed upon the village and wrote, "My surprise did not equal my astonishment. Never had my eyes rested upon a more captivating scene." He then wrote at length about how neat and clean the town appeared. He added that nearly all of Nindiri's inhabitants were pure Indian. Stillman, *Seeking the Golden Fleece*, 219–20. In early November 1850, L. N. Weed wrote favorably about the village, saying the Indian population of Nindiri grew the finest fields of corn he had seen in Nicaragua. Weed, *circa* November 8, 1850.

15. The census of 1846, according to Ephriam Squire, reported some 15,000 residents, but when Squire visited Masaya in September 1849, he produced a figure of 15,000 to 18,000. He said the shops were fine, the public build-

ings impressive, and the city's "people are regarded as the most industrious, and are celebrated throughout all Central America for the extent and variety of their manufactures." Squire, *Nicaragua,* I:211–13. Pierce wrote favorably of the town and reported that it had 13,940 inhabitants. Pierce, November 25, 1850. Scherzer pronounced Masaya to be one of the "most industrious, peaceful, and prosperous of all the towns of this much agitated and unfortunate republic of Nicaragua, in which the elements of revolution and anarchy appear as inexhaustible as the combustible matter beneath its volcanic soil." Scherzer, *Travels in the Free States of Central America,* I:68.

16. This man and his family seem remarkably similar to the "wealthy old Spaniard" and family encountered by Hiram Pierce in Masaya. Pierce, November 25, 1850.

17. Jacob Stillman thought Granada had a distinct European flavor and found the people to be very open and kind. In strolling around the suburbs and on the shore of the lake, he learned that a fair number of residents had picked up English phrases from visiting Americans and others. The townsfolk, he wrote, were "everywhere very kind, and saluted us as we passed with such English as they had acquired from their more civilized guests, and even the little ones would say smiling with genuine good feeling, 'Good-by—go to h–ll!'" Stillman, *Seeking the Golden Fleece,* 225, 227. After noting that the town had about twelve thousand people, Pierce said he liked it and was treated well there. The only sour note was his complaint about troublesome ticks. Pierce, November 26, 1850. Ephriam Squire's reaction was mixed. He liked much about the city, including the fine manners of many of its people, but he was repelled by the spirit of faction and political strife that was all too evident. Squire, *Nicaragua,* I:136–81. See also Weed, November 10, 1850.

18. This may be something of an exaggeration, but it does conform closely to an observation made by another American: "The natives are very friendly & think much of the Americans." Pierce, November 22, 1850.

19. This vessel was very common in Nicaragua and could carry sixty men. See Pierce, November 28–December 5, 1850; Squire, *Nicaragua,* I:90–94; Stillman, *Seeking the Golden Fleece,* 226–27, 231–35.

20. More commonly known as the chigger. Noted by Pierce on November 26, 1850.

21. This speculation was both reasonable and incorrect. Elephantiasis is caused by filarial worms.

22. Alligators were seen from Lake Nicaragua to San Juan on the Caribbean coast. See Pierce, November 30, 1850; Squire, *Nicaragua,* I:60, 100. While drifting down the San Juan River, Jacob Stillman wrote, "Alligators, like half-rotten logs, lay in the mud on the shore, and tumbled into the water with a sudden splash as we approached." Stillman, *Seeking the Golden Fleece,* 234.

23. Both Pierce and Squire agreed that San Carlos contained about twenty houses or huts, sported a customhouse and a small arsenal and a garrison of twenty-five men, and was in a state of general dilapidation, notwithstanding the fact that the town served as a transshipment point for cargo and as a refitting place for vessels plying the lake and river. Squire and his companions received courteous—even lavish—treatment from the officer in charge of the military post. See Pierce, December 4, 1850; Squire, *Nicaragua,* I:114–17, 119–22. Jacob Stillman prowled around the old fort, noted that compared to western Nicaragua the weather at San Carlos was sultry, and was generally unimpressed by what he saw. Stillman, *Seeking the Golden Fleece,* 230–32. The presence of a customhouse at San Carlos was dictated by the fact that the British had seized the western coast of Nicaragua, the Mosquito Coast, and had firm control of the port of San Juan, also known as Greytown.

24. Hiram Pierce thought the river was a quarter of a mile wide and had a deep and rapid current, while Jacob Still-

man merely wrote that it was wider and deeper than he had expected it to be. Pierce, December 4, 1850; Stillman, *Seeking the Golden Fleece*, 233.

25. As Parke and his acquaintances floated downstream from San Carlos to San Juan on the Caribbean coast, the first rapids they encountered were Rapides del Toro, just a few miles upstream from Castillo Viejo. The next rapids, Rapides del Castillo, were just above the old fort and posed problems for those navigating the river, usually necessitating the removal of passengers and cargo from the bungos. Several miles downstream from Castillo Viejo were Rapides de Machuca, the most formidable rapids on the river. If these patches of swift water made downstream travel exciting and even dangerous, it made travel by bungo upstream very arduous. Pierce, December 5, 1850, claimed it was said that twenty days were required to ascend the river to San Carlos in a bungo, while Ephriam Squire boasted that his party made the toilsome ascent in just six. Squire, *Nicaragua,* I:113.

26. San Juan, known to the British and to shippers as Greytown, was not very impressive. L. N. Weed, November 24, 1850, said the town had about fifty buildings, a few of which were adobe brick and roofed with tile. Most houses, he said, were constructed of reeds and had palm-leaf roofs. He and his traveling mates had heard that food was in short supply in San Juan, so they brought with them from Granada live fowl, eggs, bread, dried beef, and fruit. Writing on December 6, 1850, Hiram Pierce observed that swarms of Americans had eaten "them out of house & home, & they seem to be dependant on Grenada for their supplies, as they raise nothing about here." He also reported that the breakers were rolling within a mile and could be heard for fifteen miles inland. The day before, December 5, Pierce referred to San Juan as "a poverty stricken place containing perhaps 1,000 inhabitants." Jacob Stillman visited the port and sniffed, "A more disgusting place I never saw." He then added: "A few frame houses, and a flagstaff, from which floated the British flag,

constituted the town." Stillman, *Seeking the Golden Fleece,*
236. Visiting San Juan in June 1850, Ephriam Squire
counted fifty or sixty palm-thatched houses, which were
arranged with a moderate degree of regularity. No lands
in the vicinity were cultivated, he observed, and all the
inhabitants were heavily dependent on outside food
sources. Squire, *Nicaragua,* 1:72.

27. British interest in the Caribbean coast of Nicaragua dates
from 1630, when agents of an English-chartered company
became the first white settlers on the coast. They dubbed
the coast the Mosquito Coast, after the Mosquito Indians,
and from 1655 to 1850 Britain claimed a protectorate over
the Indians, a claim that was hotly disputed by Spain, the
Central American republics, and then the United States,
the latter fearing British hegemony over the long-
proposed interoceanic canal. In 1848 the Indians, aided by
a British force, seized San Juan and held it until 1860. The
role of British arms in this activity inflamed public opinion in the United States, and the stationing of British
warships off the port did nothing to reduce tension.
Hiram Pierce noted the British war steamer lying in the
harbor and said the town "is entirely under the control of
the English who have a small garrison here of some 20,
mostly blacks from Jamaica. With these they keep a strict
police day & night." Pierce, December 5–6, 1850. Jacob
Stillman witnessed the efforts of the authorities to main-
tain order: "On landing, we were waited on by a dozen of
Her Majesty's colored troops, called policemen, who re-
quested us, on behalf of the people of the town, to deliver
up to their keeping any fire-arms that we might have
about us, until such time as we should leave the place." He
said some of the Americans refused and the officer in
command did not force the issue. Stillman, *Seeking the
Golden Fleece,* 236. British occupation of San Juan and
other points on the coast angered many people in the
United States. As far away as Oquawka, Illinois, newspapers railed against Great Britain. A lengthy article in the
August 29, 1849 issue of the *Oquawka Spectator* complained that the British had elbowed out an American

company that was under contract to build a canal across Nicaragua. It added that Greytown was part of a Mosquito kingdom that the British had established under the nominal control of a "stupid, half-breed native" puppet. British interest in the coast and in all of Nicaragua was very real, however, and of long duration. Despite prohibitions found in the provisions of the Clayton-Bulwer Treaty of 1850, both Britain and the United States sought to exercise dominion over parts of Central America. As late as 1895 the Hatch incident provoked the British into occupying the western port of Corinto, and in 1909 a British cruiser intervened at Greytown. U.S. Marines landed in Nicaragua in 1912 and remained there almost continuously until 1933.

28. Ephriam Squire opined that British occupation of the coast had several consequences. The local folk, he claimed, adopted the trappings of British dress, or what they thought were some of the features of British dress. Streets were renamed, one becoming King Street. A regulation was promulgated that called upon residents of Greytown no longer to allow their poultry and pigs to roam the town freely. A large number of Mosquito Indians flocked into the coastal areas, blacks were brought in from Jamaica, and other people came from elsewhere—all of which tended to create a cosmopolitan admixture. Even so, the population of Greytown fell, a consequence of the decline of traffic and cargo passing through since the British occupation: "The population of the town does not exceed three hundred, having considerably diminished since the English usurpation." Squire, *Nicaragua,* I:43. In an effort to resist the British encroachment, Nicaraguans to the west tried to buy up as many foodstuffs as possible to hoist the prices the British and their coastal minions would have to pay. The British, moreover, dredged up old—and perhaps questionable—rights that formerly had been enjoyed by the Mosquito Indians under the Spanish. This was done to justify their "protection" of the Indians and to squelch international ire. Finally, prior to the occupation, San Juan was dependent upon the Di-

ocese of Nicaragua. The occupation broke ties between San Juan and diocesan headquarters, giving the Church of England a chance to become established along the coast. Squire, *Nicaragua*, I:56–79.

29. Americans found the loosely dressed, shapely, dusky females quite attractive. See, for example, Squire, *Nicaragua*, I:89, 108, and Pierce, November 24, 1850.

30. L. N. Weed, December 1, 1850, said the *Tay* arrived on Saturday.

31. Fatigue, the lengthy layover at San Juan, and general discomfort in western Nicaragua seem to have dampened Parke's initial enthusiasm for its people. His views of blacks, none too favorable to begin with, were reinforced negatively by his stay in British-held San Juan.

32. Chagres was on the Atlantic coast of the Isthmus of Panama near the mouth of the Chagres River and about eight miles west of Colón. The village boomed during the gold rush as thousands of gold seekers cut across the isthmus, but after that it fell into sharp decline.

33. The only Portobelo is northeast of Chagres in the northern part of the Isthmus of Panama. Evidently, the steamship on which Parke sailed pulled out of Chagres, ran into strong headwinds perhaps straight north of Portobelo on its way to Kingston, ran short of coal, and then turned south to Portobelo to replenish its fuel supply.

34. The flower is not with the diary.

Afterword

1. Most of the information for this section came from several sources: Frink, "Charles Ross Parke, M.D."; Robinson, *The Biographical Record of McLean County, Illinois;* Has-

brouck, *History of McLean County; United States Biographical Dictionary and Portrait Gallery of Self-Made Men, Illinois Volume; Biographical History of the McLean County Medical Society, 1854–1954;* The Banquet Manuscript.

2. The Banquet Manuscript, 5.

3. Dr. Parke was one of fourteen physicians who gathered at the McLean County courthouse on Monday evening, March 20, 1854, to organize a medical society. Two weeks later, he was one of fourteen physicians who signed its constitution. On April 8, 1861, he was elected to a year's term as secretary and on April 10, 1865, he was elected the society's eighth president, serving until April 9, 1866.

4. Becoming politically aware during the age of Jackson, Parke became a Democrat for life.

5. On the way to the Crimean War, while there, and while returning home, Parke kept a detailed and lively diary of what he saw and experienced: "Diary of Charles Ross Parke, M.D., written during his journey to Russia, and his period of medical service with the Russian Army in the Crimean War, Sept. 9, 1855–November [21?], 1856." The diary focuses on local customs, architecture, life in various cities, various classes of society, sickness, treatment of the wounded, and military matters.

6. About a year younger than Parke, Oglesby was a forty-niner and a veteran of the Mexican War. He crossed the continent with eight other men from Macon County, Illinois. By profession he was a lawyer, and by political inclination he was a strong Whig. With the imminent collapse of the Whig party in the mid-1850s, Oglesby rushed into the Republican fold. He served Illinois as a Republican governor for three nonconsecutive terms between 1865 and 1889.

7. Frink, "Charles Ross Parke, M.D.," 14.

Works Cited

Akin, James, Jr. *The Journal of James Akin, Jr.* Edited by Edward Everett Dale. *University of Oklahoma Bulletin,* No. 9. Norman: University of Oklahoma, 1919.

Anthony, C. V. *Fifty Years of Methodism: A History of the Methodist Episcopal Church within the Bounds of the California Annual Conference from 1847 to 1897.* San Francisco: Methodist Book Concern, 1901.

Applegate, George W. Letters, 1849–50. MS, Beinecke Library.

Atlas of Whiteside County and the State of Illinois. Chicago: Warner and Beers, 1872.

Backus, Gurdon. Diary, 1849. MS, Beinecke Library.

Bancroft, Hubert Howe. *California Inter Pocula.* San Francisco: History Co., 1888.

——. *History of California.* 7 vols. San Francisco: History Co., 1884–90.

Banks, John Edwin. Diary, 1849. In Howard L. Scamerhorn, ed. *The Buckeye Rovers in the Gold Rush.* Athens: Ohio University Press, 1965.

The Banquet Manuscript. Parke Collection, McLean County Historical Society, Bloomington, Ill.

Barrett, James T. "Cholera in Missouri." *Missouri Historical Review,* LV (July 1961).

Batchelder, Amos. Journal, 1849–50. MS, Bancroft Library.

Benson, John H. Diary, 1849. TS, Nebraska State Historical Society.

Bent, Charles, ed. *History of Whiteside County, Illinois*. Clinton, Iowa: L. P. Allen, 1877.

Bidlack, Russell E., ed. *Letters Home: The Story of Ann Arbor's Forty-Niners*. Ann Arbor, Mich.: Ann Arbor Publishers, 1960.

Biographical History of the McLean County Medical Society, 1854–1954. Bloomington, Ill., 1954.

Biographical Record of Bureau, Marshall, and Putnam Counties. Chicago: S. J. Clarke Publishing Co., 1896.

Biographical Record of Whiteside County, Illinois. Chicago: S. J. Clarke Publishing Co., 1900.

Boorstin, Daniel J. *The Americans: The National Experience*. New York: Random House, 1965.

The Boston Almanac. 1847–54.

Bowman, Alan P., comp. *Index to the 1850 Census of the State of California*. Baltimore: Genealogical Publishing Co., 1972.

Bradsby, H. C., ed. *History of Bureau County, Illinois*. Chicago: World Publishing Co., 1885.

Brainard, David. Journal, 1849. MS, State Historical Society of Wisconsin.

Breyfogle, Joshua D. Diary, 1849. MF, Bancroft Library.

Bruff, J. Goldsborough. *The Journals, Drawings, and Other Papers of J. Goldsborough Bruff, Captain, Washington City and California Mining Association, April 2, 1849–July 20, 1851*. 2 vols. Edited by Georgia Willis Read and Ruth P. Gaines. New York: Columbia University Press, 1944.

Burbank, Augustus Ripley. Diary, 1849–51. MF, Bancroft Library.

Burlington Hawk-Eye, 1849 (Burlington, Iowa).

Callahan, Edward W., ed. *List of Officers of the Navy of the United States and of the Marine Corps from 1775 to 1900.* New York: Haskell House Publishers, 1969.

Carnes, David. Journal of a trip across the plains in the year 1849. MF, Bancroft Library.

Castleman, P. F. Diary, 1849–51. MF of TS, Bancroft Library.

Catalogue of Medical Graduates of the University of Pennsylvania, 1847.

Chamberlain, William E. Diary, 1849. MF of MS, Bancroft Library.

Chapman, William W. Diary, 1849. MS, Huntington Library.

Claypool, Edward A. and Azalea Clizbee, comps. *A Genealogy of the Descendants of William Kelsey.* 3 vols. Bridgeport, Conn.: Marsh Press, 1947.

Colton, J. B. In *Oquawka Spectator,* October 3, 1849 (Oquawka, Ill.).

Colville, Samuel. *Samuel Colville's City Directory of Sacramento, for the Year 1854–5.* San Francisco: Mason & Valentine, 1854.

Cosad, David. Diary, 1849. MS, California Historical Society.

Coy, Owen Cochran. *The Great Trek.* San Francisco: Powell Publishing Co., 1931.

Cross, Osborne. "The Journal of Major Osborne Cross." In Raymond W. Settle, ed., *The March of the Mounted Riflemen.* Glendale, Calif.: Arthur H. Clark Co., 1940.

Daily Alta California, 1850 (San Francisco).

Decker, Peter. *The Diaries of Peter Decker: Overland to California in 1849 and Life in the Mines, 1850–51.* Edited by Helen S. Giffen. Georgetown, Calif.: Talisman Press, 1966.

Delano, Alonzo. *Life on the Plains and Among the Diggings: Being Scenes and Adventures of an Overland Journey to California.* Auburn, N.Y.: Miller, Orton, & Mulligan, 1854.

————. *Alonzo Delano's California Correspondence; Being letters hitherto uncollected from the Ottawa (Illinois) Free Trader and the New Orleans True Delta, 1849–52.* Sacramento, Calif.: Sacramento Book Collectors Club, 1952.

DeVoto, Bernard. *The Year of Decision: 1846.* Boston: Little, Brown & Co., 1943.

Dewolf, David. "Diary of the Overland Trail and Letters of Captain David Dewolf." *Transactions,* Illinois State Historical Society, 1925.

Dickinson, S. N., comp. *The Boston Almanac for the Year 1849.* Boston: B. B. Mussey, 1849.

Doetsch, Raymond N. *Journey to the Green and Golden Lands: The Epic of Survival on the Wagon Trail.* Port Washington, N.Y.: Kennikat, 1976.

Doyle, Simon. Diary, 1849. MS, Beinecke Library.

Eastin, Thomas. Diary, 1849. MS, California Historical Society.

Egan, H. In *Frontier Guardian,* July 11, 1849 (Council Bluffs, Iowa).

Emigrant Trails in Southeastern Idaho. Washington: U.S. Department of the Interior, 1976.

Evans, Burrell Whalen. Narrative, 1849. MF of MS, Bancroft Library.

Everts, F. D. Diary, 1849. MS, Beinecke Library.

Fairchild, Lucius. *California Letters of Lucius Fairchild.* Edited by Joseph Schafer. Madison: State Historical Society of Wisconsin, 1931.

Fairfield Ledger, 1901 and 1906 (Fairfield, Iowa).

Faragher, John M. *Women and Men on the Overland Trail.* New Haven, Conn.: Yale University Press, 1979.

Farnham, Elijah Bryan. "From Ohio to California in 1849: The Gold Rush Journal of Elijah Bryan Farnham." Edited by Merrill J. Mattes and Esley J. Kirk, *Indiana Magazine of History, XLVI* (September and December 1950).

Federal Census, Sadsbury Township, Chester County, Pennsylvania, for 1850.

Foster, Isaac. Diary, 1849–50. TS, Huntington Library.

Franzwa, Gregory M. *Maps of the Oregon Trail.* Gerald, Mo.: Patrice Press, 1982.

———. *The Oregon Trail Revisited.* 3d ed. Gerald, Mo.: Patrice Press, 1983.

Frémont, John C. *Report of the Exploring Expedition to the Rocky Mountains in the Year 1842 and to Oregon and North California in the Years 1843–44.* Washington: Gales and Seaton, 1845.

Frink, Dwight E. "Charles Ross Parke, M.D." TS, McLean County Historical Society, Illinois.

Frontier Guardian, 1849 (Kanesville, Iowa).

Futhey, J. Smith, and Gilbert Cope. *History of Chester County, Pennsylvania, with Genealogical and Biographical Sketches.* Philadelphia: Louis H. Evarts, 1881.

Geiger, Vincent, and Wakeman Bryarly. *Trail to California: The Overland Journal of Vincent Geiger and Wakeman Bryarly.* Edited by David M. Potter. New Haven: Yale University Press, 1945; reprint, New Haven, 1962.

Gibbs, George. "The Diary of George Gibbs." In Raymond W. Settle, ed., *The March of the Mounted Riflemen.* Glendale, Calif.: Arthur H. Clark Co., 1940.

The Gold Rush: Letters from the Wolverine Rangers to the Marshall, Michigan, Statesman, 1849–1851. Mt. Pleasant, Mich.: Cuming Press, 1974.

Gould, Charles. Diary, 1849. TS, Bancroft Library.

Granville, Ohio, Company. Diary, 1849. MS, Beinecke Library.

Gray, Charles Glass. *Off at Sunrise: The Overland Journal of Charles Glass Gray.* Edited by Thomas D. Clark. San Marino, Calif.: Huntington Library, 1976.

Gregory, J. W. *History of Schuyler County, Missouri.* Trenton, Mo.: W. B. Rogers Printing Co., [c. 1909].

Gudde, Erwin G. *California Gold Camps.* Berkeley: University of California Press, 1975.

Hackney, Joseph. Diary, 1849. In Elizabeth Page, ed., *Wagons West: A Story of the Oregon Trail.* New York: Farrar & Rhinehart, 1930.

Hafen, LeRoy R., ed. *The Mountain Men and the Fur Trade of the Far West.* 10 vols. Glendale, Calif.: Arthur H. Clark Co., 1972.

—— and Francis Marion Young. *Fort Laramie and the Pageant of the West, 1834–1890.* Glendale, Calif.: Arthur H. Clark Co., 1938.

Haines, Aubrey L. *Historic Sites Along the Oregon Trail.* Gerald, Mo.: Patrice Press, 1981.

Haines, James. Life and Experiences in California. TS, Bancroft Library.

Hale, Israel F. "Diary of a Trip to California in 1849." *Society of California Pioneers Quarterly, II* (June 1925).

Hall, O. J. Diary, 1849. TS, Bancroft Library.

Hamelin, Joseph P., Jr. Diary, 1849–50. MS, Beinecke Library.

Hannon, Jessie Gould. *The Boston-Newton Company Venture: From Massachusetts to California in 1849.* Lincoln: University of Nebraska Press, 1969.

Hard, G. C. In *Rockford Forum,* July 4, 1849 (Rockford, Ill.).

Hasbrouck, Jacob Louis. *History of McLean County, Illinois.* Topeka, Kan.: Historical Publishing Co., 1924.

Haskins, Charles W. *The Argonauts of California: Being the Reminiscences of Scenes and Incidents that Occurred in California in Early Mining Days, by a Pioneer.* New York: Fords, Howard & Hulbert, 1890.

Hillyer, Edwin. Diary, 1849. MS, State Historical Society of Wisconsin.

Hinman, Charles G. *"A Pretty Fair View of the Eliphent" or, Ten Letters by Charles G. Hinman written During His Trip Overland from Groveland, Illinois, to California in 1849 and His Adventures in the Gold Fields in 1849 and 1850.* Edited by Colton Storm. Chicago: Gordon Martin, 1960.

History of Adair, Sullivan, Putnam and Schuyler Counties, Missouri. Chicago: Goodspeed Publishing Co., 1888.

History of Adams County, Illinois. Chicago: Murray, Williamson & Phelps, 1879.

History of Andrew and DeKalb Counties, Missouri. St. Louis, Mo.: Goodspeed Publishing Co., 1888.

History of Des Moines County, Iowa. Chicago: Western Historical Co., 1879.

History of Holt and Atchison Counties, Missouri. St. Joseph, Mo.: National Historical Co., 1882.

History of Jo Daviess County, Illinois. Chicago: H. F. Kett & Co., 1878.

History of Marion County, Missouri. 2 vols. St. Louis, Mo.: E. F. Perkins, 1884.

History of Sacramento County, California. Oakland, Calif.: Thompson & West, 1880.

Hixson, Jasper Morris. Diary, 1849. MS, California Historical Society.

Holland's Sterling–Rock Falls Directory for 1875–76. Chicago: Holland Publishing Co., 1875.

Holliday, J. S. *The World Rushed In: The California Gold Rush Experience.* New York: Simon & Schuster, 1981.

Hoover, Vincent. Diary, 1849. MS, Huntington Library.

Howe, Octavius Thorndike. *Argonauts of '49: History and Adventures of the Emigrant Companies from Massachusetts, 1849–1850.* Cambridge, Mass.: Harvard University Press, 1923.

Humphreys, Alfred Glen. "Thomas L. (Peg-leg) Smith." In LeRoy R. Hafen, ed., *The Mountain Men and the Fur Trade of the Far West, IV.* Glendale, Calif.: Arthur H. Clark Co., 1966.

Hutchings, James M. *Seeking the Elephant, 1849: James Mason Hutchings' Journal of His Overland Trek to California.* Edited by Shirley Sargent. Glendale, Calif.: Arthur H. Clark Co., 1980.

Ingalls, John. *California Letters of the Gold Rush Period: The Correspondence of John Ingalls, 1849–1851.* Edited by Robert W. G. Vail. Worcester, Mass.: *Proceedings* of American Antiquarian Society, 1938.

Iowa Sentinel, 1849.

Iowa State Gazette, 1849.

Jackson, Donald Dale. *Gold Dust.* New York: Alfred A. Knopf, 1980.

Jagger, D. Diary, 1849–50. MF of MS, Bancroft Library.

Jefferson County Records. Fairfield, Iowa, 1964.

Johannsen, Robert W. *To the Halls of the Montezumas: The Mexican War in the American Imagination*. New York: Oxford University Press, 1985.

Johnson, John A. Note Book, 1849. MS, Beinecke Library.

Johnson, Joseph H. Diary, 1849. MS, Huntington Library.

Johnston, William G. *Overland to California*. Oakland, Calif.: Biobooks, 1948.

Kirkpatrick, Charles A. Diary, 1849–50. MS, Bancroft Library.

Krepps, Bolivar. Letters, 1849. MS, Denver Public Library.

Lapp, Rudolph M. *Blacks in Gold Rush California*. New Haven, Conn.: Yale University Press, 1977.

Lewis, John F. Diary, 1849. MS, Beinecke Library.

Locke, Dean J. Diary, 1849. TS, California Historical Society.

Lord, Israel Shipman Pelton. Diary, 1849–51. MS, Huntington Library.

Lorton, William Birdsall. Diary, 1848–50. MS, Bancroft Library.

McCall, Ansel J. *The Great California Trail in 1849*. Bath, N.Y.: Steuben Courier, 1882.

McLear, Patrick E. "The St. Louis Cholera Epidemic of 1849." *Missouri Historical Review, LXIII* (January 1969).

Mann, Henry Rice. Diary, 1849. TS, Bancroft Library.

Mantor, Lyle E. "Fort Kearny and the Westward Movement." *Nebraska History,* XXIX (September 1948).

Markle, John A. Diary, 1849. MF of MS, Bancroft Library.

Mattes, Merrill. "Chimney Rock on the Oregon Trail." *Nebraska History,* XXXVI (March 1955).

———. *The Great Platte River Road: The Covered Wagon Mainline via Fort Kearny to Fort Laramie.* Lincoln: Nebraska State Historical Society, 1969.

Meeker, Ezra. *Ox-Team Days on The Oregon Trail.* Edited by Howard Driggs. Yonkers-on-Hudson, N.Y.: World Book Co., 1922.

Menefee, C. A. *Historical and Descriptive Sketch Book of Napa, Sonoma, Lake and Mendicino.* Napa City, Calif.: Reporter Publishing House, 1873.

Middleton, Joseph. Diary, 1849–51. MS, Beinecke Library.

Miller, Greenberry. Diary, 1849–50. MS, Bancroft Library.

Miller, Reuben. Diary, 1849. TS, Huntington Library.

Minges, Abram. Diary, 1849. MS, Bentley Library.

Missouri Republican, 1849 (St. Louis; also known as the *Daily Missouri Republican*).

Monmouth Atlas, 1849 (Monmouth, Ill.).

Morgan, Dale L. "The Ferries of the Forty-Niners." *Annals of Wyoming,* XXXI (April and October 1959), XXXII (April and October 1960).

Newhall, J. B. *A Glimpse of Iowa in 1846.* 2d ed. Burlington, Iowa: W. D. Skillman, 1846.

Oglesby, Richard J. "Richard J. Oglesby: Forty-Niner." Edited by Mildred Eversole. *Transactions* of the Illinois State Historical Society, 1939.

Oquawka Spectator, 1849 (Oquawka, Ill.).

Orvis, Andrew M. Diary, 1849–50. MS, Beinecke Library.

Ottawa Free Trader, 1849 (Ottawa, Ill.).

Packard, Wellman. *Early Emigration to California, 1849–1850.* Fairfield, Wash.: Ye Galleon Press, 1971.

Paden, Irene D. *The Wake of the Prairie Schooner.* New York: Macmillan, 1943.

Page, Elizabeth, ed. *Wagons West: A Story of the Oregon Trail.* New York: Farrar & Rhinehart, 1930.

Page, Henry. Diary, 1849. In Elizabeth Page, ed., *Wagons West: A Story of the Oregon Trail.* New York: Farrar & Rhinehart, 1930.

Parke, Charles Ross. "Diary of Charles Ross Parke, M.D., written during his journey to Russia, and his period of medical service with the Russian Army in the Crimean War, Sept. 9, 1855–November [21?], 1856." Library of Congress.

Parkman, Francis. *The Oregon Trail: Sketches of Prairie and Rocky-Mountain Life.* 8th ed. Boston: Little, Brown and Co., 1891.

Parks, Frank Sylvester. *Genealogy of Arthur Parke of Pennsylvania and Some of His Descendants.* Washington: Published privately, 1922.

"Pawnee." In *Missouri Republican,* 1849. (According to Dale Morgan, "Pawnee" was Captain Stewart Van Vliet, the quartermaster at Fort Kearny.)

Pearson, Gustavus C. *Overland in 1849: From Missouri to California by the Platte River and the Salt Lake Trail, an Account from the Letters of G. C. Pearson.* Edited by Jessie H. Goodman. Los Angeles: Published privately, 1961.

Perkins, Elisha Douglas. *Gold Rush Diary: Being the Journal of Elisha Doug-*

las Perkins on the Overland Trail in the Spring and Summer of 1849. Edited by Thomas D. Clark. Lexington: University of Kentucky Press, 1967.

Pierce, Hiram D. *A Forty-Niner Speaks*. Edited by Sarah W. Meyer. Oakland, Calif.: Keystone-Inglett Printing Co., 1930.

Pigman, Walter Griffith. *The Journal of Walter Griffith Pigman*. Edited by Ulla Staley Fawkes. Mexico, Mo.: Walter G. Staley, 1902.

Placer Times, 1849 (Sacramento, Calif.).

Pleasants, W. J. *Twice Across the Plains, 1849 . . . 1856*. San Francisco: Walter N. Brunt Co., 1906.

Portrait and Biographical Album of Whiteside County, Illinois. Chicago: Chapman Brothers, 1885.

Prichet, John. Diary, 1849–51. MF of TS, Bancroft Library.

Pritchard, James A. *The Overland Diary of James A. Pritchard from Kentucky to California in 1849*. Edited by Dale L. Morgan. Denver: Old West Publishing Co., 1959.

Prucha, Francis Paul. *A Guide to the Military Posts of the United States, 1789–1895*. Madison: State Historical Society of Wisconsin, 1964.

Rafferty, Milton D. *Historical Atlas of Missouri*. Norman: University of Oklahoma Press, 1982.

Ramsay, Robert L. *Our Storehouse of Missouri Place Names*. University of Missouri *Bulletin,* Vol. 53. Columbia, Mo.: University of Missouri, 1952.

Read, Georgia Willis. "Diseases, Drugs, and Doctors on the Oregon-California Trail in the Gold Rush Years." *Missouri Historical Review,* XXXVIII (April 1944).

————. "Women and Children on the Oregon-California Trail in the Gold Rush Years." *Missouri Historical Review, XXXIX* (October 1944).

Reardon, Cornelius. Letters, 1850. MS, Bentley Library.

Record of the Services of Illinois Soldiers in the Black Hawk War, 1831–32, and in the Mexican War, 1846–48. Springfield, Ill.: Journal Co., 1902.

Reid, Bernard J. *Overland to California with the Pioneer Line: The Gold Rush Diary of Bernard J. Reid.* Edited by Mary McDougall Gordon. Stanford, Calif.: Stanford University Press, 1983.

Reid, John Phillip. *Law for the Elephant: Property and Social Behavior on the Oregon Trail.* San Marino, Calif.: Huntington Library, 1980.

Richmond Palladium, 1849 (Richmond, Ind.).

Riley, Glenda. *Women and Indians on the Frontier, 1825–1915.* Albuquerque: University of New Mexico Press, 1984.

Robinson, John. *The Biographical Record of McLean County, Illinois.* Chicago: S. J. Clarke Publishing Co., 1899.

Robinson, Zirkle D. *The Robinson-Rosenberger Journey to the Gold Fields of California, 1849–1850.* Edited by Francis Coleman Rosenberger. Iowa City, Iowa: Prairie Press, 1966.

Rockford Forum, 1849 (Rockford, Ill.).

Rosenberg, Charles E. *The Cholera Years: The United States in 1832, 1849, and 1866.* Chicago: University of Chicago Press, 1962.

Russell, Don. "How Many Indians Were Killed?" *The American West, X* (July 1973).

Ruxton, George Frederick. *Life in the Far West.* New York: Harper & Brothers, 1849.

Sacramento Transcript, 1850 (Sacramento, Calif.).

Scherzer, Carl. *Travels in the Free States of Central America.* 2 vols. London: Longman, Brown, Green, Longmans & Roberts, 1857.

Searls, Niles. *The Diary of a Pioneer and Other Papers.* San Francisco: Pernan-Walsh Printing Co., 1940.

Sedgley, Joseph. *Overland to California in 1849.* Oakland, Calif.: Butler & Bowman, 1877.

Settle, Raymond W., ed. *The March of the Mounted Riflemen.* Glendale, Calif.: Arthur H. Clark Co., 1940.

Shaffer, Leslie L. D. "The Management of Organized Wagon Trains on the Overland Trail." *Missouri Historical Review, LV* (July 1961).

Shaw, Reuben Cole. *Across the Plains in Forty-nine.* Edited by Milo Milton Quaife. Chicago: Lakeside Press, 1948.

Shinn, Charles Howard. *Mining Camps: A Study of American Frontier Government.* New York: Charles Scribner & Sons, 1884.

Shombre, Henry J. Diary, 1849. MF, Bancroft Library.

Shuck, Oscar T., ed. *History of the Bench and Bar of California.* Los Angeles: Commercial Printing House, 1901.

Smith, Dora Wilson. *Whiteside County, Illinois, 1850 Census.* Indianapolis, Ind.: Heritage House, 1977.

Spooner, E. A. Diary and Letters, 1849. MF, Bancroft Library.

Squire, E[phriam] G[eorge]. *Nicaragua: Its People, Scenery, Monuments.* 2 vols. New York: D. Appleton & Co., 1856.

Stackpole, William. Diary, 1849. MS, Beinecke Library.

Stansbury, Howard. *Exploration and Survey of the Valley of the Great Salt Lake of Utah.* Washington: Robert Armstrong, 1853.

Steck, Amos. Diary, 1849. MS, State Historical Society of Colorado.

Steele, John. *In Camp and Cabin*. Chicago: Lakeside Press, 1928.

Stevens, G. B. Journal, 1849. Beinecke Library.

Stewart, George R. *The California Trail: An Epic with Many Heroes*. New York: McGraw-Hill, 1962.

————. *Ordeal by Hunger: The Story of the Donner Party*. New York: H. Holt and Co., 1936.

Stidham, Joseph S. In *Richmond Palladium*, October 24, 1849.

Stillman, Jacob D. B. *Seeking the Golden Fleece: A Record of Pioneer Life in California*. San Francisco: A. Roman & Co., 1877.

Stoddart, Thomas R. *Annals of Tuolumne County*. Sonora, Calif.: Mother Lode Press, 1963.

Swagert, S. Laird. "British Comment—As of 1849–1851." *California Historical Society Quarterly, XXXII* (March 1953).

Sweet, J. H. "Old Fort Kearny." *Nebraska History, XXVII* (October–December 1946).

T., Dr. Diary, 1849. MS, Bancroft Library.

Tamony, Peter. "To See the Elephant." *Pacific Historian, 12* (Winter 1968).

Tate, H. Clay. *The Way It Was in McLean County, 1972–1822*. Bloomington, Ill.: McLean County History '72 Association, 1972.

Tiffany, P. C. Diary, 1849–51. MS, Beinecke Library.

Tinker, Charles. "Charles Tinker's Journal: A Trip to California in 1849." Edited by Eugene H. Roseboom. *Ohio State Archaeological and Historical Quarterly, 61* (January 1952).

Tipton, Lindsey. Diary, 1849. MS, Bancroft Library.

Tuttle, Charles A. Letters, 1849. Bancroft Library.

United States Biographical Dictionary and Portrait Gallery of Self-Made Men, Illinois Volume.

U.S. Bureau of the Census, Population Schedule, 7th Census, 1850, Chester County, Pennsylvania, Part 1.

Unruh, John, Jr. *The Plains Across: The Overland Emigrants and the Trans-Mississippi West, 1840–60.* Urbana: University of Illinois Press, 1979.

"W." In *Oquawka Spectator*, August 8, 1849.

Wanamaker, George W. *History of Harrison County, Missouri.* Topeka, Kan.: Historical Publishing Co., 1921.

Ware, Joseph E. *The Emigrants' Guide to California, 1849.* Reprint edited by John Caughey. N.Y.: De Capo Press, 1972.

Way, Royal Brunson. *The Rock River Valley: Its History, Traditions, Legends and Charms.* 3 vols. Chicago: S. J. Clarke Publishing Co., 1926.

Wedel, Waldo Rudolph. *An Introduction to Pawnee Archaeology.* Smithsonian Institution, *Bureau of American Ethnology Bulletin 112.* Washington: Government Printing Office, 1936.

Weed, L. N. Journal, 1850. TS, Beinecke Library.

Weekly North-Western Gazette, 1846 and 1849 (Galena, Ill.).

Wilkins, James F. *An Artist on the California Trail: The 1849 Diary and Sketches of James F. Wilkins.* Edited by John Francis McDermott. San Marino, Calif.: Huntington Library, 1968.

Williams, Walter, ed. *A History of Northwest Missouri.* 3 vols. Chicago: Lewis Publishing Co., 1915.

Willis, Edward J. Diary, 1849. MS, Beinecke Library.

Wistar, Isaac Jones. *Autobiography of Isaac Jones Wistar, 1827–1905.* New York: Harper & Brothers, 1914.

Wood, Joseph Warren. Diary, 1849–53. MS, Huntington Library.

Woodruff, George H. *Will County on the Pacific Slopes.* Joliet, Ill.: Joliet Republic and Sun, 1885.

Woodruff, Mrs. Howard W., comp. *Marriage Records: Marion County, Missouri,* Books A and B, 1827–1856.

Woods, Daniel B. *Sixteen Months at the Gold Diggings.* London: Sampson Low, [1851].

Wooldridge, J. W. *History of the Sacramento Valley, California.* 3 vols. Chicago: Pioneer Historical Publishing Co., 1931.

Young, Sheldon. Log, 1849–50. TS, Huntington Library.

Index

273

Women, 6, 9, 27, 86, 90, 92, 96, 128, 129, 133; in new roles and activities, xxiii; Indian, 28, 29, 54, 88–89; as overlanders in 1849, xxi; male relationships with, changed by the overland experience, xxiii, xxiv; in religious order in Peoria, Illinois, 140; in Russia and the Ukraine, 138; Sioux, 28; gambling, 91
"Women's work": performed by men, xxiii, xxiv
Wood, Capt. David, 83

Wood, Mr., 21
Woodburn Capt. (George W.?), 9, 12, 17
Woodworth, Messrs., 72
Woodworth, Mr., 81
Woodworth's Camp, 83, 84
Worthington, Dr. Wilmer (physician), 13

Yates, Richard (Governor of Illinois), 139
Yates, William, 87
Young, Brigham, 96
Yuba River, 80, 84, 85